Creative Cash

How to sell your Crafts, Needlework, Designs & Know-how

by Barbara Brabec

Scratch-Board Illustrations
by Alice Bidwell

BARBARA BRABEC PRODUCTIONS

■ P. O. Box 2137 ■
Naperville IL 60567-2137

CREATIVE CASH: How to Sell Your Crafts, Needlework, Designs &
Know-How, by Barbara Brabec

Barbara Brabec Productions
P. O. Box 2137
Naperville, IL 60567-2137

Printed in the United States of America
by McNaughton & Gunn, Ann Arbor, Michigan

Fifth edition, revised

Cover design adapted from needlework
designed and stitched by the author

Library of Congress Catalog Card Number 96-093448

ISBN 0-9613909-3-X

Previously published by the following:
    under ISBN 0-9613909-0-5, by Barbara Brabec Productions
    under ISBN 0-89586-129-1, by HP Books
    under ISBN 0-88453-017-5, by Countryside Books
    under ISBN 0-936930-05-5, by Aames-Allen Publishing Co.

This book is for my mother, Marcella Schaumburg,
who convinced me many years ago that
I could do anything I really wanted to do;
And for my husband, Harry,
who inspired this dedication when he said,
"Behind most successful women you'll find
an encouraging mother and an amazed husband."

Acknowledgments

I owe so much to so many people in the crafts industry that I could not begin to thank everyone here. But I'm especially indebted to dozens of magazine and newsletter editors who have given publicity to this book, and special visibility to my work as a whole. Their endorsement of *Creative Cash* has helped to make it the most popular book of its kind, and their support of my work has been a constant source of encouragement through the years.

I'm also indebted to the many teachers and workshop leaders who use this book as a text in their classes; to the countless number of specialists in Home Economics, the Cooperative Extension Service, Small Business Development Centers, and individuals in SBA and SCORE offices who keep referring budding craft entrepreneurs to this book and others I've written; and to the many free-lance writers and authors who have reviewed this book, mentioned it in magazine articles, and listed it as a valuable resource in their own books.

I owe much to my readers, too. I lost count years ago, but I know that thousands of people have sent me notes or letters in response to this book. The first mail enabled me to sigh with relief in the knowledge that I had delivered the kind of book people wanted to read. All the mail that followed helped me to become a self-supporting writer, and I will be forever grateful to everyone who has taken the time to respond to my writing through the years.

On this page in the original edition of this book, my acknowledgments included a special thank-you to Marilyn Heise, who recommended me to the publisher who wanted this book written. I also thanked my husband, Harry, who offered encouragement and advice, yet never tried to influence the direction or content of this book. As a beginning writer at that time, he nicknamed me "Agatha" (after the great mystery writer, of course), then went about with a grin telling everyone that what I was writing was a mystery to him.

My writing is no longer a mystery to anyone, but what remains a mystery to me is how this book has managed to dramatically change not only my life and Harry's, but the lives of so many of its readers as well. I now believe that *Creative Cash* has a creative spirit of its own. Long past the time when most books of its kind have disappeared from the scene, it simply refuses to die. For that, I'm truly thankful.

Table of Contents

The Story Behind This Book

There's quite a story behind this book, and I'd like to share it with you. To date, four publishers have handled this popular best-seller, and I've been two of them on three separate occasions. Therein lies my tale.

This book was published in late 1979 by Countryside Books, then a division of a newspaper publishing company in Barrington, Illinois. Shortly before my book entered production, my publisher, Steve Lang, asked me to join the company as his assistant. I was thrilled to think that I would actually have a hand in the birthing process of my first book, plus some involvement in its marketing as well. But everything changed suddenly just two weeks after I'd started my new job. Steve was among the victims of the ill-fated Flight 191 that crashed at O'Hare Airport in May, 1979.

The shock of Steve's death hit hard. He was just 34 years old, and the very heart and soul of Countryside Books. In fact, he was the only one who knew what was going on within the company, and it didn't take me long to realize that now I was the only one left who knew anything at all about the inner workings of the publishing division. And with just two weeks' job experience, that wasn't much.

With my book not yet on press, I doubted that it would be published at all . . . unless I did something about it. So I volunteered to take Steve's job and, wonder of wonders, I was given the chance even though I had no previous book publishing experience. Thus I came to be general manager of the company, and publisher of my own book the first time around.

This job was a great challenge for me, but one I met with enthusiasm and confidence. During my two years with Countryside Books, I not only made my book a national best-seller (35,000 copies, with sales to five book clubs), but also came to realize my potential as an entrepreneur. When I gave notice of my intention to leave the company in mid-1981 to start my own homebased publishing/book-selling business, the president opted to sell the book division rather than replace me. My last major responsibility to the company was to find new homes for all the books in Countryside's line. Enter HPBooks, who acquired the publishing rights to *Creative Cash* and issued a new cover edition of this title in late 1981.

By now, I was selling *Creative Cash* by mail to the many craft consumers who were expressing an interest in it. My newsletter, then called *Sharing Barbara's Mail*, was beginning to prosper. One thing led to another, and I soon began to present workshops across the country. I also contributed chapters to a couple of new books by other authors and continued to write my monthly marketing column for *Crafts*. In late 1983, I made an important business gain when I repositioned myself from a "crafts marketing authority" to a "home business development specialist." I also changed the name of my newsletter to *National Home Business Report* and circulation doubled within six months -- proving what I've said in this book about the importance of the name you give yourself, your business, or your products.

My second book, *Homemade Money--The Definitive Guide to Success in a Homebased Business,* was published in the spring of 1984 by Betterway Publications. At about the same time, HPBooks decided to let *Creative Cash* go out of print. Ironically, this decision followed on the heels of publicity I'd gotten for the book in *Family Circle* magazine. (This not only sold more than 5,000 copies in bookstores, but brought me almost 10,000 letters from *Family Circle* readers who wanted the kind of information I was selling by mail.)

Now, with 65,000 copies sold and demand for *Creative Cash* at a new high, there were no books to be found anywhere! So I naturally acquired the publishing rights and got the book back on press as soon as possible, once again becoming my own publisher.

A year later, as I was preparing to go back for a reprint of this book, a phone conversation with a publisher friend led to yet a new publishing arrangement for *Creative Cash* that was destined to last for 3-1/2 years. At the end of this relationship, I had the option of letting this book go out of print, or revising it for yet another printing under my own imprint.

I'm sure there's not another author in the world who has had the publishing experience I've just described. Believe me, it's been a thrill from start to finish, only I'm not finished yet, of course, and neither is *Creative Cash.*

Like a cat with nine lives, this book simply refuses to die and, frankly, I refuse to *let* it die because it was my "baby," and the product that got me started as a writer. As long as new readers keep telling me it's helpful to them, I'll keep it in print.

With so many excellent reviews for this book, I was reluctant to make major changes in the text. (As a wise man once said, "If it ain't broke, don't fix it.") But I have removed dated text, expanded my discussion of some topics, updated all business and marketing information, and created a brand new Resource Chapter (which readers have often told me is worth the price of the book). You'll also find some fascinating updates on what's happened to some of the individuals profiled in this book. (This illustrates better than anything how people's lives can change over a ten-year period.)

Many readers have told me how *Creative Cash* has changed their lives, and this is easy for me to believe because this book has certainly changed my own life. Perhaps you'll write some day and tell me about the business this book helped *you* start. Who knows. . . you may end up a success story in one of my next books!

INTRODUCTION

As a word, "creative" is *in* these days, but like many homemakers, it's a bit overworked.

For example, we speak of creative cooking, creative living, creative gardening, and creative crafts -- things that are possible only because we have creative minds. Now, at the risk of exhausting a word that is already tired, I give you "creative cash," a new phrase coined for the special kind of money you can make by utilizing two of your most natural resources: your designing mind and talented hands.

Of course you have a designing mind! All women do. And no woman could run an efficient home, raise children, or hold down a job unless she possessed gifted hands. I suppose there will always be women who claim they have no real talent for anything, but just for the record, I didn't write this book for them, I wrote it for YOU and everyone like you who KNOWS she has a special talent or ability -- but DOESN'T KNOW how to use it to make money.

This book tells you how to earn your share of today's "creative cash market," simply by doing things you enjoy most, and may already do best. It's filled with inspiring success stories about real people who have generously shared (without thought of monetary gain) their secrets for success, their expert advice, their best how-to-sell techniques and ideas. Perhaps you will find your counterpart somewhere in the pages of this book. If not, you will surely find valuable information, usable ideas, and a host of reasons why you should do something about your long-dreamed-of ideas.

Although this manual has been written with homemakers in mind, it is *not* for women only. In fact, any man with an artistic ability or serious hobbycraft interest would do well to read it. In an age when men are needlepointing and women are blacksmithing, who among us would dare to hang masculine or feminine tags on things like talent, ingenuity and creativity? Many husband-and-wife teams have been caught up in America's steadily-growing crafts movement, and whether you realize it or not, you may already be one-half of a poten

tial home business just waiting to be born.

Of course, you don't have to be married in order to make money from your arts and crafts, nor do you have to be a certain age, or live in any particular part of the country. If you have a good product, a market awaits it somewhere. This book shows you how to find it.

One of the most important features of *Creative Cash* is its resource chapter, the last one in the book. A quick look at it will reveal the names and addresses of many interesting art and craft periodicals and organizations, plus sources for other craft-related publications, services, and products -- some of them from individuals profiled in this book. This information makes *Creative Cash* not just a good marketing manual, but an invaluable directory of information sources unknown to the average craftsperson.

Behind the Scenes

When I first sat down to write this book, my husband offered encouragement and a little wise (though unsolicited) guidance.

"Just remember," he cautioned in his best advice-giving voice, "you're not writing for yourself, you're writing for your readers."

He was tactfully trying to tell me that most people aren't like me, don't think like me, and are certainly not going to see everything my way. True, I am too competitive, I hate to lose, and I always want the last word. Admittedly, that kind of attitude could certainly bias a book if not held in check. So, with Harry's remark ringing in my ears, I laid the framework for this book by writing dozens of letters to special contacts in the crafts field, determined to reflect not just my ideas and opinions, but the combined knowledge and experience of many talented and imaginative people across the country.

I asked for comments from individuals both famous and little known; sought advice from

9

professionals and amateurs alike; queried home-makers, craftspeople, artists, hobbyists, designers, teachers, writers, shop owners, magazine editors, store buyers, craft suppliers, manufacturers, publishers, and others whose categories escape me now. For days and days my typewriter clattered like a machine gun gone berserk, and for weeks thereafter my mailbox spilled over with some of the most fascinating mail it has ever yielded.

What did all this typewriting accomplish? You could say that I've let my fingers do the walking for you. By sharing the enlightening answers I received to questions both brilliant and stupid, I've saved you a lot of time and legwork.

I hasten to add, however, that this book is built on much more than a few dozen letters written over a period of several weeks. Success, especially in the field of crafts, doesn't come overnight in a gift-wrapped package, and comprehensive books aren't written overnight either.

This one is the result of almost ten years of diligent work and concentrated effort on my part, and an unimaginable amount of patience on the part of my husband. For five years Harry and I published a quarterly magazine called *Artisan Crafts,* whose presence in our home not only disrupted normal day-to-day living, but eventually came to dominate our lives. It was, sad to say, rather like inviting to dinner a friend who refused to leave when the evening was over. We ceased publication in late 1976, having learned by then what it really means to have a full-time publishing business in one's home, and how difficult it can sometimes be to realize a true profit from one's productive efforts.

As regards Harry's patience, let me say that not only did he have to live through the five-year period mentioned above -- which meant putting up with an ill-kept house and hastily prepared meals, to say nothing of an often nervous, over-worked and disheveled wife -- but he also had to go through what countless husbands everywhere are no doubt just encountering: his wife's search for something special to do with her free time.

Looking back, I now see that while I was happily experimenting with first one craft and then another in an attempt to develop new abilities, Harry was patiently tolerating such aggravations as glitter in his soup, yarn clippings in bed, and ceramic chips in the shag rug -- the latter often discovered at midnight by surprised bare feet on what might otherwise have been a silent run to the refrigerator. At one time or another in recent years, he has also been assaulted with the bad smell of lacquer thinner still in the air at mealtime, zonked on the nose by flying wood chips, and virtually overwhelmed by thirty-foot macrame cords being flung in frenzy. Now you know why he encouraged me to write this book. He figured it would keep me out of mischief for months.

The point of my story is simply this: Most people who are totally involved in crafts today, on either a part- or full-time basis, did not start out with that thought in mind. Like me, many began as hobbyists, looking for something special to do in their spare time, and one thing just led to another. As you will soon see from the interesting success stories herein of other men and women in America, this kind of natural progression from hobby to profession is a commonplace occurrence today.

In fact, where crafts are concerned, one thing always leads to another and, although there is always a beginning to everyone's craft life, those who are seriously involved with crafts can see no end in sight to the things they want to do in the future. And that is precisely why the word "crafts" means excitement to so many people today, young and old alike!

I believe that each person has some unique talent or ability--and that includes YOU. A serious involvement in some creative endeavor could bring wonderful and surprising changes into your life, but you will never know where your talent and ideas might take you if you don't give them a chance to grow and develop. Don't you agree the possibilities ought to be explored?.

- 1 -

So Many Crafts, So Many Possibilities

Have you ever thought about the amazing variety of art and craft activities that take place daily in every room of the American home? More important, have you considered the amount of money such activities are generating for some people?

Today, in living rooms that share space with spinning wheels and looms, yarns are spun and weavings are done for sale through galleries and shops. In the corners of rooms once used for dining will now be found cozy little offices where creative souls are writing, designing, and developing all kinds of crafty ideas for the marketplace. People everywhere are no longer just sleeping in bedrooms, but sewing, quilting and needlepointing as well.

Recreation rooms used to be a place where dad disappeared to shoot pool, or the kids went to play ping pong. Now, the whole family is apt to go there after dinner to make handcrafts that will be sold at craft fairs or shops, through a mail order catalog, or perhaps in a home-based studio-workshop. And do you realize how many cars in America are without a roof over their hoods because their garages have been converted into workshops for crafts like ceramics, woodworking, metalworking, or stained glass?

And the kitchen? Ah, yes, the kitchen. Granted, there's no time left to cook anymore, what with all this craft busyness going on, but all manner of magical things are likely to emerge from this room to end up for sale at church bazaars or local shops. It's hard to believe the number of ordinary kitchen products that are currently being used as raw materials for arts and crafts projects. Take salt and flour, for example. Once sifted to make cakes, these ingredients are now mixed to make ornaments for the Christmas tree. And bread dough isn't something you bake and eat, it's something you shape and paint in pretty colors to hang on a tree. Macaroni that once stuck in the pan now sticks instead to a variety of box tops and containers. Apples once peeled for pies are now carved into dolls. Seeds are dried to make beads, and eggs have become a favorite craft medium for thousands of devoted "eggers." Once served sunny-side up to contented husbands everywhere, eggs are often served scrambled these days because that's the only way to keep the shell intact for decorating.

Finally we come to the smallest room in the house, only to discover that even the bathroom does double duty as a workroom from time to time. I'll bet more than one person goes to the bathroom daily to dye yarn or dip batik. . . and it's anybody's guess as to where the finished products go.

That leaves us with the back yard and it, too, has become a working area for many people who use the sun as a tool to dry driftwood and weeds for decorative wall plaques, flowers for sachet packets, or herbs for gourmet cooking. Still others make sun prints or "weather" their growing collection of barn siding.

What does all this light-hearted patter prove? Simply that "arts and crafts" not only have become household words in recent years, but in many cases have actually taken over entire houses in the process. Don't you agree that anything that takes control of one's home at least ought to contribute to its support? But how? Wouldn't it be wonderful if you could wave a wand over your home and magically transform all its *busyness* into *business?*

Perhaps this kind of magic isn't as impossible as it seems. Although I'm no magician, I've certainly pulled more than one trick out of my sleeve in

11

12

Arts and crafts have not only become household words in recent years, but in many cases have actually taken over entire houses in the process. Activities such as those depicted in our imaginary cutaway house often generate a considerable amount of extra income for a family.

the past, and I'll bet you have, too. In effect, this book is your trick-up-the-sleeve, your key to success in the marketing world of arts and crafts. Once you've read it, I predict you'll be so inspired about your ideas and the possibilities that exist for bringing them to fruition that you won't want to sleep for weeks, let alone cook or clean house. Until now you may have lacked the incentive or know-how to get your ideas off the ground, but no more. *Creative Cash* shows you how others have achieved success in arts and crafts businesses, and it will convince you that your dreams can be realized too.

Your "Ladder of Success"

Have you ever wondered where you stand in today's art/craft world, as compared to others? If so, you might try thinking about your position in terms of standing on a ladder. Imagine that the first rung is for all the beginners in this field. (And for now, let's think of "beginners" as being only those who are non-sellers, since they may already be professionals when talent and ability are considered.)

The top rung of our make-believe ladder would naturally represent the full-time professional sellers -- the artists, craftsmen, designers, teachers, writers, shop owners, and others who have become successful in their chosen fields -- those who have "made it to the top of the ladder."

Between the top and bottom rungs, then, are the many different steps to be taken on the way up. You and only you know where you stand right now, and where you would eventually like to be. The real purpose of this book is to get you moving towards the goal you want to reach, whether it's halfway up the ladder or all the way to the top. Once you have started the climb it will be up to you to find the rung that's right for you and your individual lifestyle.

As you begin, remember that it always pays to be professional in your approach to selling. If you get started on the right foot, it will be easy to keep moving forward in a professional manner, and soon you will find yourself reaching for new heights on your own ladder of success.

Who Are You and What Do You Do?

If someone were to ask you that question, what would you say? Before you can properly promote or advertise yourself or your products, you must know the answer to this question. You should be able to sum it up in a few words, such as: "I am a designer who creates patterns for toymakers," or, "I am an artist who specializes in miniature paintings," or, "I am a woodworker who designs and makes decorative objects," etc. Once you have decided who and what you are, it will be easier to explain it to others, and especially useful when you sit down to write your first classified ad, press release, or copy for your brochure or catalog.

In writing this book, I tried to visualize its readers and the thousands of things they were making and hoping to sell. I finally gave up because that is as impossible as trying to define the words "artist" or "craftsman."

My husband once said that the definition of a craftsman cannot be put down as simply as you would the 12 points of the Scout law (a scout is trustworthy, loyal, helpful, etc.) and he was right. Still, many people take delight in trying to define the word, such as Raymond Martell, a jeweler craftsman who once told me, "If a person thinks of himself as a craftsman, then he or she *is* a craftsman." Someone else remarked that a craftsman is someone who loves to talk to you with his hands, and another observed that a craftsman is someone who wouldn't sell an elegant hand-woven wall hanging for less than $500, but would give it to a friend without hesitation.

If you prefer to be more technical, you can consider the following broad categories that define individuals who pursue crafts on a vocational basis. These definitions emerged from a planning study sponsored by the National Endowment for the Arts:

- **ARTIST CRAFTSMAN** -- A craftsman who works to his own design concept and makes one-of-a-kind-objects.
- **DESIGNER CRAFTSMAN** -- A craftsman who works to his own design concept and makes prototypes for small and large industry.
- **PRODUCTION CRAFTSMAN** -- A craftsman who works to his own design concept, or to the design concept of another individual, period, or group, and who makes multiples of an object.
- **ARTISAN** -- A craftsman who works to the design concepts of another individual, period, or group, and who makes one-of-a-kind, prototype, or multiple objects.

Further classifications were also made by the study group, based on the style of design a craftsman uses -- contemporary, ethnic/folk, traditional, restoration crafts, and crafts made in industry.

In this book, I have used the terms "craftsmen" or "crafts professionals" when speaking about men or women who have made crafts a part- or full-time profession; "craftspeople" when referring to a group of individuals whose interests and approaches to crafts may be quite varied; and "crafters" when speaking of craft or needlecraft hobbyists. In magazines and books today, the terms "artists" and "artisans" are often used as substitutes for the above words, thus my use of the word "artist" does not necessarily mean one who paints, any more than the word "artisan" suggests a lack of artistic ability (as implied by the NEA planning study mentioned earlier).

Once, when this topic was being discussed at length in *Artisan Crafts,* Jude Martin, a Tennessee toymaker, offered the following solution to this problem with a charming two-line poem that read: *"I is. . . a CraftsMs."*

If you occasionally feel left out of a discussion when I use certain terms to describe a group of creative men and women, please forgive me and try to remember that it is often difficult for today's writers and magazine editors to find the one word that will properly describe everyone, without offending or excluding anyone. As I said before, there are so many crafts and so many possibilities.

Enough chatter! Let's get down to work. If you are not yet selling what you make, perhaps you have reached the stage where you're beginning to wonder what you're going to do with everything you're creating. If so, you may soon have to make a decision: Stop producing, or start selling!

- 2 -

Stop Producing or Start Selling!

If you have already begun to sell your crafts or needlework, this chapter will help you gain perspective on the manner in which you first entered the marketplace, and point out a few things you may have overlooked in the beginning.

If you're a prolific producer who hasn't yet begun to sell, you'll know exactly what I mean when I say that my mother's home is decorated in "Early Barbara." And many of my friends have things made in that period before I began to sell, just as your friends probably have your handmade gifts in their homes. Isn't it logical to start selling when you're producing so much you can't give it all away? It seemed that way to me several years ago when I was going through this phase.

Although the idea of earning extra money was appealing to me, my real motivation to sell came when I looked around, saw all the stuff piling up, and heard my husband say, "It's nice, but what do you plan to *do* with all of it?" Like so many people before and after me, I had reached what I call the "crafts saturation point." I simply had to stop producing or start selling. Of course, stopping was out of the question because I was having too much fun producing. Thus I began to sell in order to make room for all the new things coming, and also to earn enough money to buy the supplies and materials needed to make them. (Does this story sound familiar?)

Like all beginners, I soon learned that making things and selling things are two different things entirely. It's rather like the fisherman who, when asked if the fishin' was good, replied: "Oh, the fishin' is easy, it's the *catchin'* that's hard."

Is there some special secret to selling? Rosemaler Carolyn Handy has an answer to that question. She thinks selling is "nothing more than having a product that is attractive, well executed,

priced right, available, and presided over by the craftsman who is happy to serve the customer." But she also says it is amazing how many people, in trying to sell, fail to observe any of the above. "The creative person, if he is to find homes for his creations, must meet the consumer halfway. As in any new area of endeavor, the early days of selling a craft can be trying, and it does take time to find the best places to sell, learn what the public wants, and decide who and what your customer is."

Another woman wrote, "Selling one's work is a natural step in looking for a response to one's creative efforts." She also told me she entered her first craft show a good distance from home because she "...sure didn't want to take a chance locally where those I knew could see me fail." She didn't fail, but this lack of confidence on the part of beginning sellers is easy to understand. For every person who has immediate success with selling, there are surely hundreds of others who have to struggle for it on a trial-and-error basis.

The Importance of Quality

This is as good a time as any to begin harping on something that is always going to be important to your selling success, whether you are trying to market handcrafts, needlework, designs, publications, services, or know-how. That something is QUALITY. Remember when I said that if you had a good product, there was a market for it somewhere? The key word, of course, is "good."

What constitutes quality in crafts and needlework? You'll get varying answers from different people, just as you would if you were to ask them if something was expensive. That which seems expensive to me might be cheap at half the price to

15

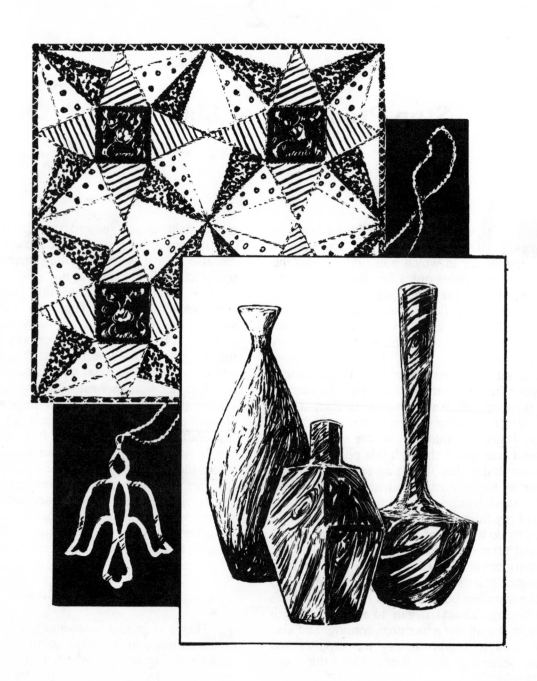

you, or vice versa. Thus, the word "quality" will mean one thing to a New York gallery owner who features designer crafts, and something else entirely to a small town shop owner who sells a variety of local handmades. My dictionary defines quality as "a peculiar and essential character; an inherent feature; superiority in kind; a distinguishing attribute," and these are certainly good thoughts to keep in mind when you are creating anything for sale.

If you have any doubts about the quality or salability of your work, look around and see how it compares to the work of others. Visit craft shows, browse in fine gift and craft shops, and make a study of mail-order catalogs. By all means, read several books and magazines pertaining to your field of interest, giving special attention to the advertisements and photographs. Soon you will begin to understand what the word "quality" means to various buyers, and in the process gain a better idea as to where your particular products fit in today's marketplace.

I must inject something at this point. I respect all forms of creativity, whether they are called art, craft, handicraft, hobby, or profession, and I would never deliberately imply that what one person does is any less important or special than what another might do, since anyone who has discovered the pleasure of working with his or her hands is a very special person indeed. However -- and this is a BIG however -- there are certain handmade products that have little, if any, commercial value, regardless of how well they are made. For example, if you are currently making things from kits, or creating scrap crafts and other items that might be described by some as "artsy-craftsy," don't be surprised to find there are few markets for them outside the range of church bazaars, home boutiques, and homemaker fairs.

But look at it this way: If you are clever enough to create charming handmades out of scraps or hobbycraft materials, then it follows that you are also clever enough to make some real, honest-to-goodness handcrafts from more durable materials. And the list of acceptable materials is endless, as anyone can see by noting the wide variety of items for sale at any quality craft shop or fair.

Needleworkers should also realize that no commercial market exists for finished needlework made from a kit. I'm not downgrading needlework kits by any means -- merely stating that today's sophisticated shop owners have no desire to purchase *for resale* any item that is not originally designed, and this applies to both needlework and crafts. But this does not mean that needleworkers have no markets for their work, only *different* ones. As needlework shop owner Connie A. Stano

states: "A woman can, indeed, make a career from needlework, but it takes great motivation, not to mention experience and some creative ability. If the needlewoman is willing to work by herself in her own community, it would be possible to be very busy today merely by running an ad in a local paper offering to finish kits, or frame or design custom pieces."

Your work may be the best of its kind, or it may be not nearly as good as your mother has led you to believe. While compliments from friends and relatives are good for the ego, such praise is only an indication that your work might sell, not a guarantee. Always remember that the marketplace is the *only place* to test the quality and salability of your work. If it's good and you are reaching the right market, your work will sell. It's as simple as that. Not so simple, however, is the task of finding the right market for your product and the best way to sell it. This is what is known as "market research," and every successful seller understands its importance.

Market Research

Doing market research is rather like being a detective, in that you must turn up a few clues in order to solve the mystery. To take some of the mystery out of selling, you must first discover who your potential customers are, and how large your potential market is. While doing this you should also be considering the various selling methods open to you (direct selling at shows or by mail order, indirect selling in shops or through a sales representative, etc.) and whether, in fact, you have a salable product at all.

To begin, ask yourself a few questions. Do people really need what you're making? If so, how many people? What kind of people? Where do they live? Can they easily get what you make from someone else, perhaps at a lower price than what you would have to charge to make a profit? Or, if people don't really *need* your product, do you think they might simply *want* it? For example, no one really needs another ceramic coffee mug, more handwoven place mats, or three more pictures for the wall, but there will always be people who want such things. In fact, most people today buy hand-crafts not because they need them, but simply because they want them, and prefer them to mass-produced merchandise.

Once you have determined who your customers will be, you must tailor your marketing appeal and your product to that group. It will always be the market itself that determines your product, and nothing will kill the success of a product faster than its being the wrong product for the intended audience. Your success in selling, and thus your profit, will largely depend on how well you have done your market research. Having the best product in the world is useless unless you also have an interested market for it *and* a way to reach that market.

Most craftspeople make a habit of producing what they want to produce; then, when it's finished, they try to find a buyer for it. That's backward thinking, especially if you really want to make money. First you should find out what the marketplace wants or needs, then try to produce it. Otherwise you'll have to create your own market, and this is difficult to do.

After you have decided which products you are going to sell, and to whom, you must give serious thought to the production methods you will use and be prepared to handle a large order should it come your way. Will you be specializing in one-of-a-kind creations, making multiples of one or more items, or working as a small manufacturer using assembly-line techniques? If you plan to be a small manufacturer, will you do everything yourself or hire outside help?

Qualities Needed for Success

It's true that market research is not required if you want to make only what *you* want to make, and sell just for the fun of it. But if you're serious about selling -- and making a profit -- you should make every effort to enter the crafts marketplace in as professional a manner as possible. Why? Because there is a great deal of competition in this field, and to succeed you must know what you're doing. Besides, there are already too many amateurs trying to sell these days, and too many truly talented people who will not succeed in their attempt at business simply because they failed to grasp the importance of such things as market research, record keeping, and the promotion of one's business. Collete Wolff, a successful toy designer, agrees.

"The craft field doesn't need any more amateurs," she says. "Granted, everyone has to start somewhere, and everyone is an amateur at the beginning. But to become a craft professional, in the best sense, with something to contribute and with something to express -- that's for the FEW, not the many. There's a big difference between the hobbyist and the professional. It's attitude, it's intention, it's point of view, it's the ability to conceptualize, it's the grasp of techniques required to produce, and it's the ability to organize and understand business practices. It's also a level of understanding about aesthetic values. To be a professional, a person has to be a self-starter.

Disciplined. Industrious. I would never encourage anyone to become a craftsman just because he's creative."

True, creativity alone is not enough to insure success in business, but it's a good place to start. "Creativity and enthusiasm," says crafts editor Sybil Harp, "are two absolutely essential qualities that one must possess to be successful in the craft field. But they are not enough. Since crafts are also a business, some business sense, or at least an understanding of basic business principles, is essential, as is the know-how to translate all that creativity and enthusiasm for crafts into services that will be marketable to craft manufacturers, merchandisers, publishers, organizations, educators, and others commercially involved in crafts."

Sybil also points out that the craft industry is full of individuals whose interest in crafts has advanced from hobby to career status. "My own observations over the years have convinced me that the most effective and successful people in crafts today are those who began as hobbyists," she says. "They are the people with originality and enthusiasm who love the field more for itself than for its lucrative possibilities."

By heeding the words of experts such as Sybil Harp and Collete Wolff, and following the professional guidelines offered by others in this book, you will automatically place yourself several jumps ahead of many so-called professionals today. Not only will you increase your chances for success, but you will greatly enhance the possibilities of *making a profit* from your art or craft business.

Blending Business Into Your Lifestyle

Most people think in terms of making a profit when they start selling artwork, needlework, or crafts, but not everyone sells just for the money. The need for extra income is only part of the picture for many women today who are simply searching for something special to do that will make them feel more satisfied as individuals. In fact, my correspondence with married women, particularly those between the ages of 40 and 50, often reveals restless feelings about this.

Most women agree there should be more to life than having a nice husband, home, and family. They think there ought to be something special just for them, something that would let them have a private and fulfilling life of their own -- within the confines of marriage, of course. Using their artistic talents and creative abilities often seems the most natural way for them to go because an involvement in this field can easily be worked into their normal day-to-day routine of homemaking and family responsibilities. But such women are usually quick

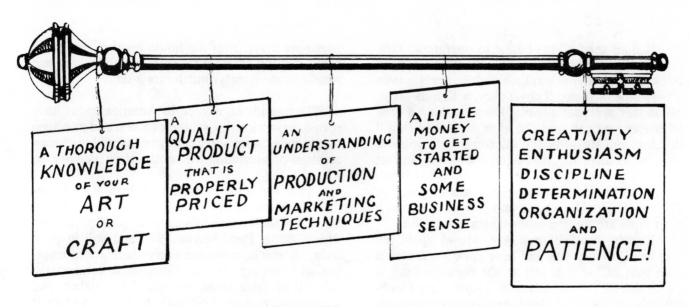

WHAT YOU NEED TO MAKE THE PROGRESSION
FROM HOBBY TO PROFESSION

to point out that they don't want to do anything that will seriously disrupt normal family living or create unnecessary problems for, or with, their husbands. They simply want to do something creative that will prove satisfying and perhaps profitable as well, reasoning that this will make them better people/wives/mothers. I couldn't agree more.

It was sheer boredom that sparked the creative streak in homemaker Joni DuBus. When she was about 40, she suddenly realized she was bored. "Our children were getting older and would soon be finished with school," Joni remembers, "and when I looked at my friends whose children were already gone, I saw the void in their lives." This was a void Joni planned to avoid in her own life.

Handthrown pottery was something she had always wanted to do, so she signed up for a class at a local art center. That did it. That class changed her whole life. Before long, she was selling 800 to 1200 wind chimes a month and turning away new accounts because she couldn't produce enough to keep up with the demand for her work-- even with the help of four part-time workers.

Of course, the development of Joni's business wasn't as easy as the above paragraph makes it sound, although it did grow right from the start. The hard times were in the beginning when Joni was still learning her craft, had to cash in her savings bonds to get the money to buy her potter's wheel, and then had to save all her craft income for months in order to get the down payment for the $3000 kiln she "just had to have." She had it completely paid for three months after she brought it home, however, and perhaps the most traumatic thing about this purchase was the effect it had on her husband. "When the kiln was delivered," Joni says, "my husband almost passed out. He had never seen one before, and he wasn't all that excited about it (to put it mildly.)"

Blending several tons of kiln into the DeBus lifestyle surely took considerable effort on the part of everyone in the family, but Joni says it was worth it. She adds, though, that she would not suggest her business for anyone without "nerves of steel, a back like a horse, and a good business head." Joni's enthusiasm for her business was obviously catching. When her husband, Bill, retired from the police department, he went into full-time work as a manufacturing jeweler, a craft he had apprenticed for many years earlier. Now both Bill and Joni have workshops in their home and love it, although they do tend to work too many hours.

"Working at home isn't always as good as it's cracked up to be," Joni warns. "You spend half, or perhaps three-quarters, of your life in jeans and sweatshirt, and you tend to work on weekends, nights, and holidays to get orders out. You have very little contact with the outside world. My days are not eight-hour days; more like fourteen or eighteen."

19

It does take a lot of time to operate a crafts business based at home, and for those who happen to have children and too little time to operate even a part-time business, Ruby Tobey, a Kansas artist, offers this practical advice: "Keep working a little whenever you can and the ideas and abilities will develop, and soon the day will come when you will have more time. Just don't quit completely and let your craft or ability get rusty. One day the kids will be a little order, or the other job less demanding. Or, you might be like me and just learn to work your craft around the other things in your life."

Ruby's three children have grown up in the middle of her artwork and have always accepted it as a part of her life, just as she does. But she is quick to add, "Serving God and raising my family will always be first, so I have to fit my work around that."

Carol Bernier's three children have always had an active part in the goings-on of her household and the retail shop she operates in her New Hampshire home. "Their chores make them aware that they belong and are important to the functioning of this house and family," she writes. "They have pride in our property and business because they work within it. We have made them aware that the little they do is vital." Carol also emphasizes the importance of keeping the business (shop or office) apart from the living quarters because children need to play and fight and can't lead a sterile life because a customer or client may come through the door at any minute. And she adds that a husband who can't feel free to put his feet up or have a beer when he wants to will soon come to resent the business that is interfering with his happy home life.

Incidentally, if you, as a wife, are seriously thinking about starting a home business in partnership with your husband, think twice. As another woman reminded me, "Being in love with a man who goes away from the house eight to ten hours a day is a lot different from loving and liking one who is home twenty-four hours a day."

Thousands of women in America today have sorted their priorities, set their values, and managed to pursue a career successfully without abandoning children or alienating husbands. How *do* they do it?

That question so intrigued Jean Ray Laury that she wrote a book on the topic and called it *The Creative Woman's Getting-It-All-Together-At-Home Book*. Published in 1977 and still in print today, it tells how women everywhere are attempting, with varying degrees of success, to combine the roles of creative artist, mother, homemaker, and wife. Jean, one of America's most beloved craft and needlework writers, is a delightful example of an all-together woman whose multifaceted career of writing, designing, lecturing and teaching has been a natural outgrowth of her many artistic interests and skills. Her book, based on letters from fiber artists all over the country, sparkles with excitement and offers help and encouragement to women everywhere who want desperately to "do something," yet have too little time and not enough space in which to work. Reading Jean's book is like being part of one of the greatest women's meetings in the world, in which everyone is sounding off for the first time in her life to someone who really understands what she is saying.

Maintaining your home, caring for a husband or family, and running a business as well, can be a real challenge, and not every woman can -- or should try to -- cope with such stress. For those who feel up to it, however, the possibilities are exhilarating and practically unlimited, as the following chapters clearly illustrate.

- 3 -

Pricing Is Everybody's Problem

Arts and crafts have played such a vital role in my life that if someone were to ask me to visualize the proverbial pot of gold, I'd probably see in my mind's eye a ceramic pot sitting on a handwoven rug with a rainbow of batik spilling into it. I do, however, tend to get practical when I think about what's in the that pot: money, money, money -- and I don't mean golden guldens. GREEN is my color, and LOTS is the quantity I prefer. But alas, in order to make lots of money, I must first have "lots of something" to sell. Having that, my problems won't be over because I will still have to *price my products to sell*

Basic Pricing Formulas

Putting just any price on something is easy, but determining the right selling price is not so simple, as most craftspeople will agree. The *right selling price* must be high enough to cover your costs and allow you to make a profit, yet low enough to attract customers. Some people just use common sense when it comes to pricing their work; others use a basic pricing formula, such as this: Labor + Materials + Overhead = Wholesale Price. Wholesale price doubled (sometimes tripled) = Retail Price.

For the benefit of those who do not understand the various elements in this formula, let me explain them briefly. *Labor* represents the value placed on the time you, or someone else, spends in making the article. (See "A Matter of Values" later in this chapter.) The *materials* figure should include the cost of all raw materials used to make what you sell. *Overhead* includes all operating costs not directly related to the production of what you make, such as rent, utilities, telephone, transporta-

tion, freight charges, office supplies, selling expenses, and so on. *Wholesale price* is the price at which you will sell your products to someone else who intends to resell them, such as a shop owner. *Retail price*, as you know, is the price eventually paid by the customer who takes your product home.

Understanding the individual elements in various pricing formulas is one thing, but understanding how craftspeople use specific formulas to establish prices is another thing entirely. Here, then, are some examples.

Lois Moyer is a creative homemaker-turned-kit-manufacturer whose basic pricing formula would be helpful to anyone who wants to produce an item in quantity for sale at wholesale prices. She simply calculates her actual costs for each item, then multiplies that amount by at least two, and sometimes three, to arrive at her suggested retail price. Then she uses her common sense to decide if the item will sell at that price, making any necessary adjustments. Her wholesale price is half the retail price, and there is a sufficient amount built into this price to allow for a 10 percent commission to sales representatives, and an additional 10 percent for volume discounts if necessary.

In applying this formula to your business, it's important to remember that actual costs include not only materials and labor, but overhead and selling expenses as well. Although Lois started her business with just one basic kit idea, she has since developed a complete line of kits now being sold by a team of sales representatives. This kind of growth would have been impossible if Lois had not made allowances for all her costs from the very beginning.

Author Merle Dowd explains it this way: "Unless you consider all the elements involved in pricing, you will experience problems in attempting

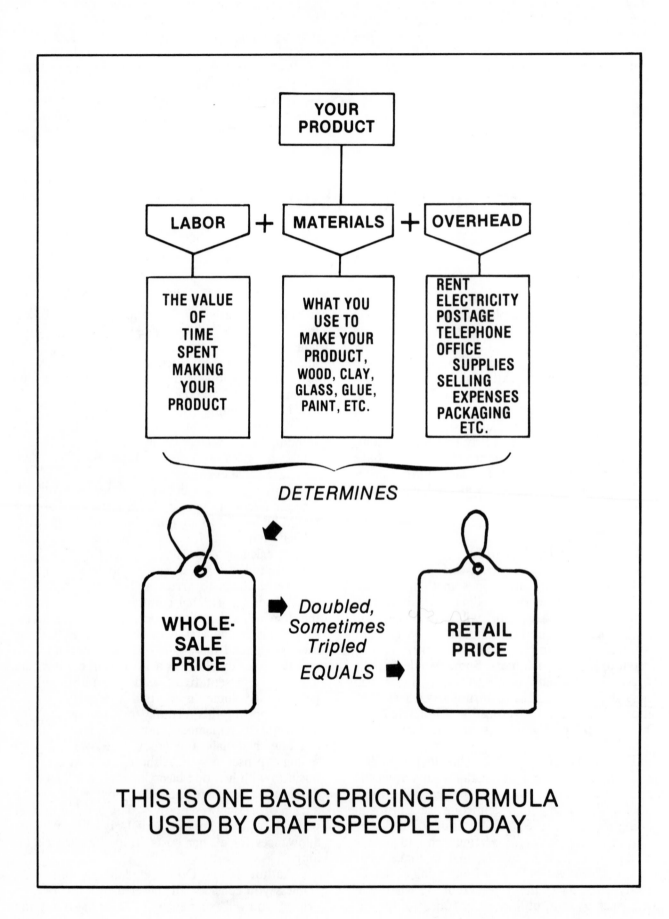

YOUR PRODUCT

LABOR + **MATERIALS** + **OVERHEAD**

| THE VALUE OF TIME SPENT MAKING YOUR PRODUCT | WHAT YOU USE TO MAKE YOUR PRODUCT, WOOD, CLAY, GLASS, GLUE, PAINT, ETC. | RENT ELECTRICITY POSTAGE TELEPHONE OFFICE SUPPLIES SELLING EXPENSES PACKAGING ETC. |

DETERMINES

WHOLE-SALE PRICE

Doubled, Sometimes Tripled **EQUALS**

RETAIL PRICE

22

THIS IS ONE BASIC PRICING FORMULA USED BY CRAFTSPEOPLE TODAY

to move from minor selling on your own to a larger volume distributed through the mail, a retail shop, or on consignment. But if you consider all of these elements, you can operate flexibly and share earnings according to the marketing functions you perform."

The Common-Sense Factor

Here's another formula used by a successful jeweler-craftsman who wholesales a line of silver rings. Ray Martell begins with the cost of materials and adds labor costs calculated at the rate he would have to pay someone else to replace him at the bench. Then he adds 40 percent of the labor-plus-materials figure for overhead, and doubles the whole thing for retail price. "Then," quips Ray, "I throw the whole thing out and figure what I can get!"

Once again, we have run into the "common-sense factor" that is so important to the pricing of any handmade article. Craftspeople aren't born with common sense when it comes to pricing; they have to acquire it much as they acquire their craft skills. Ray adds to his knowledge in this area by keeping loose-leaf folders into which he pastes, by category, advertisements of local jewelers and department stores, etc. "Whenever I am pricing," he says, "I look through the ads and my prices go up!"

If you do not produce in great quantity, nor sell at wholesale, the above pricing methods may seem unsuitable for you, or just too complicated. In that case, you might consider this common pricing formula, which has been used by many craftspeople through the years:

Cost of Materials X 3 = Retail Price

Ruby Tobey, the Kansas artist mentioned in the previous chapter, says this is a good rule-of-thumb method for her, although it doesn't always work. "On some items the cost is low for materials, but the time involved is high, so I must price according to that. On other items I am lucky to get three times the cost of materials." Because Ruby had a realistic view of both pricing and selling, she makes a lot of "bread-and-butter-items," things which can be easily produced and sold at a good profit. "When I try something new," Ruby says, "I try to find a way to make it as cheaply as possible and still have a quality item. Otherwise, I just forget about making it for sale. If I want to keep selling and working, I have to think at least part of the time in terms of what will sell and not just what is art."

Those who are timid about pricing may seek advice from shop owners. While some shops do not want the responsibility of pricing a craftsperson's work, others will offer advice when asked. As a former shop owner, Bucky King was often called upon for advice in pricing and, as a professional textile craftsman, she certainly understood the problems of the beginning sellers who came into her shop. Often, Bucky told me, if they were young and without a known reputation, she advised them to price their articles at half of what they felt they were worth. "In this way," she explained, "their work would usually sell, and their personal morale was encouraged. As their rate of sales increased, we advised a price increase in accordance with sales, perhaps making suggestions as to what we felt would sell best in color, pattern, and design."

Bucky added that they did not use pricing formulas as such, but always treated each craftsperson as an individual, using their combined common sense in arriving at a price for each item.

Ayn Chase, who owns a seasonal craft shop in Oak Bluffs, Massachusetts, is an enterprising artist-craftswoman who produces a variety of items for sale to the tourists who throng to Martha's Vineyard each summer. Primarily a weaver, Ayn brings her common-sense judgement into play when she prices her own work because she is used to hearing such remarks as, "How can you sell these at such low prices?" and, conversely, "Your things are lovely, but I can't afford them." With these comments in mind, Ayn says she often tries to imagine herself in the buyer's shoes, "to see if my prices are too high for me if I were to buy the same item."

Another craftsman and shop owner I once knew in the Ozarks operated in much the same way, except that she used "plain horse sense" to figure out a price. "Regardless of the cost of materials and time," she said, "if the item is priced so high it will not sell, then it should not be made for sale or bought for resale."

A Matter of Values

Everyone who sells is aware that the cost of materials must be carefully considered when pricing, but often it is the labor factor that determines the selling price of a handmade item. Have you ever wondered why the same type of handmade article sells for one price here, and another price there?

This confusion is easily explained when you consider that no two people picked at random will ever place the same value on their time. The decision as to what your time is worth is a personal one, and it may be influenced by any number of factors, such as your education or degree of skill, your age, your reputation (if any), your previous salaried job experience (if any), the area in which you live, the demand in your area for what you make or do, and your need for money. Finally, there is the matter of *ego*. Bucky King notes: "As age and reputation increase, the tendency to placate the ego rears its ugly head, and one's prices seem to soar along with ego. Flexibility is very important here, because inflated self-esteem can put a mighty big hole in your balloon."

Who and what you are will always affect the prices you charge for your work, just as it will affect the prices you are willing to pay for the handwork of others. If you are married, I wouldn't be at all surprised to hear that your husband doesn't agree with you on the topic of what your time is worth. This is particularly true concerning the pricing of handmade articles. A man will always argue on the basis of his working experience and salary, while a homemaker will naturally tend to think in terms of what she would ordinarily be doing with her spare time if she weren't making something for sale -- such as keeping an eye on the baby, watching television, reading, puttering with a hobby, or simply waiting for a casserole to come out of the oven.

While this kind of logic is immediately understood by women everywhere -- and is okay for those who just want to earn a little pin money -- it's not at all practical for professionals or those who aspire to be professional in their approach to selling. Time is a precious commodity that should never be given away carelessly. Thus it is important for all serious sellers to set some sort of value on their time -- even if it's only a couple of dollars an hour -- and try to work out prices accordingly.

If you think $2 per hour seems low, consider that professional artists and craftsmen often have difficulty in getting even this small amount for their time. "You never get the value of your time for your work," says Bucky, who now lives and works on a ranch in Wyoming. "The minimum wage may be $3.50 per hour, but just imagine anyone paying me $350 for 100 hours of work! As a fiber artist I am expected to receive only $2 per hour because, even though I have just as much ability as any ditch digger, cab driver, or salesman, the public does not pay for art by the hour."

Bucky also reminded me that there is yet another factor to be considered when crafts and needlework are being priced for sale: *the love factor.* As she explains, "Most of us would continue to produce if we never sold another piece, simply because we love what we do. I use no formula to price what I make because *love* goes into my work. It is design and pattern, informed with sensitivity. But I am not a dreamer either, so I put realistic prices on items that are for sale."

As an exhibitor in numerous nationally recognized exhibitions, Bucky's prices are usually estab-

lished by what other professional textile craftsmen charge. "Most of us are fortunate to get $200 to $400 for a medium-sized wall hanging," she says. "As spinner, even if we get $1.50 for an ounce of handspun wool or silk, we are underpaid for our efforts in shearing, washing, carding, spinning, and dyeing the thread -- *but we had the love of doing. We don't get paid for love.*"

A decorative painter wrote, "I love to paint and I'd rather paint and sell it than paint and look at it. My husband and I both figure our costs by time and material and take that into consideration when pricing our merchandise. We have been told time and again that our prices are too low, but we are getting a fair return and we are selling."

It's certainly true that if you are doing what you want to do, on a schedule of your own making, you will be content to accept a lower hourly rate of pay than you might demand if you were working for someone else. As another woman put it, "You don't punch a time clock in this kind of work, so I don't think time should be counted."

Needleworkers, perhaps more than others, realize that time cannot be considered in terms of so many dollars for so many hours spent. As a needleworker myself, I work primarily at two times: when I'm "watching" television, or when I'm traveling. To my way of thinking, the hours spent in these activities would normally be time wasted, so when I eventually complete a piece of needlework in the process, I always feel I've gained something in the bargain. Thus, to needleworkers everywhere who take great pride in doing quality work, the hours spent are not important. If a great deal of needlework can be turned out in a year during spare-time hours, that's a bonus, indeed. And if it can also be sold at reasonable prices to appreciative buyers, so much the better.

The Psychology of Pricing

The craft seller should understand that all buyers have preconceived notions as to what any item should cost. When you take this fact into consideration, you are applying psychology, as well as common sense, to your pricing formula. Perhaps one of the first things all craft professionals learn is that certain items must be priced to compensate for others. Quite often an item that takes a lesser amount of time and effort to produce can be priced higher than something that may have been twice as difficult to make and took three times as long besides. Always try to find out what "the going prices" are for items similar to those you produce, and never feel guilty about taking a larger profit on something you have produced easily and quickly,

To make the job of finding supplies easier, read one or more craft periodicals regularly, and gradually acquire a well-rounded library of supply catalogs and directories. Membership in craft organizations or cooperatives might also be helpful inasmuch as such groups can often buy at quantity discounts and pass savings along to their members.

because sooner or later you will have to take a loss on something that should be priced higher, but cannot be, for one reason or another.

You should also realize that certain prices -- such as $2.29, $4.88, and $7.98 -- are just plain bad for handcrafts. That's because they sound like amounts one might expect to pay for items in a discount house. This is a good example of the psychology of pricing. It's difficult to explain, but after you have sold many things, you will begin to notice that items with a certain price sell better than others. If you will look closely at the price tag on handcrafts the next time you go to a large, professional show, you will probably note an interesting pattern emerging -- a pattern that will offer a reliable guideline for pricing your own products.

Guidelines are important, but in the long run, you must not forget that *the customer is King.* He is not concerned with how long it takes to create an item, nor what it costs to make. His decision to buy, or not to buy, is based simply on what he is willing to pay to own the item. If he wants it badly enough, he will find the money to buy it.

Buying Supplies Wholesale

The price you pay for materials can greatly affect the selling price of your products, so it's only natural for you to ask, "Where can I get it wholesale?" Many of you already have discovered one thing: The fact that you can use craft or needlework supplies in quantity does not necessarily

entitle you to buy them at wholesale prices. You may have discovered, too, that the solution does not always lie merely in obtaining a resale tax number. (See Chapter 14.) Most manufacturers and wholesalers in the craft supply industry do not wish to sell to individuals because it is too expensive for them to handle small orders, and they also want to protect their "legitimate dealers" -- those who own retail establishments. Their point is well taken if you consider the situation from the dealer's viewpoint. How would you feel if you were a struggling craft supply shop owner who learned that an individual working out of her home was able to buy the same supplies at wholesale that you were selling in your shop? You, as a retailer, would have enormous overhead costs to contend with, while the individual would not. To shop owners, this does not seem fair at all.

From the crafter's viewpoint, however, I know how frustrating it is to have to buy materials at retail prices when it also means the price of your finished products must be raised to compensate for the higher cost of materials. Often this will make craftwork too expensive to be readily salable, if salable at all. Thus many individuals soon discover they cannot afford to produce certain objects for sale.

No one has all the answers for the problem of how and where to buy raw materials and other craft supplies wholesale, but here are some helpful guidelines. First you must learn who makes or sells what you need. The logical place to begin is with trade magazines and directories, of which there are literally hundreds. Trade magazines are not found

25

on newsstands, but are available by subscription and often found in libraries. You would be wise to subscribe to several trade publications as your business grows, not only to gain industry insight and information, but to locate new suppliers, sales reps, and so on. (See the Resource Chapter of this book for selected trade periodicals of primary interest to craft producers.)

Before I go any farther, let me explain something that has confused craftspeople for years. You need to understand that there are *two types* of craft suppliers: those who will sell to homebased business owners, and those who won't. Most of those who won't are the major wholesalers and manufacturers in the craft supply industry who for years have traditionally sold *only* to store owners. For at least twenty years that I know of, craftspeople have been moaning about their inability to buy at wholesale from such suppliers, but this has had little effect on company policies. Until recently, that is.

Sponsors of the HIA shows (Hobby Industries of America) have *finally* acknowledged that craft designers and "converters of craft materials for the gift market" comprise a legitimate market that HIA has never officially recognized. Although such buyers no longer have to go through all sorts of machinations in order to gain entry to an HIA show, it is still up to individual exhibitors as to whether or not wholesale orders will be accepted from them.

Meanwhile, this problem is also being addressed by the publishers of *Craft Supply Report,* a quarterly trade magazine aimed specifically at the gift producer market. The February issue of this magazine is the annual *Craft Supply DIRECTO-RY,* which lists companies that have indicated an interest in selling wholesale to legitimate home-based craft businesses. Although some suppliers have set high minimum order requirements to discourage hobby sellers, this should not be a problem for serious craft businesses. The A-to-Z supply categories are similar to what one will find in other trade directories aimed at craft retailers, so it's easy enough to track down the specific suppliers needed. (See Resource Chapter.)

Another important industry guide is *Profitable Craft Merchandising,* a monthly trade magazine for craft supply shop owners. Each year, subscribers to this periodical receive an annual directory of all the manufacturers, wholesalers, publishers and trade organizations in the craft supply industry. While some of the suppliers in this directory may not sell to you, others will.

In addition to the craft industry suppliers mentioned above, there are thousands of other manufacturers and wholesalers in this country who will welcome your orders, provided you are a legitimate business with a resale tax number and can also meet their minimum order requirements. Many of these suppliers advertise in trade journals, or you can track them down by studying *Thomas' Register of American Manufacturers,* a directory available in most libraries. Its several volumes include a listing of products in alphabetical order with the names and addresses of companies who make them. In some cases, you may be able to buy directly from a manufacturer; in other cases, you will be referred to a dealer or jobber near you.

When writing for a company's wholesale catalog (which may cost $3-$4), it's important to type your letter on business stationery. You cannot hastily scrawl a hand-written note on yellow tablet paper and expect a supplier to believe you are a likely prospect for a good order.

If you find you cannot meet the high minimums required by some suppliers, check to see if the company sells through a dealer or jobber in your area. If your business is just too small to meet everyone's minimum requirements, ask your local craft or needlework supply shop if it can offer any kind of discount, should you decide to buy in quantity. But be sure to approach such shop owners as a crafts professional -- *not* as a crafts consumer. Telephone first to set up an appointment for a discussion of your needs.

When it comes to buying supplies, it may pay you to belong to an art, craft, or needlework guild, since membership in such organizations often provides special opportunities for obtaining supplies and materials at wholesale or discounted prices. If there are no organizations like this in your area, you might give some thought to forming a special cooperative organization in order to buy materials in bulk. (See Chapter 15 for the how-to's of this.)

Tracking down wholesale supply sources is one of the most frustrating jobs you will have, but you can do it. All it takes is time, patience, and an unending supply of stamps.

A final tip: Do not build a business around a single source of supply which might dry up or go out of business when you least expect it. Always leave yourself an escape route by having other supply sources in reserve.

- 4 -

What To Do When Your Work Won't Sell

"What do you do when your work is good, and still won't sell?" a beginning seller asked me one day. The question was not new to me, so I naturally had a few answers ready and waiting:

1. Make something else, or
2. Change your prices, or
3. Change the function of your product, or
4. Change the materials being used, or
5. Change your colors or designs, or
6. Change the name of your product.

Make Some Changes

Let's discuss the above suggestions one by one, as I did in my meeting with Pamela Milroy, owner of Global Designs. Our conversation, summarized below, may give you a few ideas that can be applied to your own selling problem, if indeed you have one at all.

First, let me describe Pamela's product. She makes Christmas ornaments using styrofoam balls, stainless steel pins, high quality glass beads, sequins, and velvet trims. She creates her own designs, which are basically geometric. In the beginning she was making huge ornaments the size of basketballs, reasoning that they would be great for display purposes in department stores, restaurants, and fancy shops. When Pam's grandmother saw them, however, she told her they wouldn't sell, and she was right. "I have to sell them for $75 each wholesale," says Pam, "and I realize now that no matter how much I enjoy making them, no one's going to pay that much for them."

When I suggested she make something else, Pam explained that simply wasn't the solution for her. She happens to like making this type of ornament and doesn't want to make anything else. (She

is fascinated by spherical shapes and enjoys working with the many beautiful beads and trims she uses.)

We agreed that her pricing logic was correct, so we proceeded to talk about the idea of making decorative home accessories (global-shaped, of course) that would be suitable for display all year long, instead of just during the holiday season. For example, not Christmas tree ornaments, but small sculptures perhaps, with her ornamented balls speared with a stainless steel rod and mounted on an appropriate base.

"But who would want glass-beaded ornaments with velvet ribbons sitting on their coffee table all year?" Pam asked, adding they would certainly be great dust catchers.

"Right," I agreed, "so why not think about changing your materials? Instead of glass beads, you could experiment with handmade ceramic beads or metal beads; instead of velvet ribbons, try metallic trims."

I also suggested that Pam give some thought to changing her colors and doing ethnic, rather than Christmas designs. Then we talked about how to create such designs when one is not an artist. (See end of this chapter.)

Finally, Pam and I discussed how a change of name can affect an item's salability. For example, you can get only so much money for a Christmas ornament, yet if you make something ornamental and call it *sculpture*, people will automatically pay more for it. And, sometimes, what you call yourself can affect the salability of your work. Or, as E. J. Tangerman, a well-known woodcarver, once said: "If you're a 'primitive' carver, you can charge three times what you would if you just admitted you are crude."

27

My interview with Pam ended on a high note. She had gained new perspective on her particular selling problem, and I had gained a new idea for my book. Later she told me she was concentrating on making regular-sized ornaments that could be wholesaled, and also experimenting with the idea of making mobiles from her smaller ornaments, a possibility that presented itself during our conversation.

Improve Your Marketing Strategy

If you have a selling problem, it may be necessary to change not only your product, but your marketing strategy. Perhaps you can learn from the experience of a woodcarver friend of mine.

In the early days of editing *Artisan Crafts* magazine, I was doing some whittling on the side and became acquainted with Dave Leitem, a fellow woodcarver from Pennsylvania. He really had selling problems. Like Pamela, Dave had great confidence in his craftsmanship, but was frustrated by his lack of ability to sell what he was making. We corresponded for some time and it became something of a personal challenge to resolve Dave's marketing problem.

Because he was so emotionally involved with his work, Dave couldn't see certain things that were evident to me, so I offered some suggestions that he considered, tried, and eventually profited

from. Some craftsmen go through life with their heads stuck in the sand, unable or unwilling to change anything, but not Dave. He experimented with different types of ads, wrote and rewrote price lists and brochures, and kept trying new techniques of selling at craft shows and approaching buyers. Eventually he achieved the success he so desired.

A newspaper article about Dave's latest accomplishments accompanied his last letter to me. His now-successful woodcarving business has been expanded to include the carving of candles, and his whole family works with him on this, much to his delight. With an annual income from crafts now substantial enough to support his family, Dave's new problem is no longer in selling, but in meeting the demand for his products. Now that's a problem any craftsman welcomes, and can solve for himself.

The right solution to a selling problem may be difficult to find. In addition to some of the things already discussed, you might consider changing your marketing outlet. If you are selling in shops, perhaps your product is better suited to sell at craft fairs, or vice versa. Or maybe you have a perfect mail-order product and just don't know it. Have you ever wondered why you can't buy the same things in a Sears store that you can buy in the catalog? Sears must have a good reason for selling certain items by mail and others by sight and sound and touch. Try to relate that reasoning to your product and see what happens.

Let me regress for a moment and return to a point I made earlier; namely, "make something else." Do you realize that the item most in vogue at the time is the one that is going to be hardest to sell? That is, if wooden toys, soft sculpture, or teddy bears are currently the most popular items being produced by hobbyists, you will probably have difficulty selling such crafts unless you are doing something entirely different from everyone else. If your aunt or your neighbor can make the same things you are making, why would they, or anyone else, need to buy them from you? Or, as one macrame artist puts it, "The secret to marketing any craft is constructing an item that few other people are willing to attempt."

Get A Good Gimmick

If you insist on making what everyone else is making, then, to sell, you must at least *do something different* with your craft to make it stand out from the crowd. In that case, perhaps a good gimmick will solve your selling problem.

A gimmick, according to Webster, is "an important feature that is not immediately apparent," or "a new and ingenious scheme or angle."

Every successful seller has a good gimmick, and it need not be cheap, faddish, scheming, deceitful, or tricky, as the word sometimes implies. The clever gimmick once used by a weaver I interviewed illustrates my point.

Bonny Cook Lowry used to have trouble selling her work, until she accidentally discovered *fur weaving*. When she found out that this type of weaving required nothing more than an ordinary loom and a second-hand fur coat, she decided to try it. "I was happily surprised that my very first pieces were salable and did sell immediately," Bonny recalls. "Suddenly I was being asked to demonstrate at craft fairs and to enter craft shows and special exhibitions. Then came the one-man shows."

Why? Because, quite accidentally, Bonny had developed a *good gimmick*. "When ecology became the resounding cry across the country," she said, "I thought sure the demand for articles woven of fur was doomed. Quite the contrary. Because I primarily use second-hand fur, people considered that I was recycling. Another unexpected gimmick." Bonny went on to write a book about her craft, illustrating once again how one thing always leads to another.

Gimmicks come in all forms, and Ruby Tobey discovered one that increased her sales considerably. Because she lives in Kansas and paints American scenes in blue, she calls her china painting "Kansas Delft." The name caught on and she can't keep enough painted because many people who collect genuine Delft or the Copenhagen Blue now buy her things to add to their collections. Ruby followed up on this idea by introducing a new line done in browns, called "Dirt Farmer's Delft." (Both names have been protected by trademarks.) As Ruby says, "It's coming across new ideas like these that makes working fun." And it's good gimmicks like these that put additional cash into one's pocket!

Sandy Mooney accidentally discovered her gimmick while demonstrating batik at a local fair. She was then making charming character dolls, pillows, scarves, aprons, and "whatever else I could think up that could be translated into batik." One customer, amused by her colorful display of life-sized stuffed batik dolls remarked, "They're great, but you should make some of them into hookers." Sandy thought that sounded like fun, so she made one a few weeks later. "For some reason," she said, "she looked like the great grandmother of all the madams instead of the beautiful sexy gal that I had in mind. Someone bought her (perhaps as a gift for a grandfather) and after several more tries, I finally came up with a good-looking sexy lady."

One of Sandy Mooney's "Ladies of the Evening."

Sandy went on to include several naughty ladies in her slide presentations for fair jurying, and without question, these unusual "Ladies of the Evening" played an important role in helping her gain a reputation as a professional craftswoman.

The unique gimmick used by tinsmith Horman Foose illustrates the old saying, "Necessity is the mother of invention." The Pennsylvania Dutch have a wonderful taste treat called funnel cakes, a fried pastry sprinkled with powered sugar. To make it, a special batter is poured into a funnel while the bottom is kept closed with one finger. Then, placing the filled funnel over a skillet of hot oil, the batter is quickly released and spiraled outward from the center to form a flat, circular cake that's served hot. But just any old funnel won't do -- the hole must be a particular size, and a handle on the funnel is also required for efficiency. And Horman Foose makes and sells that special funnel, including

29

the recipe for funnel cakes along with it. Of course, the funnel is just one of dozens of items in his line, but it is his gimmick nonetheless. Whenever possible, Horman and his wife, Maria, demonstrate two crafts at once: She makes and sells the cakes, and he makes and sells the funnels. (And to taste a hot funnel cake is to want the recipe and the special handcrafted utensil it requires.)

Action is often the most important quality of a clever gimmick, and a good "spiel" delivered with flourish will often sell more crafts than superb craftsmanship. Remember, in order to sell, one must first capture the attention of the buyer. Blacksmith Harry Houpt certainly knows how to do that. I met Harry when he was demonstrating at the annual Kutztown Folk Festival in Pennsylvania. He always drew large crowds with his rhythmic "musical anvil," which he played with a hammer before fanning the forge and demonstrating his blacksmithing skills. Then he would make a miniature horseshoe (a good gimmick in itself), all the while talking about life and the lessons it holds for all of us. Everyone would listen, especially the children, one of whom would be the lucky recipient of the newly-created horseshoe.

Bill Reed, a quiet-spoken fellow from West Virginia, built his successful woodcarving business bye developing a delightful line of rocking horses. Actually, they weren't horses at all, but fanciful mules, cows, buffaloes, giraffes, and other critters such as a rocking duck and a log hog. Cleverly displayed in a rail-fence corral, these handcarved animals always drew a great deal of attention at a show. But an even greater number of prospective buyers were lured to Bill's stand whenever he brought his "big beast" to the show with him. This was a wonderful rocking mule that stood almost six feet high, and anyone who thought he could mount the magnificent monster was cordially invited to climb aboard and have a picture taken. True, people often left Bill's exhibit empty-handed since not everyone had a need for a rocking animal, but they never left without a wonderful memory that would be shared with friends, thus providing splendid worth-of-mouth advertising for a modest woodcarver who seldom tooted his own horn.

As Bonny Lowry reminds us, "Gimmicks are great for publicity. They stir the imagination of the customer. Just as fingerprints set each individual apart, but do not make the person, gimmicks set apart similar crafts, but do not make the craft. It still takes the craftsman."

When crafts editor Sybil Harp saw Bill Reed's giant rocking horse at a crafts fair, she decided to accept his invitation to "mount up" and have her photograph taken. This is the artist's version of that photograph.

30

Gimmicks will never replace fine craftsmanship, but they can certainly increase sales. With a little imaginative thinking on your part, you can probably come up with a good gimmick that will boost your sales. Don't be afraid to experiment with this idea as well as the other suggestions in this chapter.

Develop Creativity and Design Ability

Your craftsmanship may be superior, but if your designs are poor (or worse, copied from other craft sellers) you may experience difficulty in selling, particularly to established shops and stores. Sophisticated buyers can spot copied designs and kit products a mile away. If you are serious about selling, don't waste your time copying the designs of others. Create your own and be done with it.

What? You say you're just not that creative? Nonsense. You may not be an artist, true, but there is a streak of creativity and artistry in each of us. In fact, creativity may be merely the discovery of something that's been there all along. Perhaps you ought to think more like Oscar Wilde, who once said "An artist is not a special sort of man, every man is a special sort of artist."

You *can* learn to apply your natural creativity to your crafts or needlework, and here are a few tips to get you started. The first thing you must do to sharpen your sense of creativity and design is develop a "seeing eye." In other words, don't just *look* at something, really try to *see* it. I'm sure that in the past you've looked at clouds and seen something in their formations, such as an animal or a tree, but have you ever really seen the intricate patterns in a seashell, the veins in a leaf, or the interesting design on your window as the setting sun casts a shadow of bare branches?

Designs are everywhere for the taking. You need only train your eyes to see them. Why, one winter morning I looked out the window and saw, sticking to a tree, a clump of snow that looked exactly like the face of a pompous old woman. She had a double chin, a pointed nose, and a mop of hair so amusing I had to sketch her quick before she melted. (My husband thought I was a bit daft, of course, since he couldn't see a thing.)

Another day, while baking cookies, I noticed the design my electric beaters left in the dough and saw not cookies but a "kookie" owl perched on a branch, surrounded by swirling leaves. The cookie baking had to wait until I captured this rare bird on paper for a future piece of needlework. The interesting thing about these designs (shown at right) is that I couldn't have created them without the help of an outside spark of nature. I'm just not an artist, you see.

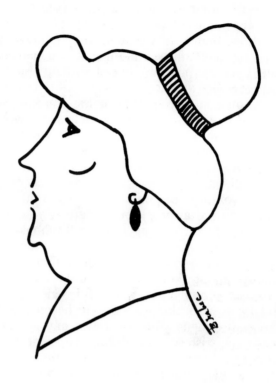

Above, "Snow Lady" design captured by the author one morning during breakfast. She was hiding in the guise of a clump of snow on a nearby tree, patiently waiting to be found by someone with a "seeing eye."

Below, an owl who suddenly swirled into the author's view as the electric beaters came out of a batch of cookie dough.

31

Try capturing a few designs of your own some day. It's not as difficult as you might believe. All of us drew things as children, and although your drawing may still be child-like, it is nonetheless a talent you can use and, like everything else, it will improve with practice.

You won't see anything unless you really look, and ideas won't come to you unless you work to get them, so it may be necessary for you to study some design books to get started on the road to creativity. (Any library will have books on design that will help you unlock your artistic talents.)

If you need inspiration for designs other than what you see around you in nature, you will be delighted to learn there are literally thousands of copyright-free designs available to you today, and you don't have to visit a museum to find them. I'm talking about the amazing world of the *Dover Pictorial Archives,* a wonderful series of high-quality paperbacks, each of which contains hundreds of designs you can use in any manner or place you wish, without further payment, permission, or acknowledgement. If you claim you "can't draw a straight line," you'll really appreciate these books, and you'll soon discover that you *can* add your own ideas to a design or pattern created by someone else. Remember that every artist through the ages has studied the work of others for inspiration and ideas, often lifting or adapting the best ideas of someone else for his own use. You can too.

There is an increasing interest these days in ethnic designs, and the Pictorial Archive books offer a real treasure of usable patterns, ideas, and authentic motifs from many cultures, such as the American Indian, Japanese, Chinese, African, Mexican, Russian and East European, North African, Egyptian, and so on. There are also books on American folk art, flora and fauna, geometric design and ornament, and Art Deco.

Here's how to use design books like this in an imaginative way. Study their overall content, then select several motifs or ideas you like. Next, consider how you might mix, match, or blend one or more in an unusual arrangement or design, and don't hesitate to make changes in the process. Before long you will find that you have created a design of your own. It's important to remember that the designs suggested for one medium are often perfectly suited to others; thus one person's "original" macrame hanging may actually have been inspired by an ancient Egyptian weaving or ceramic pot, and a colorful quilt pattern may have been lifted from an unusual stained glass window somewhere in Europe. Many is the time I've looked through a book labeled "For Needleworkers" and seen remarkable designs that could just as easily be used by rugmakers, handweavers, mosaicists and decorative painters, to name just a few. In turn, designs on ancient ceramic pots, Indian baskets and African masks (all neatly captured for you in the Pictorial Archive books) lend themselves beautifully to needlework and a variety of crafts such as jewelry, papier mache, woodcarving, weaving, macrame, beadcraft, etc.

In summary, to become more creative you must first open your mind to the possibilities, and the best way to do this is *to open a few books.* See the Resource Chapter to order the Dover books, and in the meantime, give some thought to this idea, suggested by an unknown poet: "The universe is full of magical things patiently waiting for our wits to grow sharper."

NOTE: For more information about what makes a design "original," refer to "Getting Designs and Ideas Published" in Chapter 9.

Illustration opposite page: Examples of copyright-free art from the Dover Pictorial Archives, taken from the following books:

(A) Art Nouveau Floral Ornament In Color
(B) Designs from Pre-Columbian Mexico
*(C) Russian Peasant Design Motifs
    for Needleworkers & Craftsmen*
(D) Japanese Design Motifs
(E) Early American Design Motifs

A

B

C

D

E

33

Country Crafts
Shop

34

- 5 -

Putting Your Home To Work For You

Perhaps you'd like to have a shop of your own but just can't afford the large investment required to open a retail establishment. In that case, you might give some thought to starting a shop in your own home. Many people have done this successfully on a temporary or permanent basis, beginning with a very small outlay of cash. Later I will discuss the legal aspects of having a shop in your home but, for now, read the following success stories to discover some good ideas that may work for you.

Before starting any kind of home shop or business, you ought to give some honest thought to this question, posed by Ginny Wise: "If big money profits do not materialize, will there be other satisfactions that will make it worth the time and effort?"

Home Gift Shops

Ginnie is a busy farm homemaker who has had a gift shop in her home for several years. Called Wises-on-High-Banks, it is filled with nature crafts made by Ginnie and her husband Ernie, a plumber by trade. The Wises' 240-acre farm in Ohio is their "raw materials factory" since it contains 65 acres of river bottom that floods yearly, yielding many pieces of driftwood each spring. This driftwood, and other wood weathered by the elements and gathered from the ravines and hillsides, is combined with dried mosses, wayside grasses, pods, and rocks to make a variety of natural gift items for their shop.

Although the shop is located off the beaten track, it still attracts its share of customers. The rustic beauty of the surrounding countryside often lures shoppers to its door, and of course the Wises advertise regularly and have a good brochure. In addition to exhibiting and selling at fairs and shows, the Wises invite various clubs to hold their meetings in their home. Afterwards, Ginnie gives a little talk about the farm, shows some of her craft work, and invites her visitors to browse in the shop before they leave.

35

Do the Wises consider their home business a success? "Yes," says Ginnie, "but our success has not necessarily been in terms of making money. It is more in terms of *saving* money, in that when we go to art and crafts shows this is our vacation, so we have a paid vacation with possibly some profit in it, too. We save money by having an avocation that more than pays for itself; it saves in that it substitutes for an active club and social life, and since craft work can be good therapy, I suppose one could say that it possibly saves on medical bills as well. More important, however, is the return I've had in terms of newfound self-worth, along with the ego-stroking that most of us need from time to time. The enjoyable friendships and acquaintances we have made through our craft is another good return on our investment. And, of course, ranking right up at the top would be the added sense of togetherness and closeness that my husband and I have realized as we have worked and traveled with our craft."

Dreams can, and do, become a reality for those who are not afraid to try. The Wises know that, and so does Miriam Fankhauser, another homemaker who always wanted a shop of her own. In fact, she had its name (and her first daughter's name) picked out long before she was married. Her mother's love of dolls started it all.

"I think I never quite outgrew dolls," says Miriam. "At any rate, I started making them, and when I began to shop for my baby girl, I realized I could design and make dolls that were more durable and beautiful than any I could buy."

One thing led to another, and Miriam finally opened her "House of Pearl" shop in the basement of her home. "I had a corner of collectible fashion cloth dolls, three styles of doll heads, a few toys, and several other items," she recalls. "In 2-1/2 years, the shop grew from a 10 x 12 foot area to a 10 x 40 foot showroom, with muslin and felt dolls, pin cushion dolls, a larger selection of children's toys, and a variety of doll furniture, including swings, highchairs, rocking and swinging cradles, canopy beds, and toy boxes." Miriam hired a craftsman to do all the woodcutting, but she did all the sewing herself. "While my success is not yet guaranteed, I have no doubt I am going to do exactly what I have set out to accomplish."

Miriam taught school for 7-1/2 years but, having resolved not to teach while her children were growing, she became a "complete homemaker" after her first daughter was born. Still, she is a woman with an alert mind that must be constantly challenged and this, plus her interest in dolls and designing (she is also a certified interior decorator), just naturally led her to start her own business. Miriam's positive attitude reflects the feelings of

many talented and ambitious homemakers today who have recognized that they *do* have certain creative abilities, and *do* have what it takes to meet a new challenge head-on. Philosophizing, Miriam sums it up like this:

"There are many things I am still trying to resolve, but I know this: When we venture into something new, we must not become discouraged, we must love what we are doing, and we must want what we are doing badly enough to keep trying until we realize our goals." With enthusiasm she adds, "God bless every homemaker who dares to venture from her four walls, her TV serials, and her boredom into a world of unlimited horizons."

One of the most interesting and amazing success stories I uncovered in my research for this book was that of Carol Ann Bernier. Married to Emery Bernier, a noted stained glass artist-craftsman, Carol is the mother of three children. The Bernier family lives in a wonderfully big house in Wentworth, New Hampshire that serves as both home and shop. Called The Bernier Studio, it boasts 10 rooms, of which five are devoted to the works of more than 150 artists and craftsmen. There is also a book store, an antique shop, a gourmet room, and a women's clothing boutique.

Carol is currently managing The Bernier Studio and often travels the country in search of unique handcrafts and gifts. She also lectures on the art and technique of stained glass windows, as well as on crafts and craftspeople in America. She is the author of *Stained Glass*, and her articles have been published in leading trade magazines.

She is also a member of several business organizations and the president of one, as well as treasurer of the Wentworth Women's Club and president of her high school alumnae association. On top of all this, Carol somehow manages to remain a contented, well-organized homemaker whose house is as neat and uncluttered as her shops. "The one rule we have in our house," she says, "is NO CLUTTER. No one can leave anything lying around, whether it's school books, toys, or clothes. This is an indispensable rule for the working mother. It lifts your spirit. Without clutter, a house always seems to look clean, even when you know that up on that third shelf you could probably write your name in the dust."

It seemed improbable to me that a high school graduate who began her business career as a bank teller and secretary could have accomplished so much, so quickly, in a field so unrelated to what she had been trained to do. "How were you able to do it?" I asked, and in a fascinating nine-page letter I wish I could quote in full, she told me. Perhaps Carol's story will help you realize your own potential for success.

It all started with her husband, Emery. Employed for 13 years as a stained glass artist for a Boston firm, he had often talked about starting his own business, but just didn't want to make that break from a steady income to "maybe's," as Carol called it. Once, while browsing in a small gift shop, the Berniers saw some cheap Mexican stained glass window mobiles, and Carol decided then and there that if those things would sell, Emery's superb work should sell easily. But he wasn't convinced.

"I decided I had to step in," Carol recalls. "I took a few days off work and experimented myself. I'm no artist, but I drew a star, a tulip, a candle, and a small heart, then proceeded to put into practice all I had watched Emery do during the three years we'd been married. I cut the glass (crudely), got lead around it, soldered, and there they were. Oh well. But they were as good as the Mexican stuff. Nothing compared to what Emery would have produced, but I had hounded him enough. He had to be convinced they would sell, and if he wouldn't do it, I would."

With shaky knees and shallow breath, Carol entered her first gift shop trying to look very businesslike. She didn't even know about markups, but when she walked out of that shop she had an order, and that was the start of The Bernier Studio. Emery than had the push he needed and together they started to build their business, with Emery producing, and Carol out looking for buyers. Eventually, Carol talked Emery into leaving his steady job and working on his own.

After a couple of good years, and the birth of one child, Carol started thinking of her own shop. "Why not?" she thought. "Other shops sell our stained glass; let's sell our own." They attempted a shop in their home, but felt the "vibration of the town selectmen," so they decided to move. It was then that they found their current house in Wentworth which, coincidentally, had been used as an antique shop by the former owner. "Antiques?" thought Carol, her curiosity aroused once again. "What a wonderful thing to sell!"

Although she knew nothing about antiques, except for the few auctions and flea markets she had attended, her business sense told her that the woman who had lived there before surely had some steady customers who would be coming back for antiques, so she'd better have some for sale. With her usual determination, she proceeded to learn the antiques business and soon became a self-taught expert. (She stayed away from expensive items, starting with bowl and pitcher sets, cups, china, and small woodenware.) "It was fun, interesting, and challenging," Carol told me, "and, actually, I did very well."

Another two years passed successfully for the Berniers, and soon Carol, ever the adventurer, felt an urge to expand a bit. "Why not handcrafted gifts?" she mused, thinking they would fit in well with their handcrafted glass. Off she went in search of craftspeople. Then she heard about gift shows. "Maybe there might be something there," she told herself, and sure enough, she discovered several gift lines that worked well with the crafted items. She even found some new craftsmen being represented at these shows. Eventually the lines grew and Emery had to stop creating stained glass from time to time to take up hammer and nails and open another section of the house or barn.

In time, Carol decided to try selling women's apparel. As usual, she started very small, offering a total of 40 dresses in assorted sizes plus a few blouses and skirts. To her amazement they sold rapidly. Once again Carol considered the possibilities. "Why not?" she thought. "Let's really get into it. Expand. Transform another section into an adaptable room and stock it with women's apparel."

Naturally, Carol has done well in this area, like all the others, because she is sensible and has a good head for business. But she admits that buying clothing is quite different from buying gifts and crafts. "There's a lot to learn," she says, with a warning to all aspiring business people that boils down to this: ASK QUESTIONS. "Never hesitate about asking questions," she advises, "and then listen -- really concentrate -- on what is being said. And see, don't just look. Absorb as much as you can. It's amazing, the wealth of knowledge that can be gained by just noticing things and people."

Like all people in business, the Berniers have had a few failures along the way. But, as Carol says, "In the long run everything we did or attempted to do has been an education. We feel we are better prepared for what the future may bring because of all the things we have gotten involved in to date."

I asked if they had any advice to pass along to those starting new businesses, and got these do's and don't's from them:

• Make the most of your time
• Be organized
• Keep your studio or workshop clean and orderly
• Keep good records
• Don't overextend yourself financially
• Don't borrow money thinking you'll sell or do very well
• Don't talk yourself into a project by looking at only the good, and overlooking the bad.

What I found especially interesting about Carol's success story was the fact that her primary goal in the beginning was not to become a success herself, but to help her husband achieve recognition. "Very few people have Emery's talent and qualifications," she told me. "I knew what he could do. I was and am very proud of him and his skill, and I wanted people to know about my special husband. He just wouldn't blow his own horn, so someone had to do it for him. Who was better qualified than I, his wife?"

As a postscript to this story, I want to tell you how this energetic gal copes with life and "gets it all together." As determined and self-confident as she is, even Carol has her "downs." But she knows how to get over them, and other women might do well to follow her lead when they find themselves ready to throw in the towel.

"If I really hit a stumbling block," says Carol, "a good outburst of emotions -- alone -- really helps. That includes having a good cry. It might seem foolish, but expressing how disappointed I am in the outcome of a situation by getting angry with myself and crying, has always worked very well for me. I tell myself, 'Carol, you are failing. Go ahead and cry and be angry with yourself. Get it out of your system, then get up and fight back. There must be something you overlooked, so find it!'"

Right on, Carol!

Holiday Boutiques

If the idea of a permanent shop in your home is not desirable, or even possible, perhaps the idea of a temporary shop, such as a holiday boutique, would appeal to you. Here are several examples of boutiques and craft sales that different women have operated in their homes with considerable success. (Additional information about this topic appears in *Creative Cash's* companion book, *Crafts Marketing Success Secrets*, listed in the Resource Chapter.)

One-day Christmas boutiques are now quite common all over the country. For this book, I interviewed a group in the Chicagoland area to learn more about the boutique they have presented for several years. The spokesperson for this group said that she is one of six women who plan and organize the sale, which until recently has been held in a different woman's house each year. She said they simply divide the various jobs to be done and share in any expense involved. For example, one will handle the bookkeeping, another the distribution of flyers in the neighborhood, a third will mail announcements to their mailing list, and so on.

That mailing list, by the way, is the group's most valuable possession, and the real key to their continued success. In the beginning, they asked all visitors to sign a guest book with their names and addresses, but later found this wasn't necessary since most buyers paid by check and they could just as easily take the addresses from the checks before they were deposited. A file card is made for each buyer, and each year's purchases are noted. (Since many of the buyers on the group's choice mailing list make annual purchases in amounts as high as $80, these names are like gold to the craftswomen involved.)

Total sales have increased steadily through the years, partly because new items are offered each year. In time, this group decided to hold its show in a local church, rather than in one of the women's homes. After so many years of having home shows, the women who started this had literally "had it" and decided to go the church route from that point on. Although new sellers will be allowed to exhibit in the future, this particular group is reluctant to bring any new women into their "working nucleus," for various reasons. Rather than ask anyone else to share the responsibility and expense of the show with them, they will simply charge a small exhibitor's fee in the future.

In considering your home as a possible "one-day shop," do consider how this activity may disrupt normal family living, and think about such things as traffic patterns, both in the house and on the street. There is also the matter of the legality of it all, which seems to fall into a mysterious "grey area." Since people everywhere are doing this sort of thing, the question of whether it's legal or not doesn't seem to matter to most. It often seems to depend on the kind of neighborhood you live in, the type of neighbors you have, and how strictly

local laws are enforced. My advice is to check into the matter carefully before you make definite plans to hold such a sale in your home.

If local officials don't know what a "holiday boutique" is, you might compare your event to a garage sale that is held once a year for a short period of time. One boutique owner I interviewed told me about a particular problem she encountered when she began to check into the legalities of home shows. The lawyer she contacted told her that as long as she used a private invitation and served only cookies and punch, such a sale in her home would be within the law. But she decided to go one step further. "Since I hold an occupational license to make and sell my crafts and greeting cards, I decided to get a final word from the zoning folks who issued the license," she told me. "Am I ever glad I did! I learned that, in Caddo Parish in Louisiana, a home sale is totally against the law, and if I had been caught holding such an event, I would have lost my business license. I can hold such a sale anywhere else (a public building), but not in my home."

The thing to remember here is that laws are different from city to city, so it's always wise to ask city officials before proceeding with such an event. Remember, too, that even if such an event is legal, it takes only one complaint from a neighbor to close you down. That's why most people planning this type of event make it a point to first check with their neighbors, extending them a special invitation to attend the gala event, and telling them there will be a lot of cars parked on the street that day.

Turning your house, or that of a friend's, into a one-day Christmas shop will most likely prove to be profitable the first year, and even more profitable each time the event is repeated in the future. That's because such events quickly develop a following of interested buyers who tend to return each year with new friends in tow.

Everyone I've ever talked to about holiday boutiques also emphasizes the "fun aspect" of such an event. Who wouldn't have fun arranging and displaying beautiful gifts and decorative accessories in a home boutique? The addition of little extras, such as homemade cookies and cinnamon-orange tea brewing in the kitchen, will make the day even more enjoyable for everyone involved.

39

If you can't arrange a group sale, don't be afraid to try this idea by yourself, especially if you have a good supply of merchandise to sell. Your one-day sale could even be held in the evening, and need be nothing more elaborate than setting up a special room as your display area and inviting a few friends over for coffee and Christmas craft

Planning to turn your living room into a holiday boutique for a day or more? If so, this illustration provides some ideas on how a variety of crafts might be arranged around your regular furniture. If an Easter boutique is preferred, the Christmas tree could be replaced with a gold-painted tree branch hung with Easter Eggs.

shopping. I started selling in just this way, inviting about a dozen friends over one evening early in December. To my surprise, I sold almost $100 worth of crafts, and that gave me all the encouragement I needed to walk into a local shop soon afterward to show the owner what I had to sell.

Carol Reeves, a macrame artist and teacher, had 15 shows in her California home before she discontinued them. "I simply lost interest in doing them," she said. But Carol's regular customers missed her shows so much that she finally decided to have another boutique after all.

In the past, Carol's boutiques have been similar in nature to the one already discussed, except for the fact that she managed them by herself and generally had two-day sales twice a year. Her shows were presented in May, just before Mother's Day, and in November, in time for the Christmas season. Occasionally, she also had a summer boutique, or a "Mini-Boutique" just before

Christmas. These were usually held on a Friday and Saturday afternoon from noon to 4 p.m. "It was fun," says Carol. "We served refreshments, and the boutiques always had the air of a party."

Carol always invited several other craft sellers to participate with her, selecting those whose products complemented her macrame work. "Sellers brought their work to my house on Thursday and I arranged it throughout my living room and dining room, and on the patio in warm weather," she said. "Individual sellers marked their own items with the retail price. For my effort, I kept 20 percent of the price of items sold."

Part of that amount helped defray Carol's expense of invitations, postage, and refreshments. The remainder was profit. Naturally, Carol advertised her shows locally and sent out invitations to prospective buyers. Her mailing list numbers more than 400 names, but she estimates that only a quarter of those invited each year will actually come.

Ruby Tobey has an interesting variation on the theme of home boutiques. Once a year, usually in the third week of November, she has a week-long open house in her basement but, unlike Carol, she sells only her own work. She can do this because she produces a variety of items, including a unique line of china painting, an annual calendar with poetry she writes herself, and note papers printed with her drawings. Like the other women I've discussed, Ruby also has a good mailing list of interested buyers, and she advertises in the local paper. (Of the 500 names on Ruby's mailing list, she estimates that about a quarter will actually attend, which coincides with what Carol Reeves reported. This, then, would seem to be a good figure to remember when estimating the number of buyers you might expect for your event.)

What are the advantages of an open-house boutique? Ruby said her sales are always good, but more important, the boutique gives her a chance to get to know people better -- people she might not meet otherwise. She enjoys having the undivided attention of her customers, too. "This is the one time all year that the audience is all mine -- not shared with others as it is as a craft show." And with a chuckle Ruby adds, "Probably the best thing about my open house is that we get the basement cleaned really well once a year."

Bonny Cook Lowry and her mother, Bessie Cook, are certainly pros when it comes to running a Christmas shop in their home because they did this every year for ten years in their Bainbridge Island home in Washington. Called "The Country Craftsmen," the shop was discontinued with sadness when Bonny and her mother moved to Long Beach, where they opened a year-round shop by the same name. (Bonny, you'll recall, is the enterprising fur weaver you met in the preceding chapter.)

"We made and gathered for our show all year long," says Bonny, "and we also displayed the works of many other craftspeople." Unlike Ruby's open house, however, their shop was open for two months, and occupied half the house. Their clever use of folding screens, collapsible shelves, and tables made it possible for them to make interesting and unusual displays, and their shop was a welcome event to the local residents each year.

As you can see, there are many variations on the theme of home boutiques. Since there are no hard-and-fast rules here, your event will be special simply because you are a unique individual with good ideas of your own. This is the kind of home-based business that can only grow more profitable with each passing year, so "go with the flow!"

If zoning laws permit the hanging of a sign in a window of your home, you might wish to design one that emphasizes your particular skills or the products you wish to sell. This macrame teaching sign suggests one way this can be done.

Teaching in Your Home

Any creative person with a flair for teaching and an extra room, basement, or garage, could easily turn that space into an income-producing area by starting an arts and crafts class or workshop. I'll be talking more about teaching in general in another chapter, but for now, I want to tell you about Carol Reeves' approach to teaching in her home.

"Most of my teaching has been at home around the kitchen table, and these classes have been fun for everyone," she says. "Initially I advertised in the local papers, but most people have found me by word of mouth."

Carol sets aside one night a week for her classes, and occasionally her studio becomes a "field trip" for other macrame classes in the community. Instructors from the junior college, the

41

school district adult education program, and the city parks and recreation department bring their students to see her work, buy the macrame supplies she sells, and perhaps learn a new knot or two.

"I like to teach people individually," Carol explains, "assisting them at their level of expertise with the project of their choice. Whenever I have more than six or eight students, I have someone help me teach. There is a fee per class and students may purchase materials from me or bring their own." The casual atmosphere of Carol's classes makes it easy to make new friendships, and some of her students return every year.

Carol sells craft supplies to her students, as well as by mail order. The advantages of doing this are obvious. By acting as a dealer (buying craft supplies for resale), Carol gains in two ways: (1) she is able to buy her own materials in greater quantity and at lower prices than she would normally have to pay; and (2) she can realize a good profit (approximately 40 percent) on all the supplies she sells.

As was previously discussed, in order to buy at wholesale prices, you need a business name, a resale tax number, and a professional image. But, even without these things, as a teacher you may find that many suppliers will at least offer you a special studio discount of 10 percent or more.

Obviously, not everyone is qualified to be a teacher, and even those who are may have no desire to teach. But it cannot be denied that teaching is an excellent way for a talented and creative woman to earn extra money in the comfort of her own home. In addition, teaching often serves as a springboard to other interesting sideline activities, such as lecturing or demonstrating one's art or craft -- topics I will soon be discussing in greater detail.

The Party Plan

Have you ever attended a Tupperware Party? If so, you already know what party plans are all about. This method of selling works well for handcrafts, as Joan McGovern explains.

"Basically, I take my samples and catalog into people's homes, present them, and take orders," says Joan, who had this idea a long time before starting her business, The Final Touch. "My husband talked me out of it at first, but I kept turning it over in my mind, becoming more and more fascinated by the idea. I finally decided I had nothing to lose except time, so I tried it."

Joan has been involved in crafts for as long as she can remember, but only in the past few years has she started to market anything. After selling for a while, she decided that selling her own crafts was just not interesting enough. "I wanted to get more involved in the craft world," she said, "and market other crafts besides my own."

Financially, a shop was out of the question, but Joan reasoned that if clothing, jewelry, and kitchen items could be sold through the party plan, why not crafts? After months of searching for just the right crafts to sell, Joan asked various craftspeople to send a sample of each item they wanted her to market for them, plus a color photograph and all pertinent information as to sizes, colors, etc. (She found everyone willing to do this, by the way, although some did not have photographs to send, and she had to take a few pictures herself.) With the color photos, she then made up a catalog which she knew would be necessary since she couldn't carry everything with her when she went into homes.

At this point she had everything she needed to start selling -- except a place to go. (Exposure was, and still is, a problem for Joan who says, "Who has ever heard of The Final Touch?") Of course, Joan started where all beginning sellers seem to start -- with friends. Eventually she arranged a number of bookings and also found a demonstrator who began to give parties for her. Together, the two women worked outward from their combined circle of friends, and Joan's business began to grow.

In presenting her parties, Joan follows the basic concept of the party-plan type of selling in that she first finds a hostess who will volunteer the use of her home and provide both guests and refreshments. Then Joan, as the demonstrator, presents her line of crafts and gives her demonstration -- usually a talk about the people who make the crafts, or any interesting techniques that may be involved. Afterwards, the guests are invited to examine the merchandise on display and place orders for what they want. (Note: Guests do not pay at this time, but rather when the merchandise is delivered.)

Joan explains that there may be variations between the sample and the item people will receive, pointing out that no two handmade items will ever be exactly the same. And, she tells them that it may take four to six weeks to receive orders, since craftspeople will be making each individual item to order. Joan's hostess receives a small gift (usually something Joan has made herself) plus a 10 percent credit on sales (payable in gift merchandise, not cash). Joan also gives additional credit to the hostess if future bookings are realized as a direct result of the demonstration in her home.

The continued success of this type of selling depends, of course, on being able to continually find new hostesses who will bring in new guests to buy the merchandise. Even more important to

*Women who enjoy meeting new people and talking about handcrafts
would find party-plan selling an enjoyable way to earn money.*

Joan, who wants to expand to other states, is to find reliable and competent demonstrators from all areas of the country.

After each party, Joan sends the orders out and the craftspeople ship the items directly to her as soon as possible. When everything is received, she delivers the order to the hostess who, in turn, is responsible for getting the items to the individual buyers and collecting payment. When Joan receives full payment, she pays the craftspeople. She told me that this has always gone smoothly for her, even though she works primarily with people she has never met personally.

"One problem I foresaw, which never came to pass, was unreliability on the part of craftspeople to meet deadlines, but everyone has been more than cooperative, and all orders have been filled satisfactorily and on time. In fact, in most cases we exchange little personal notes as the orders go back and forth, and I find I am dealing with a wonderful group of people."

If you like the concept of the party plan, you have two alternatives. You could consider becoming a demonstrator for one of the commercial craft party plan companies who regularly advertise in national magazines, or set up your own operation. But remember that it takes *work*, not only to

43

organize such a business, but also to find reliable craftspeople who will be able to fill the orders you take. How did Joan find her suppliers?

First she located a directory of professional craft sellers (see the Resource Chapter for such directories currently known to the author), and sent many letters explaining her plan. Then she placed an ad in a major crafts magazine, which brought an overwhelming response. She was thus able to find several good craft items to add to her line. Between periods of letter writing, Joan also went to many craft fairs, often finding one or more new craftspeople at each show who were interested in working with her. When I interviewed Joan for this book, she was selling the products of more than 50 craftspeople. "I'll always be searching for new crafts because I will always need new items to show established customers in the future," she says.

How much money can be made with the party plan method? This will vary greatly depending on (1) the kind and price of merchandise being offered for sale; (2) your own sales ability (demonstrating is easy; skillful *selling* takes practice); and (3) the number of people in attendance. Joan says it takes at least ten people to make a sales demonstration profitable for her.

One of the best things about starting your own party plan business is that it requires a small outlay of cash at the beginning. Joan's only expenses were for photos, albums, ads in local papers, business cards, order blanks, and "lots and lots of stamps and stationery."

Don't overlook the fun aspect of this kind of business, either. "My demonstrations are usually on a week night," says Joan, "so my husband stays home with the children. It gets me out of the house to meet new people, talk about my favorite topics, have cake and coffee, and have a good time in general."

Home shops, holiday boutiques, teaching workshops, and party-plan selling can all be fun and profitable, but maybe you'd rather keep your home life a bit more serene and do your selling elsewhere -- perhaps at the fair? It has a special lure of its own, and it's certainly a great way to break into the crafts business with a minimum of splash. (Which means you can get your feet wet without committing the rest of yourself.)

Beginning sellers will find in the next chapter a vivid description of the many pleasures and possibilities of craft fair selling, while seasoned show-goers will discover some tips and ideas on how to increase sales.

Update on Businesses Mentioned in This Chapter

To illustrate how things change, here are a few notes about some of the people who contributed to this chapter:

• **Ruby Tobey** says her goals have changed some since she was interviewed for this book. She still presents her open houses (in 1990, she was planning her 23rd annual sale) and sells at fairs, but her main concern in recent years has been to become more professional about her business. "When I started out to be an artist, I did not realize it must be a business, too, so I have learned to be my own tax person, bookkeeper, public relations person, promoter, etc. -- in addition to learning how to be a better painter." Ruby is also teaching these days, and writing articles for the painting magazines.

• Several years after I interviewed **Miriam Fankhauser,** she wrote to say she had returned to substitute teaching on a regular basis, putting her business on the back burner. "We stretch only so far," she said. "I love it all and have lots of energy, but there are limits, and at the moment my business is being sacrificed. As our lives take turns, we must turn with it."

• I've lost touch with **Joan McGovern, Carol Reeves, Bonny Cook Lowry** and **Ginnie Wise,** all of whom moved without notifying me of their new address. If you happen to know any of these women, ask them to get in touch. I'd love to have updates for the next printing of this book. (I did hear through the grapevine that Ginnie closed her gift shop to become involved in other activities.)

• And **Carol Bernier?** When sales of crafts began to decline a few years ago, she branched out into a field that really boomed: weddings. She eventually opened a shop in a nearby town, offering a line of wedding dresses, accessories, and various personalized bridal services. Meanwhile, she continued to manage husband Emery's stained glass studio, selling his windows and restoration services. In her home shops, she carried a complete line of crafts, gifts, and books.

I could not reach Carol for a personal update, but I did track down the fellow who bought Emery Bernier's stained glass studio in 1984. He said that Carol and Emery had sold all their shops that year, and moved away to retire on the profits they'd made. As Paul Harvey would say, "Now you know the *rest* of the story."

Carol once told me that the secret to her success was her willingness to change with the times. As I see it, however, she achieved success because she always believed in herself, never gave in to her fears, and never let a lack of knowledge stop her from doing something of interest to her. She simply made it a point to learn what she needed to know, then proceeded accordingly.

- 6 -

The Lure of the Fair

I have a friend who has a successful husband and a profitable home business of her own, yet she works two days a week in a bookstore for the minimum hourly wage. For a long time I wondered why she did it since I knew she didn't need the money. When I asked her, she gave me a grin and this perfectly logical explanation: "Because I love books and people and all the nice things that can happen in a bookstore. Besides, I'm sick and tired of doing volunteer work, and this is my new lifeline with the outside world."

Many people sell at craft fairs (my friend included) for the same reason -- because they love crafts and people and all the wonderful things that can happen at a fair, which is their lifeline with the craft world. A good fair, festival, or show (call it what you will) is a joy for one and all because it offers so many opportunities to see, to touch, to learn, and to be entertained. Those who participate in shows go not just to sell their wares, but also to meet other creative people, to exchange information and ideas, to observe new techniques, and perhaps just to have a pleasant vacation away from their studios and workshops. In particular they enjoy the special pleasure that comes from selling something they have made themselves, and then seeing that pleasure reflected on a buyer's face.

Pleasures aside, there are several real advantages to craft fair selling. To begin with, fairs are the most profitable way for the majority of craftspeople to market their work. When you sell at a fair, you are selling direct to the consumer, which means you are also eliminating the "middle man" -- the shop owner who generally takes a 25 to 40 percent commission on consignment sales, the wholesale buyer who expects 50 percent off the retail price, or the sales representative who requires a 10 to 20 percent commission.

Fairs will also provide you with an excellent way to test prices, gain confidence in selling, and meet the kind of people who can help your business. In fact, the contacts made at a fair are often more valuable to craftspeople than sales themselves. For example, you might meet one or more shop owners who will want to carry your work, be given a commission to do some special job, catch the eye of a writer or photographer who will give you free publicity, or be invited to participate in other shows and events.

Another advantage is that many fairs and shows offer prize money or special awards that are important to a craft seller's ego or reputation.

Professionals and hobbyists alike share similar advantages in craft fair selling, but when they also share tables or booths in the same show, there's bound to be some incompatibility. Like oil and water, craft professionals and amateur craft sellers don't mix well. For this reason, many of the better shows today are juried. "Juried" simply means that certain standards have been established for each show, and hopeful exhibitors must meet those standards to be accepted into the show. As a seller, however, the most important thing is not just that your work be up to the standards required for a particular show, but that the show itself meets *your* requirements.

Entering shows on a hit-or-miss basis can be a total waste of time, financially speaking, so it's wise to enter juried shows whenever possible, or at least have a clear understanding of the type of work that will be exhibited in any show you plan to enter. Simply ask yourself, "Is my work in the same category?" Of course, the standards committee of a juried show may sometimes answer that question for you by refusing to accept your work for exhibit and sale, but in that event, it's decidedly to your advantage. What's the sense in exhibiting in a fair that won't show your products to best advantage, or attract the kind of buyers you seek?

No one knows just how many selling crafts-people there are in America today or how many craft fairs are held annually, but experts claim there are more than 6000 fairs and as many as 52 million Americans who consider themselves "handcrafts-men." Although I can't verify these figures, I do know from traveling all over Europe that America is unique in all the world for both its abundance of fairs and its number of selling craftspeople. With so much competition and so many shows to choose from, how do you pick the few best suited to your needs, let alone *find* them?

Finding the Right Shows to Enter

There is no single source for information on all the art/craft events held annually in the U.S., but I have listed several of the most well-known "show calendars" in the Resource Chapter. Note that many art/craft magazines and newsletters also include show listings as a special service to readers. If you're looking only for fairs and shows in your immediate area, be sure to send for my special *Directory of Show Listing Periodicals,* which includes all of the state and regional show calendars known to me at any given time. (I keep this information on computer, and am constantly updating it for my readers.)

A subscription to one or more of these show calendars will keep you informed of events coming to your area. Some of the show calendars merely list an event's name, date of show, and who to contact for entry information, while others include special evaluations of shows based on reports from exhibiting craftspeople.

Care should always be taken in choosing which shows to enter, particularly flea markets and small local shows. Such events, when not juried, can often demean the quality of a good craftsman's product. You should also be wary of shows that appear to use artists and craftsmen as a drawing card, but seem to be promoting other things, such as antique shows, concerts, outdoor picnics, horse races, or carnival-type attractions. Look instead for shows that emphasize arts and crafts for sale, and try to get into shows where the number of craft sellers per craft will be limited. This will automatically cut your competition and entice buyers, who will have a wider variety of crafts from which to choose.

"It certainly is important that you select shows with care," says rosemaler Audrey Punzel, "or you may end up wasting your time." Audrey subscribed to two show-listing publications when she first began to sell at fairs, but even that didn't provide any guarantees. "Picking the right shows was mostly a matter of chance at first," she says, "but before long, other artists shared their opinions and soon there were no more 'lemons.' One thing we did learn was that the big celebration with the beer tent and carnival rides was not conducive to good sales."

Another artist puts it this way: "I started out going to all the art fairs I could, just to try them all. Now I have reached the point where I attend only four or five of the bigger ones, about two in the spring and two or three in the fall. It's not that I think I'm getting too good for all the small town shows I used to attend, but rather that I just can't afford to go to the ones that don't pay. Sometimes I could stay home and work all day and be further ahead than if I were sitting at a show and not selling."

Any widely publicized craft fair will attract an interesting variety of exhibitors, including craft professionals who rely on such shows for their entire living, part-time craftspeople who have other jobs and count on craft fairs for extra income, and homemakers and hobbyists who are trying to break into the field or gain additional selling experience. The real beauty of a crafts fair is that it is based on the principle of free enterprise, so the spirit of competition is keen. It's every man for himself, or woman, as the case may be. Even though you may feel like a complete amateur in a class all by yourself, if your work is good, you can easily compete with anyone else in the show -- provided you go to that show prepared.

Many do not prepare for their first selling experience, as evidenced by a letter I received from a woman who was chairing a Chamber of Commerce spring festival of arts and crafts. "I sure could use your book right now," she wrote. "All these little ladies are pulling their patchwork pot covers, quilled flower pictures, and string art from boxes to enter in this festival. They have no idea about pricing, setting up a booth, or displaying. They are too bashful to submit articles and photographs for publicity. They don't even know to ask questions about sales tax, labeling of certain fibers, the ethics of copying the work of others, or using kits."

Obviously, there are many things beginning sellers should know before they enter their first show, and the rest of this chapter is devoted to a discussion of points that are applicable to both small and large fairs. If you aren't a beginning seller, you have probably worked out most of your big problems by now, but there is always something new to be learned, so don't overlook the many professional tips and guidelines which follow.

47

Craft fairs are a way of life for countless American craftspeople, and they remain as popular today as they were thirty years ago. They are a joy for participant and visitor alike because they offer so many opportunities to see, to touch, to learn, and be entertained. Experts say that this method of merchandising is one of the fastest growing trends in small business commerce, generating $5 billion or more annually. No one knows for sure how many shows take place each year, but it has been estimated that there are over 20,000 invitational shows alone.

What to Know Before You Go
(Or, What to Ask Before You're Sorry)

Let's assume you want to enter a local, indoor, one-day show because it seems right for you and your products. In order to be prepared for all the possibilities, you should ask the following questions before you enter the show:

1. Do you think you will sell enough to cover your expenses and make a profit? If not, will the experience and publicity you receive compensate for any financial loss?

Consider not only your time, but the entry fee or sales commission that may be taken at show's end, plus all expenses such as gas, food, and parking. Find out if there will be additional expenses for extra lights, security, insurance, etc. Remember Ruby Tobey? She says, "Many people say if you break even at one of the art fairs you can count it good because you are getting publicity and exposure for your work. I guess I would agree, but that would depend on the distance you have to travel and how much work it is for you to set up your display. Anyone who attends many art fairs soon learns that he must have many small items that can be sold fast to earn back the cost of the entry fee, gas, food and, in my case, a baby sitter."

2. Are you planning to do the show alone, or will you have the help of a friend?

If you think you can do a show alone, think twice. It's possible, of course, but difficult. Have you figured out how you're going to get everything

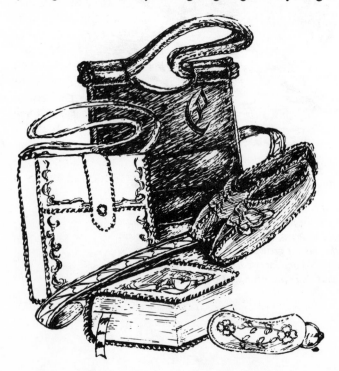

48

loaded into your car, van, etc., then get it unloaded at the show, and finally get everything home afterwards? (Prior to the show, inquire about the facilities for parking and unloading.) Think about who will help you "cover base" during the show while you take a break or have lunch. When the crowd gets heavy, you may need someone to help watch for shoplifters, keep children's hands off fragile merchandise, or package sold items. Remember that craft fair selling, normally tiring in itself, is all the more so because it involves the emotions of the seller.

3. Will tables and chairs be furnished, or will you have to bring your own? If you have things that must be hung, will a wall unit be provided?

Perhaps you will have to construct special displays for yourself -- an added expense, but well worth it if you plan to do several shows. Find out if you will have sufficient lighting for your exhibit, and electrical outlets if needed. (For more information on how to display your merchandise, see "How To Plan a Good Display" later in this chapter.)

4. How many people are expected to attend the show, and will you have enough merchandise to last? How much is enough?

There are no easy answers here, because even professionals can miscalculate in this area. So much depends on variables such as the weather, the publicity given to a show, or the individual whims of buyers. When possible, talk to other craftspeople who have been in the show you plan to enter. If such guidelines are unavailable, simply take twice as much merchandise as you can reasonably expect to sell and hope for the best. Better too much than not enough.

For many years, Audrey Punzel sold most of her rosemaling at craft fairs. She was often joined by her husband, Ray, who made much of the woodenware she painted. They carried a lot of work home with them after their first three-day local show, which brought them only $200 in sales. In later years, however, they would often gross $1000 per day in the larger shows. They confirm that selling experience is the best guide for determining merchandise requirements for any show. (That's another good reason why you should always keep good records of what you sell and where.)

5. Do you have a variety of products priced in a broad range?

What you sell may depend entirely on the price range of your merchandise. Says Audrey, "We've always offered items priced from $1 to $70, with a few special things (such as trunks) priced as high as $300. And we've also carried what I call 'loss leaders,' popular items that are real bargains."

Audrey shares a story to prove the wisdom of this practice: "A customer timidly stopped one time at a distant show, browsed and finally bought a $3 napkin holder. A few hours later she came back with her husband and bought a $60 table. I feel she never would have stopped if I hadn't had that $3 napkin holder that appealed to her." This story was continued at another show when, once again, Audrey met the same woman. "She stopped and introduced herself, saying she had $200 to spend this time. In the end, her order came to more than that, and it was all a chain reaction starting with a three-dollar item."

6. Are you going to sell at retail prices only? If so, what will you do if a wholesale buyer approaches you?

You are the only one who can determine whether it is possible, or desirable, to sell at wholesale prices or not, but whatever your decision, make it *before* you go to your first show, and set your retail prices accordingly.

If, like many craftspeople, you feel you simply cannot wholesale your work, perhaps the method used by the Punzels would work for you. Audrey explains: "In the beginning, we were concerned that if we priced our merchandise too high, we'd have to sit and wait for the occasional customer, and this would be discouraging. For this reason we did not wholesale. Instead, we developed a policy of giving 10 percent for cash (or payment within ten days) for those who bought $50 or more for resale. They were then free to put any price on the items warranted by their trade area. I recall one gift shop owner who bought a small clock for $18 and sold it for $32.50. She also bought a purse for $22.50 which she retailed for $35. Since she constantly reordered these items, I know they moved well. To protect our relationship with shop accounts like this, we were always careful not to supply more than one gift shop in an area, thus avoiding any hard feelings over pricing."

In later years, Audrey changed her wholesale policy. "We continue to wrestle with this wholesale-retail business," she told me. "I'm convinced that the way we did it (less 10 percent) was the way for us to start, and I'd do it again. We have raised our prices now and wholesale at one-third off. No objections so far, and we're picking up new wholesalers all the time."

SPECIAL NOTE: Ordinarily, shops need to mark up merchandise a full 100 percent to cover the many expenses involved in running a shop, but, occasionally, as in the case of the Punzels, shop owners realize that certain items are going to sell very quickly in their area at a higher price than the craft seller is asking. In order to carry these items (which will be an attractive addition to their stock), they are sometimes willing to take a smaller mark-up, and a lesser profit.

Unfortunately, some craftspeople react badly to a situation like this. Often, when a shop owner indicates that merchandise can be sold at a higher retail price, the seller gets greedy and raises retail prices accordingly. But this can be a bad move, indeed, for now the seller finds he cannot move items at this higher price, and in addition, he has lost the shop as a customer. Don't let yourself become this money-hungry. Be content to receive the price you know will yield a satisfactory profit, and when you find a shop owner who can help you sell your work, understand that he or she, too, is entitled to make a profit from the sale of your merchandise. That's the American way.

Finally, let me remind you that nothing upsets a shop owner more than discovering that a craftsperson is wholesaling an item at, say, $10, and selling it at craft fairs for the same price. If the shop offers it at $20, then the craftsperson should also sell it for $20. *It is unprofessional to do otherwise!* I urge you always to maintain your retail prices because, like the shop owner, you also have selling expenses that must be offset, and the time spent at a show (away from your studio or workshop) should yield some profit for you. Craft sellers are self-defeating if they decide to become wholesalers and then go out to a fair and sell at less than retail prices. They are then underselling their dealers. Only by maintaining your retail prices at all times can you hope to realize the profit that is rightfully yours, and only by operating in a professional manner can you hope to maintain good business relations with your shop customers.

In addition, you should not discount your prices. *Your work is worth as much at the end of a show as it was at the beginning.* If you don't sell it, simply take it to another show and try again.

7. What if a shop owner asks you to place your work on consignment, or a customer wants a custom-designed item?

Before deciding whether or not to place your work on consignment, you should carefully weigh the many advantages and disadvantages of this type of selling, which is discussed in detail in the next chapter.

If you decide to take a custom-design order, remember that some people will order something, then decide later on they don't want it -- after you

| WOULD YOU GIFT WRAP IT PLEASE? | WHAT • $25? WHY I COULD MAKE THIS MYSELF! | COULD YOU MAKE IT IN PURPLE? | DO YOU HAVE A PRICE LIST OR BROCHURE? | I ONLY HAVE $3. DO YOU TAKE CHARGE CARDS? | THE SHOP IN TOWN HAS ONE JUST LIKE THIS ONLY CHEAPER. | I THINK IT'S GOING TO RAIN! |

have spent several hours and perhaps many dollars in materials. That's why it's a good idea to do one of the following things where customer orders are concerned: Either ask for a down payment sufficient to cover your actual costs (to be kept if the customer cancels later on), or make sure your custom-designed item is such that it can be easily sold to someone else.

8. How are you going to keep track of your sales at the show? Do you have a sales slip book? Sacks and wrapping paper?

Keeping records of your sales is very important (both for tax reasons and for projecting future merchandise needs for other show), and you can buy the necessary sales slip books at stationery stores. For each item sold, you should write a sales ticket for the customer, and make a carbon copy for your own records. Show the name of the item sold (or its code number, if you have assigned one to it and recorded this information elsewhere), then the price, how much tax is being charged, and finally, the total.

It's a good idea to take inventory at the beginning and end of each day you participate in a fair. Compare this to sales made that day, and the money in your cash box. This will help you determine if anything is missing, and it will also give you a quick picture of what's selling best.

Once your sale is made, you can wrap or bag it in a number of ways. You'll find some bag sources in the resource chapter, but if you need to begin less expensively, use lunch sacks or even plastic bags for small items, or wrap things in tissue and tie with colored yarn. Some craftspeople simply use newspaper tied with twine because they know craft fair buyers aren't that fussy about how something is wrapped. The important thing is whether they can get it home safely or not.

9. What about a money box? Will you accept checks? Credit Cards?

You can easily make a simple money box. One idea is to use a cigar box and add cardboard dividers secured with tape to keep coins and currency separate. Even better, use a fishing tackle box, which you may already have on hand. Keep your money box closed unless you are making change, and always be careful to keep bills out of the box until the financial transaction is completed. (This will protect you in case a customer becomes confused about the size of the bill he gave you.) Be sure to take sufficient change with you because you probably won't be able to get it at the show.

Decide prior to the show whether you will accept checks or not, and what identification you will ask to see. Here are some tips to help you avoid bad or phony checks. First, in accepting a check from anyone, try to "feel" the transaction by looking the customer right in the eye when you take the check. Dishonest people may tend to break eye contact (although shy people tend to do the same thing).

If you feel uncomfortable about the check for any reason, ask for a little more information than usual. At least, get the customer's driver's license number and telephone number, and check the number on the check. (Low numbers indicate a new account while high numbers suggest stability.)

In the past, it has been common practice to ask customers for a credit card number as a credit reference. But many consumers now refuse to do this--and rightly so--because giving their credit card number to another individual leaves *them* open to fraud. Having this number does a crafts seller little good since a bounced check can't be covered by charging the same amount to a customer's credit card. Therefore, what you might want to do is simply ask to *see* a credit card for reference, but not copy the number.

Your use of a credit card to charge customer purchases during a show is another thing entirely. Although you may want to do this, you may find your bank reluctant to issue you a merchant bank card. (Homebased businesses of all kinds are considered risky by most banks.) In addition, even if you can get a card, it's mighty hard to pick up the telephone and check a customer's credit when you're at a crafts fair.

Phony checks are another matter to consider. A thief gone straight has explained that real checks are perforated on at least one side, while phony checks are usually smooth on all four sides. Real checks are printed with magnetic ink that doesn't reflect light (check those numbers in the lower left-hand corner of the check). The print on a phony check will look shiny and slightly raised because of the copying process used. If you're *really* suspicious about a check, dampen your finger and rub it across the ink. If it rubs off, look out!

10. Will you demonstrate your craft at the show, or wear a costume?

Demonstration of one's craft is sometimes required, other times not permitted or even advisable. When allowed, and when you feel a demonstration will help your sales, by all means demonstrate! Generally speaking, an active crafts seller will always outsell the one who merely sits on a chair in the corner, reading a book or showing no apparent interest in whether customers buy or not. Naturally, if you plan to demonstrate, you must also plan to have some sales help. You can't do both efficiently.

11. Do you have printed business cards? A price list or brochure?

Any seller who doesn't have a business card or some kind of printed literature with his name and address on it is telling the world, "I'm unprofessional!" Even if you have to hand-print a few cards to get started, take *something* to your first show with your name and address on it, so you can hand it to interested people who request it. As soon as you can afford it, have printed cards made. They need not be expensive to be effective. (See "Promotional Materials" in Chapter 12.)

Business cards distributed at a fair may lead not only to additional sales from shop owners and individual buyers, but may also be retained by members of the press and others who have attended a show for "research purposes" of one kind or another.

If you are selling several standard items, you definitely need a price list and brochure, particularly if you wish to sell your work by mail. These can be handed out to people who stop at your booth, but do not buy. Since not everyone buys on impulse, this may lead to mail order sales long after the crafts fair is over.

12. Are you aware of the many laws and regulations that apply to art and craft sellers?

Clearly, may sellers and show promoters operate in defiance of the law. Some are aware of laws but choose to ignore them; others are simply ignorant of the law, forgetting that old saying, "Ignorance is no excuse."

If your state has a sales tax -- and most do -- you *must* collect (and later pay to the state) sales tax on all your sales. There are also regulations that affect the raw materials you can use in your work, the labeling of your products, and consumer safety laws. Are you familiar with them? Have you registered your name with the county clerk?

If you choose to ignore the laws applicable to sellers, then you must also be prepared to pay the penalty, which could be something as simple as having your booth closed down at a show, as bad as a stiff fine, or worse. (For more information on this topic, see Chapter 14.)

All of the foregoing questions are as applicable to local, indoor, one-day events as they are to shows of longer duration that are either outdoors or out of town. However, there are a few additional things to consider here, namely:

13. If your display is to be left overnight for any reason -- either indoors or outside -- have you considered the possibility of theft or damage?

I recall one couple who told me they entered a large shopping mall show and lost everything when the mall caught fire one evening. They never thought it would happen to them, so they had no insurance for such a thing. Do you? (If you ever need to get fabric fireproofed for a show, your local dry cleaner can probably do it for you.)

Damage to craft work sometimes comes in strange forms. I recall the time when a friend of ours was exhibiting corn dollies in a week-long, out-of-doors festival. One morning when she opened her tent, she found that squirrels had had a field day chewing on items displayed on a table. She lost a lot of work as a result.

Finally, a gentle reminder that you can be held liable for any damage, injury, or sickness caused by one of your products. Discuss this topic with your insurance agent, and also refer to Chapter 14.

14. If exhibiting outdoors with no protection from the elements, will you be prepared for wind or rain?

Any outdoor show is a calculated risk, and many people have had their entire stock ruined in an unexpected rain or wind storm. It won't happen to you, however, if you take steps to prevent it.

15. If exhibiting outdoors in a tent, have you considered that it might leak?

Never leave your work unprotected at night. Even new tents have been known to leak, and water can also seep in under the tent flap, ruining anything on the ground. It might be wise to take duckboards with you, as well as large, waterproof coverings.

16. What major expenses will be incurred by an out-of-town trip?

Sometimes it is more profitable to exhibit in small local fairs than to travel out of town to the big shows and incur the accompanying food, gas, and lodging expenses. When traveling in a van or trailer to save on expenses, remember that you will still need a place to camp, and reservations must be made accordingly. Don't forget to allow for changes in weather and take appropriate clothing so you won't have to buy something you don't really need. Some people also carry portable fans or heaters with them in case of extreme weather conditions. At any rate, make sure you take sufficient funds with you -- or have access to additional cash -- should you incur unexpected car trouble, illness, or serious injury.

And there you have the most important things to think about before you enter a craft show. As a seller, you may never make a shot heard 'round the world, but if you want to make a good bang, you'll need the ammunition for it.

Setting Up a Display

How you display your crafts at a fair is up to you. You can either do it like an amateur -- and realize sales accordingly -- or try to emulate the professionals and perhaps reap large profits, even in a small, local show.

Like commercial gift items, crafts and needlework need to be beautifully displayed in order to attract the attention of buyers, and you can get some good ideas for your table or booth simply by browsing in a nice gift shop. Note the interesting shelf arrangements, display cases, and background walls. They will probably give you several ideas for displays you can easily make, using inexpensive materials.

What constitutes a good display? You need to show enough work to demonstrate the range of items available, and enough to allow customers to browse without being overwhelmed by too many choices. "It's not necessary to put everything you brought to a craft fair on the table at one time," says one professional.

There are several things to consider when planning a display. Let's begin with the size of your selling area. The average display area at fairs is about ten feet square, and depending on what you are selling, you may or may not want your customers walking within this area. Therefore, you should design your booth to keep customers exactly where you want them -- whether it's in front of you, down the center of your booth, or all around you. Do remember that not everyone in a crowd will be honest, and a poorly designed booth will be a real temptation to any thief, to say nothing of mischievous children. Since small, expensive pieces (such as jewelry) are the things most likely to be taken, they should always be kept in a suitable display case, or at least on a table near you where they cannot be touched without your knowledge. (Instead of just laying jewelry on a piece of black velvet, for example, you might make a sturdy, velvet-covered display board that allows for tying items down, to be removed only when sold.)

A good display must be strong and sturdy in order to stand up against the press of the crowd, the whoosh of the wind, and the weight of your merchandise. At the same time, it should be lightweight, or at least portable enough to be easily carted to and from fairs. Ideally, your entire booth should be designed so it can be set up or broken down and packed by one person, since you may not always have someone around to help you.

If you plan to exhibit at outdoor shows, you might consider using cinder blocks as the basis for shelves to hold pottery or glassware. Although they are heavy to lug around, they can make a sturdy and attractive display. Be sure your display unit doesn't end up top-heavy. You wouldn't want it to fall over after it's loaded with your crafts, ruining them and possibly the booth of another craftsman as well.

I'll never forget the sight and sound of a stained glass display I once saw fall over when a hard gust of wind hit it. My heart ached for the craftswoman who lost hundreds of hours of work in a few seconds. You should realize that you *can* buy insurance against such disasters. (See Chapter 14.)

A common type of display unit, equally as good indoors or out, is the A-frame structure, which resembles a tall saw-horse. Such units are especially suitable for things that must be hung, and it's always easy to add shelves when needed. Collapsible metal bookshelves might also work for you, and I'm sure you have seen shelves made by placing boards on the steps of two step ladders. In fact, Audrey and Ray Punzel built their entire display unit around this idea. (See next page.) I asked them how they did it, and what suggestions they had to offer to other craftspeople.

"Be original and practical," Audrey told me, "and be sure your display fits the type of merchandise you're selling. Our ladders and planks would hardly be suitable for fine jewelry."

The Punzels began building their display by staining two ladders and two planks. Then they framed two pieces of pegboard, mounting them (with carriage bolts and wing nuts) to the top plank between the ladders. A brace and bracket centered in the back holds them up and together. Audrey rosemaled the ladders and the planks, and they themselves became a conversation piece. This, plus a card table and chairs, was their original display.

"Then," says Audrey, "we added more items because we needed more space." First they framed two more pieces of pegboard and added "wings" at each end, mounted with pin butt hinges. The wasted space between the legs of the ladders was put to use by framing two more triangle-shaped pieces of pegboard. These held movable shelves, and could also be utilized for hanging things if the shelf items moved faster than the hanging items.

The Punzels' next display project was a combination cart and table, designed by Audrey. "My husband has always called me the Head of Design," she says, "and he's the Head of Manufacturing. According to him, if I designed a dinghy, we'd end up with the Queen Mary." Audrey explains how her "Queen Mary Cart and Table" was built:

"Ray had steel plates welded to the frame of one-inch conduit. Two fixed and two swivel casters

were mounted on the plates, and a plywood bottom was attached. Angle iron was welded across the top of each end to hold the table top." (The board is loose, and when used as a cart, it is just dropped to the bottom. The Punzels load it with their boxes of merchandise and wheel it into their van on two wooden rails they made to hook over the back bumper.) "When we unload," says Audrey, "we roll it out to our site, unload the boxes, raise the board to table top height, and put our fitted cloth over the top. The table is also used for display and we have hidden storage space underneath."

If you don't have a van or station wagon, getting your display and merchandise to a show may present a problem, but you can work it out. An automobile can hold an amazing amount of goods when properly packed, and your goal is simply to design a display that will collapse and fit into the space you have available. When packing space is a problem, you might think about using small barrels or boxes that will hold your merchandise en route to a show, then double as display props in the booth itself. Boards placed on two boxes or barrels make very good shelves to hold merchandise.

By the way, did you note Audrey's mention of a *fitted* cloth used over her table-cart? Although this isn't necessary, it would certainly add a tailored look to any display table. A table covering should at least come all the way to the floor or ground. This not only looks better, but also enables you to use the area under the table for storage. Be sure to select a material that complements your crafts or needlework, remembering that the background should never overshadow the work itself. Suitable fabrics for table coverings might be felt, burlap, velveteen, or simply a colored sheet or bedspread. Or perhaps a large straw mat on top of your table is just the thing that's needed to give your crafts the proper background. Experiment to achieve the best results.

Always think CONTRAST when planning a display. Consider placing smooth surfaces against rough ones, and vice versa. Vividly colored items will look best on subdued or natural backgrounds, while items with little color will be more noticeable when placed against a brightly colored or rough-textured background. (Weathered wood, burlap covered walls, and painted pegboard have long been favorite backgrounds for craftspeople, but perhaps you can come up with something more original.) Glass looks terrific on bricks, and silver jewelry always looks impressive when displayed on black velvet or plexiglas, which also complements many other crafts. A sheet of plexiglas, when placed on blocks of wood or bricks, can make a stunning display prop, and if you can also figure

53

This display unit, shown as it might look in the early stages of being set up, was designed by Audrey and Ray Punzel of Wisconsin. Ladders were stained and ornamented with rosemaling similar to the painted designs on their products, and pegboard was cut to fit the ends of the ladders. The combination of shelving placed on the steps of each ladder, with framed pegboard walls behind and a covered table in front, gives plenty of space to display a variety of differently shaped items. This type of display also allows for gradual enlargement as one's business grows.

out how to include battery-operated lights in special displays such as this, it would add considerably to the overall effect of your booth -- particularly when you end up in a dreary tent some day.

If you don't want to build your own props, visit flea markets and used furniture shops for things that will serve your needs. All it takes is a bit of time and imagination. You could probably do wonders with an old hat rack, trunk, or antique shelf unit. Also keep your eyes open for interesting nature items, such as small logs, driftwood, or gnarled branches. All would add flavor to many craft and needlework displays. (See illustration, next page.)

As you can see, ingenuity is the key to good display planning, along with originality and practicality. Your work may actually be judged by the overall quality of your display, so make it as sturdy, functional, clever, and eye-catching as you can.

Your Personal and Professional Image

Good displays are vital to success in selling, but it takes more than that to be a successful seller. Also needed are craftsmanship, showmanship, and salesmanship, to say nothing of a neat appearance.

Your appearance is certainly important to your professional image, and when exhibiting your work, it is wise to dress in a manner appropriate to your craft. For example, if you do contemporary work, regular clothing would be fine. If rustic or country crafts are your specialty, however, jeans and a plaid shirt or other homespun costume would probably look better. If you happen to do a traditional folk art, a colorful native costume would attract extra attention. When there are two or more people in a booth, something as simple as matching aprons, shirts, or hats can be a real eye-stopper. If needlework, quilting, or macrame happens to be your specialty, you might do some fancy stitching on your blouse, make a patchwork skirt or jacket, or macrame a fancy vest for yourself. Above all, be neat and clean. As Audrey Punzel says, "Your 'bag' may be jeans and a disheveled appearance, but most customers are neat, and they will appreciate neatness in you."

Also consider that a growing number of people are not smoking these days, and the person who insists on smoking in a booth should figure on losing a lot of sales from nonsmokers, many of whom simply won't go near anyone who is apt to blow smoke in their direction.

Next to neatness, friendliness may be most important. Sellers who sit in their booth with arms crossed, staring at the crowd with a bored expression (or worse, reading a book) are *not* radiating interest and friendliness. As one buyer commented, "These actions almost dare customers to stop, and they usually don't. It takes action to get attention. Paint, whittle, tie knots, move about -- *but do something* -- and smile!"

Carol Bernier, the shop owner and crafts buyer you met in Chapter 5, told me that too few craftspeople ever greeted her as she approached their booth. "It's amazing what a smile and a cheery hello can do," she said. "For one thing, it stops me for a moment. If I seem slightly interested, why doesn't the person then say something like, 'Do you like the color?' or 'That's one of my new designs,' or *anything* to make me feel at ease and encourage me to pause and look around." More often than not, Carol said, craftspeople usually just sit, and stay sitting.

"Sometimes, in shopping for crafts at a fair, I have literally had to step over and around craftspeople who were sitting on the floor or ground, talking to other craftspeople and completely ignoring interested buyers. Here I am, *a buyer*. Grab me, *sell* to me! Don't ignore me!"

Carol says she cannot overemphasize the importance of a businesslike image, and she advises sellers to make the most of their time at a show and do what they originally set out to do: SELL. "You can talk to friends and read books after the show," she concludes, "when you've counted up all the sales you've made."

Yes, I know it's hard to sell, especially when you are so emotionally involved with your products, as all creative people are. But you must develop a different attitude at a fair and remember that, here, you are a salesperson first, and an artist or craftsperson second.

Some people avoid contact with the public simply because they are shy or lack confidence in their work. Others just don't want to hear the usual discouraging remarks such as "Oh, I can do that myself," or any of a hundred other comments made by thoughtless people. Negative feedback is one of the few disadvantages of direct selling that you will have to learn to accept. Although it hurts to hear it, it can sometimes be helpful when it reminds you that there is still room for improvement in some areas.

Carol Bernier has an interesting viewpoint on this topic that might help you cope with negative feedback. "Just because someone makes an unflattering comment about your work, it isn't the end of the world," she emphasizes. "A person may make a comment, but he or she is still a potential buyer. If not at this show, perhaps later when needs have changed or your work has improved (if it truly is shoddy). Or maybe the next time you will have colors and styles to the customer's liking. But if you reciprocate with a nasty remark to this potential buyer, it could influence future sales. Try to remember that you can't please everyone all the time."

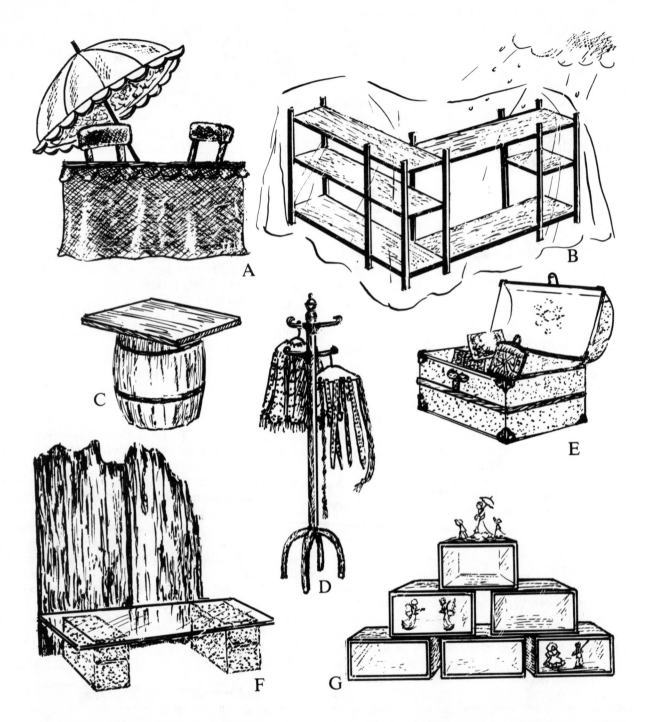

A few display ideas that could be used at a crafts fair. (A) If you don't have a shady spot at an outdoor crafts fair, an umbrella over your table will provide welcome relief from the hot sun. (B) Don't forget that it could rain. Take a large plastic cover to throw over your display. (C) An old barrel could serve as a container when carrying crafts to the fair, then do double duty as a display unit once you're set up. (D) An antique coat rack might add atmosphere to a crafts display, as would an old trunk (E) that could be filled with things like pillows, quilts, dolls, or toys. (F) An interesting piece of driftwood, a couple of bricks, and a sheet of plexiglas make an eye-catching display for a variety of crafts, as does an arrangement of boxes or cubes (G).

Even Zeuxis realized this way back in 400 B.C. Once, when he was criticized for something he had done, he said (smugly, I'm sure), "Criticism comes easier than craftsmanship." Remember that the next time you overhear a discouraging word, and smile to yourself. For all you know, your most appreciative buyer could be right on your critic's heels.

Besides looking good and acting friendly in spite of what people may say, what else can you do to create a better image of yourself? In addition to demonstrating your craft, or at least looking busy in your booth, you should have printed sales literature and business cards to give to interested people. And, hangtags on your work that tell buyers who you are and what makes your product special can add considerably to your professional image. You can design these yourself and have them printed quite inexpensively.

It is also important to stay in tune with the times. You need to study the new trends in crafts, gifts, toys, decorative accessories, clothing and colors to keep up with your competition. If you are like most craftspeople, you will tend to return to the same fairs year after year, particularly if they prove financially successful for you. In that case, some of the people visiting these shows may be customers who bought from you in previous years. If you want them to have something to come back for each year, you will have to add new items to your line from time to time, or at the very least change your colors, patterns, or designs so your work will look different to those who know you.

REMEMBER: If a field is to yield a good crop every year, it must be cultivated with care. And when you have learned how to cultivate repeat customers at a fair, you will have learned an important secret in making more money from your crafts.

Special Exhibitions and Prize Money Opportunities

There are some people who will never produce enough work to sell at a craft fair, but who would nonetheless enjoy having it seen and appreciated by others. For such people, exhibitions may be particularly appealing. And, when the possibility of cash awards exists, the temptation to exhibit one's work may be even greater.

Hobbyists and professionals alike enter exhibitions for similar reasons: to gain prestige or recognition in their field, and to compete for money awards. I know little about this from experience, which is why I asked a nationally-known textile artist to comment on this topic. Bucky King, who thinks of herself as a "threadbender," teacher, designer, producing craftsman, and lover of fibers,

has had her work exhibited throughout the United States and the United Kingdom. I asked her to explain the types of exhibitions craftspeople and needleworkers might enter.

"Basically, there are two distinct kinds of exhibitions," Bucky wrote. "There is the juried show, and the nonjuried show. The juried exhibition may be open nationally, regionally, or locally. (This is always stated in the prospectus, as are all the rules for submission.) The best of these always offer good money prizes and are worth the trouble to seek. Selections are made by qualified jurors. The juried show for the professional craftsman offers recognition, not just in prizes awarded, but in the prestige of being accepted and the good publicity this brings. It also furthers sales, because of the publicity. The craft collectors in this country frequent these shows and are influenced by the work presented. Galleries go to these shows looking for future work for their shops, and magazines such as *American Craft* review them, thus providing more free publicity and recognition for the craftsman.

"Amateurs usually have their work juried out of such shows," Bucky notes, "partly because the competition from professionals is keen, and partly because they submit unprofessional slides. In fact, about 80 percent of the national and regional open juried shows are by slide submission simply because it is easier to mail back the many rejects in the form of slides than it is to mail back the actual work itself."

There is always an entry fee for exhibitions, which you do not get back if your work is rejected, thus entering exhibitions can be expensive, particularly when a professional photographer must be hired to take slides. And without good slides, one has little chance of getting into a good show. In addition to professional slides, what else do jurors look for? Competence, for one, says Bucky. A command of your materials and the use of proper techniques. Innovative designing. "Work that looks like things already on the market won't measure up here," she warns.

The other type of show is the nonjuried show, where everything submitted is hung or displayed, and might win a prize if it is offered. "About 70 percent of all the needlework shows in the United States are nonjuried," says Bucky. "Awards, even money prizes, are offered, and everything submitted is shown. The jurors simply select the best pieces and award the ribbons or prizes accordingly. Naturally, since these shows lure many hobbyists, the quality of design is sometimes quite poor, although techniques may be excellent."

Juried exhibitions, then, are best for the more professional craftsperson or needleworker, while

NEEDLEWORK EXHIBIT

while the hobby-crafter or less experienced needle-worker should try a nonjuried show for her first fling. Adds Bucky, "This is a good way to start, particularly if recognition is all the person cares about, and for many this is all that is important -- to see their pieces hanging or displayed somewhere."

Perhaps that's why so many hobbyists exhibit their work at county or state fairs. Thousands of people will thus see an individual's work, and the craftsperson's family will take special pride in any blue ribbons that may be awarded here.

National and regional exhibitions and competitions are generally listed along with regular craft fairs in the various craft marketing periodicals and show calendar publications. (See Resource Chapter.) Study the listings, then write for additional information (called a "prospectus") before deciding whether you want to take this particular step on your crafts ladder of success. A word of warning: When it is necessary to submit the actual work itself, instead of slides, think twice before you mail your most prized creation to an exhibition, since the possibility always exists that you will not get it back in the same condition as you sent it. The exhibition committee may not handle it as carefully as it should, and if you aren't insured and your work is damaged or stolen, guess who loses?

Granted, this sort of thing is probably the exception, rather than the rule, but it is a possibil-ity that must be considered, and it would be remiss of me not to mention it. In the end, it all comes down to how much you desire recognition and the possibility of cash awards for your work. Many people enter exhibitions on a regular basis, often to excellent advantage with no problems whatsoever. If you are primarily interested in selling one-of-a-kind pieces, or doing commission work (versus selling in a variety of shops), regular exhibition of your work could greatly enhance your image and increase your sales.

Exhibitions aside for the moment, there is yet another way to win recognition and prize money, with no entry fees and little risk involved. You might enter some of the contests advertised in women's magazines such as *Woman's Day, Family Circle,* or *Good Housekeeping,* etc. Here, men and women alike can vie for cash awards and the chance of having their work featured in an upcoming issue of the magazine, which is great for both the pocketbook and the ego. Occasionally such contests are given publicity in craft or needlework journals, but generally one learns of them simply by being a regular consumer magazine reader.

Magazines readers are obviously interested in such contests. My research for this book revealed that one *Good Housekeeping* quilt contest attracted almost 10,000 entries. A *Woman's Day* crochet and knit design contest received more than 25,000 entries, with 51 winners and a First Prize of $1,000. Several years ago, after a *Family Circle* needlework contest drew over 60,000 original designs with its offer of $10,000 in prizes, 200 semifinalists were asked to send their actual creations, and many winners were then selected and featured in the magazine.

Wholesale Fairs and Gift Shows

This section is for those readers who have considerable product to sell at wholesale prices, and who may be dreaming about, or actually gravitating toward, bigger and better shows. Tremendous sales possibilities await the craftsperson who can meet the challenge of the big handcrafts fair, and there are many to choose from these days.

When this book was first published, the major marketplace for contemporary crafts in the United States was the Northeast Craft Fair in Rhinebeck, sponsored by the American Crafts Council. In 1977, that show reported sales of $2 million, with public attendance of 44,000 and 2,000 registered wholesale buyers. More than 2,000 craftspeople applied for the 500 available booths in this show. In 1983, sales had increased to $6.1 million, and public attendance had risen to 50,000.

I haven't kept tabs on the sales figures of wholesale shows through the years, except to note that they have risen steadily. "The business of contemporary American crafts is booming, if record sales at the annual American Craft Enterprises Fair in Baltimore can be cited as an accurate indicator," reported *In Business* magazine (Summer, 1989 issue). Sales for 1989 were close to $16 million. Some exhibitors reported average sales at the $40,000 level, so you can see we're not talking kid stuff here.

Says Carol Sedestrom Ross, president of American Craft Enterprises, Inc. (the marketing arm of the American Craft Council), "We attribute this success to the fact that crafts are the only beautiful objects left to buy that are truly made in America, which is one reason why our shows are getting more successful."

In a smaller show in Illinois recently that's typical of many shows across the country, 139 exhibitors reported sales of almost a million dollars from a buyer base of just 11,000 people. You need to understand that it is *contemporary* crafts of the highest quality (original designs only) that are selling at shows like these. Craft categories in such shows usually include glass, fiber, jewelry, wood, leather, metal, basketry, paper, and mixed media.

Of course, you should not even consider entering a major wholesale show unless you're an experienced seller who's fully prepared for all possibilities. In order to produce crafts in quantity, one has to have a certain psychological makeup. It can get to be very much like factory work after all, and few genuinely creative people can be production craftsmen for long. Those who can, however, may often sell as much as half (or more) of their annual production at one trade fair. They will work for months beforehand to build inventory, then go to the show and completely sell out their stock, returning with enough new wholesale orders to keep them busy for weeks thereafter. Then the cycle begins anew.

Many craftspeople have gone into trade shows not really expecting to sell much, only to be bombarded with orders and placed in a panic situation when they suddenly realize they have taken more orders than they can possibly fill. On the other hand, an exhibitor might not receive many orders at all. Either way, doing a trade show can be something of a shock, as indicated by the letter I received from Mark Davis, a Wisconsin craftsman who offers a superior line of wooden toys. After exhibiting in his first commercial gift show, Mark wrote, "I tried my first trade show in Kansas City, and it will be the last, as I lost my shirt on the deal. I can't compete with plastic imports."

Later, Mark tried one of the larger craft trade fairs and reported, "I didn't do real well, but I've received several orders since, and the experience really opened my eyes. I see that I have to clean up my act. For this to work, I must have a totally professional image and look as if I know what I'm doing -- brochures, invoices, letterhead, price lists, etc."

As you can see, even a professional craftsman can find a trade show intimidating, and entry into such a show is for the few, not the many. However, if you would like to learn more about trade shows, simply read the appropriate trade magazines. For instance, craft shows are listed in the various periodicals serving this field, most notably of which is *The Crafts Report*. Gift shows are listed in trade magazines such as *Gifts and Decorative Accessories* or *Sew Business*. Information about craft supply trade shows are found in magazines such as *Profitable Crafts Merchandising*.

59

Also refer to "Exhibiting at Trade Shows" in Chapter 10, since it contains the advice of some women who took their kits to a major trade show and gave their businesses a tremendous boost as a result. They agree it wasn't an easy job, but they are proof that the average craftsperson is often equal to such a challenge.

Whether situated in a rural or urban area, the typical crafts shop in America is likely to be owned by people with a special interest in handcrafts and the American craftsman. Often the owners of such shops are crafts professionals themselves.

- 7 -

Selling Through Retail Outlets

Craft fair selling isn't the answer for everyone and, for some homemakers, it may even be impossible because of family obligations that require their constant presence at home. Marketing through retail outlets is always a possibility, however, and particularly desirable for those who wish to spend most of their time designing or producing instead of selling. An extra advantage of shop selling is that it can be done entirely by mail -- a real plus for those who live in rural areas.

But inexperienced sellers often have a poor understanding of how shops operate, and thus, a poor understanding of how to deal with them. In fact, many craftspeople think shop owners are taking advantage of them when they take a 100 percent markup on their work. Let me set you straight on that right now. Financially speaking, most craft shop owners are in the same boat as sellers. Their profit margins are slim, their hours long, their problems many and complex.

In my experience as a crafts magazine editor, I often had the opportunity to study both sides of this picture and came to understand the problems faced by craft sellers and shop owners alike. Therefore, I chose to present in this chapter a picture few sellers have seen before: the craftsperson as he or she appears to the craft shop owner. Later on you will read what some shop owners have to say about dealing with craftspeople, what they expect of them, and what frustrates them most. Then you will learn what you should expect of them, and what precautions you should take when entering into any new shop relationship.

Shops and Galleries: How They Differ

Perhaps a general discussion of the difference between shops and galleries will help sharpen your focus at this point. Galleries aside for the moment, there are two basic kinds of shops with which you will probably be dealing: *craft* shops and *gift* shops. While both may carry handcrafts and imports, gift shops are generally associated with the commercial gift industry, craft shops with the handcrafts industry. What this means is that the owners walk different paths, read different publications, go to different shows, etc.

Gift shops and boutiques can be started by anyone with sufficient capital to buy inventory but, often, such people have little knowledge of crafts. It's true that many gift shops now carry a line of handcrafts, but often this merchandise is purchased from craft professionals who exhibit at wholesale craft shows or have sales representation at leading gift shows or merchandise marts. This is not to say that the average craftsperson cannot sell to commercial gift shops -- only that handmade items are going to have competition, and it's important to deal with shop owners in a businesslike way.

Craft shops are usually started by people with a special interest in handcrafts and the American craftsman, and, often, the owners of such shops are craftspeople themselves. Of course, some are simply business-minded men or women who are dedicated to the idea of helping craftspeople market their work.

As for galleries, there are two kinds. One kind offers only fine art and the other sells art plus crafts or sculpture, weaving, needlework, etc. Art and craft galleries usually operate on a consignment basis similar to regular craft shops, with their primary difference being the way merchandise is displayed. Also, special exhibitions and sales are held from time to time to promote the work of one or more artists or designer craftsmen represented in the gallery. Art galleries prefer to work only with

full-time professionals, but craft galleries are usually interested in contact from any fine artisan or craftsperson.

Craft shops may operate on an outright-purchase basis, consignment arrangement, or a combination of both, but commercial gift shops and other retail outlets usually buy outright. If a craft shop takes work on consignment, a commission of between 25 and 40 percent of the retail price is usually taken by the shop. Galleries may take an even larger commission.

Some craft shops work on a different basis, called "guaranteed sales," whereby the shop owner buys the craftwork outright with the understanding that the craftsman will exchange any pieces that have not sold after a certain length of time. In some ways this is similar to consignment, except it's better because you get your money before the work is actually sold. But if it doesn't sell, and the shop has kept it in good condition, you will be expected to replace it with other work of the same quality and price. Or, if you guarantee sales on wholesale orders, it would mean that if your work does not sell after a specified length of time, at a specified price, it can be returned to you (in good condition) and you will allow credit for it on the shop's next order.

The Consignment Controversy

Many professionals will advise you against consignment selling, arguing that shop owners who won't (or can't afford to) buy your merchandise outright will not work very hard to sell it, and will often ruin it in the process. Yet, for the beginner, consignment selling may be the best (or only) way to get started.

Since I have had both good and bad experiences with consignment, I am not going to advise you one way or the other. But I am going to present a picture of this type of selling from the viewpoint of both seller and shop owner, and show you the advantages and disadvantages to both. Then you can decide for yourself if consignment is the route you want to go.

First you should understand the basic difference between selling your work outright and consigning it. When you sell outright, you relinquish all control over your merchandise. Once you have been paid for it, the shop owns it and can sell it for any price it wishes. When you consign merchandise, however, you are merely transferring it to another who will act as your sales representative. Thus, you remain the owner of all consigned goods and will not receive payment for them until sometime after they have been sold. This can often take months, which is why some craftspeople prefer to wholesale their work. Even though their profits may be smaller, they at least get their money in hand as soon as possible.

What are the main disadvantages of consignment selling? We might begin with the increased bookkeeping and paperwork involved. For the craftsperson, it's more than would be required for wholesaling, and for the shop, it's enough to give a trained accountant a headache. Considering that most shop owners aren't accountants, one can imagine their problems in keeping everything straight, particularly when they are just beginning in business. A new consignment shop may begin with as few as twenty-five consignors, but, as business grows, this number may increase to as many as five hundred people -- all of whom are bringing in dozens of items that must be specially coded, inventoried, priced, and displayed. Ledger sheets must be accurately maintained for each consignor in order to make monthly reports and payments, checks must be written, envelopes addressed, etc. Meanwhile, the shop may be plagued with telephone calls and letters from craftspeople who want to know if this or that item has been sold and how soon will they get their money?

As the legal owner of the merchandise until it is sold, the consignor is naturally the one most concerned about it. And with good reason, for when many items are placed on consignment in several shops, it can mean that a great deal of capital is tied up in inventory. If the craft seller happens to be dealing with an undercapitalized shop, it is quite possible that payments for work already sold will be late, or not forthcoming at all.

Judy Bridge offers an example of what can sometimes happen in consignment selling. She told me how she got started selling, and what problems she encountered: "My little sock babies have really done well for me," she wrote. "It all began when I prayed and asked the Lord to help me sell my things. Next day in the mail came a copy of a crafts magazine with an article on where to sell your crafts. Now is that an answer to prayer? Wow! So I wrote to 18 shops and got 17 replies. Everyone wanted my dolls. I was so excited! The following month I did the same, and before I knew it, I had to hire someone to help me keep up with all the orders."

Sounds too good to be true, doesn't it? Judy sold some of her dolls outright, and consigned many others. Unfortunately, her experience with some of the consignment shops wasn't too good. Eager to get started in selling, Judy was not too selective. She wrote to all shops listed in the article she read, and practically all indicated an interest in her work. So she followed through and sent merchandise accordingly. Then she wrote: "I'm getting to the point where I don't want consignment any more unless the shop sells well. Right now, I'm stuck for quite a bit. My dolls are inexpensive, but they add up. I have had some shops who took half a dozen, and I've never heard from them since. A bunch of these shops can hurt, so I'm weeding out and putting them aside. I've written two or three times; I can do no more. That's where the losses

come in, and that is definitely a problem when you consign by mail. You don't know where the shop is or the people who run it. I've had shops that have had four owners in less than a year."

I've heard Judy's story dozens of times from other craftspeople, so I know this sort of thing happens with regularity. Yet, there are many good consignment shops out there somewhere, if one could only find them. Later in this chapter you will learn how to do this.

Always a problem is the shop that fails, and there was a time not so long ago when more shops seemed to be failing than succeeding. To read now a crafts directory published only a few years ago is to hear the death knell of hundreds of small shops that tried but failed to make a go of the retail crafts business. Perhaps too many were like the person who once wrote to me saying: "I am just starting an arts and crafts store on a consignment basis, only handmade articles. I have very limited funds. I really don't know what I am doing. I have always sewn and done a lot of crafts. We do not have a shop of this kind here. I really believe it will work."

It didn't. When you encounter this kind of new shop, be especially cautious in dealing with it. Good and honest intentions do not make a craft shop successful. If you happen to be dealing with a shop when it goes out of business, you should realize that, as the legal owner of consigned merchandise, you have the right to take possession of your own work. (Here's one example of where accurate records on your part could make a big difference.)

A Special Note About Consignment Laws: Theoretically, consigned goods remain the property of the seller until they are sold to the retail customer, and in normal situations, there are no problems. According to the Uniform Commercial Code (which has been adopted by most states), if an establishment goes bankrupt, consigned goods may be subject to the claims of creditors, and be seized by such creditors unless certain protective steps have been taken by consignors. (A standard consignment contract is not enough to protect one in this instance.)

Several states have now adopted consignment laws designed to protect artists and craftspeople. To the best of my knowledge, these states are: California, Colorado, Connecticut, Illinois, Iowa, Kentucky, Massachusetts, New Hampshire, New Mexico, New York, Oregon, Texas, Washington and Wisconsin. Each state's law offers varying degrees of protection, so obtain complete details about this from your own state legislature for maximum protection of your goods. Also note that some state laws protect "art" only, excluding protection to items which fall outside the area of painting, sculpture, drawing, graphic arts, pottery, weaving, batik, macrame, quilting, "or other commonly recognized art forms."

If the shop you are dealing with is miles from your home or out of state, it can be very difficult to get your work out of a shop that goes belly up. And if you eventually get it back, and it's damaged, what can you really do about it, except weep? Getting your money for items already sold can be next to impossible once a shop goes bankrupt and, regrettably, many people have been losers here. To lessen your chances of this happening to you, remember this important rule for consignment selling: Never consign more than a few items to a new or unknown shop until you have developed some kind of satisfactory relationship with it, based on prompt payment after your first shipment of merchandise has been sold. This is usually a good indication of whether you're dealing with a responsible shop or not.

Now that I've talked about the bad side of consignment, let me show you its good side. There are advantages to both sellers and shop owners, of course. From a shop's standpoint, the acquisition of merchandise on consignment means that less capital is needed to get started, and the shop does not have to worry about risk of loss if the goods do not sell. Craft sellers benefit because they can (1) consign merchandise of their choice without the pressure of meeting a deadline date; (2) control the retail selling price of their work; and, (3) use consignment to test the marketability of new or untried items. In fact, consignment selling is often the best or only way to market work of limited production, or expensive, one-of-a-kind crafts and needlework.

Many craftspeople have one or more consignment shops that regularly sell their work, and they usually enjoy a satisfactory relationship with them. Ruby Tobey is one of those people. "I like working on consignment," she says. "It just happens to fit my way of life. I need the money for supplies, but I do not have to have a regular dependable income. I like to try new things and I feel that a shop is more willing to take new things and try them if it does not have to pay for them first. I do not like to be obligated by orders for so many dozen of any item. To me, it is much easier to do the work as I like, send it out to my shops, and around the first of the month, several checks come in."

Ruby has found through experience that the shops that do best at selling her things are small craft shops usually owned by two or three women who are eager to make a go of their business. "Such women soon become firm friends," she says. "They keep in touch, send out checks regularly, let me know what is selling, pass on orders and sug-

gestions, etc." Ruby does advise, however, to be cautious about starting with a new shop unless you know the owner.

Some craftspeople believe it unwise to consign work to any shop that isn't at least two years old. But, as you probably realize, many shops could not open at all if not for craftspeople willing to consign to them. Since many new consignment shop owners work especially hard to make their business a success, you should not automatically refuse to consign in a shop just because it's new, but you should check it out carefully and test it with a small consignment of merchandise to begin with. Given time, it could turn out to be an excellent outlet for you.

One new shop owner I interviewed told me she could not have opened if not for consignments, and her words echo those of many shop owners I have communicated with in the past. "We intend to try just as hard as all the others," she said, "and depend on getting trust from craftspeople. With this, our very good location, and a lot of hard work, we believe we will succeed. I love what I'm doing and I love most of all the people who are taking a chance with me by consigning these first years while we find our market and get the experience we need to make the right buying decisions."

You will notice that this shop owner said she loves "most of the people," not *all* of them. She and scores of other craft shop owners do not love consignors who make promises and don't come through; those who send shoddy merchandise after promising good things; or those who take their work from a shop only two or three days after consigning it (perhaps to take it to a crafts fair). "People like this are breaking their contract with me," the shop owner says, "but I let them do it because I know they'll be nothing but future trouble for me. I hate the sight of my 'blackball file' (as I call it) that holds the names of people who do marvelous work, but who can't be trusted."

Although as a seller you may feel that shop owners are the ones not to be trusted, I hope you are at least beginning to realize that consignment selling is a two-way street, and a cooperative form of marketing that will not succeed unless both parties work together. Here are some additional tips that might make consignment work better for you:

1. Don't consign your work to a shop that normally buys most of its products at wholesale, or one that seems primarily interested in selling supplies, imports, or commercial gift lines.

2. Your products will sell better in any shop when several pieces are displayed. If the choice is between several shops who only want a few pieces,

CONSIGNMENT AGREEMENT AND REPORTING FORM

I.
NAME OF SHOP _____

ADDRESS _____

CITY _____

STATE _____ **ZIP** _____

NAME OF CRAFTSMAN _____

ADDRESS _____

CITY _____

STATE _____ **ZIP** _____

AGREEMENT NO. _____

AGREEMENT DATE _____

REPORTING DATES	AMOUNT PAID CRAFTSMAN

This consignment agreement is between the shop and the craftsman shown above. The shop agrees to display the consignment items properly and to maintain them in good, saleable condition for a period of _____ weeks, or until _____ (date). The shop will receive _____ % of the retail selling price of any item it sells.

II. ITEMS PLACED ON CONSIGNMENT	RETAIL PRICE	DATE SOLD	AMOUNT DUE CRAFTSMAN	DATE PAID
1.				
2.				
3.				
4.				
5.				
6.				
7.				
8.				

III. **TERMS**

    a. The items listed may not be sold for less than the retail price indicated. If any are sold for more, the craftsman is to receive his share of the higher selling price.

    b. If shipping is involved in getting the consigned material to and/or from the shop, the shop and the craftsman will share the cost of shipping equally.

    c. Unless this agreement is renewed, the craftsman agrees to pick up any unsold items, or have them shipped to him by the shop, within 15 days after the termination of this agreement.

    d. Any item which cannot be returned to the craftsman in perfect condition at the termination of this agreement will be considered sold and the craftsman will receive his share of the purchase price for it.

    e. Beginning 30 days after this agreement, and monthly thereafter during the term of this agreement, the shop will report which items, if any, were sold, and will attach a check to the craftsman in payment of his share of the items sold since the last report.

Signed: _____ Date _____ _____ Date _____
FOR THE SHOP: NAME AND TITLE   CRAFTSMAN

© 1973 by the Guild of American Craftsmen

This consignment agreement form might be used as the basis for creating a form suited to your own individual needs. (Form copyright 1973 by the Guild of American Craftsmen. Used by permission.)

or one or two who will take a good supply, pick the latter, and offer a wide price range in the articles you consign. Obviously, the less expensive pieces will sell first, but your higher-priced pieces will encourage the sale of the lower-priced items. (Of course, I am assuming you will have investigated the shop thoroughly before consigning any substantial amount of merchandise to it.)

3. Promote the shop or gallery that is handling your work. If you exhibit at a craft fair, print flyers saying your work can also be found at certain shops and, by all means, make sure your retail prices for craft shows are the same as those of your shops.

4. Finally, keep careful records and get everything in writing. Read all consignment agreements before signing them. If the shop does not offer a regular consignment form, you can prepare one of your own, or use a printed form such as the one pictured on the previous page. Basically, a consignment agreement should cover the following points:

INSURANCE: As the owner of consignment merchandise, you must be concerned with risk of loss. Your work could be damaged or completely ruined, stolen, or destroyed by a fire or flood. A shop's insurance may or may not cover consignment merchandise -- be sure to ask. You may have to take out an insurance policy of your own. (See Chapter 14). If you are sending your work to the shop by mail, who will pay for the postage and insurance? (Both ways. See "Return of Unsold Merchandise," right.)

PRICING AND SALES COMMISSION: Consignors are usually expected to set the retail price on their merchandise, but sometimes a shop will ask consignors simply to tell them how much they want for an item and they will set the retail price accordingly. This arrangement, or the exact percentage the shop will retain as its sales commission, should be clearly stated in your agreement.

PAYMENT DATES: How and when will you be paid? Monthly payments to craftspeople are customary for many shops, but there are many ways to keep consignment sales records, and the method of payment should therefore be spelled out in your agreement. In addition to a check each month, you should receive a report of the specific items sold so you can adjust your inventory records accordingly.

DISPLAY OF YOUR MERCHANDISE: Will your crafts be properly displayed and not left in the storeroom after you bring them in for consignment, or carelessly placed in a display window for weeks

at a time, to be faded by the sun? Discuss the matter of display in advance, noting in your agreement any special requirements you may have.

RETURN OF UNSOLD MERCHANDISE: How long will your work be on display, and how will unsold work eventually be returned to you? Will it be mailed back at your expense? If it's a local shop and you can pick it up in person, must you claim it by a certain date or forfeit ownership entirely? (Some shops have a clause stating that if unsold merchandise is not claimed within 30 to 60 days after a notice has been sent, the shop can assume ownership of it and dispose of it any way it wishes.)

And there you have my case for an against consignment selling, still a controversial issue in today's craft world. Says one shop owner I spoke with, "A craftsperson won't get fleeced if he or she reads the contracts presented for signature and understands what is being signed. Properly and legally handled, consignment can bring more money and more orders to the working crafts professional than guaranteed sales or wholesale selling. Sixty-six and two-thirds percent is still better than 50 percent."

Wholesaling

Consignment selling has its problems, but so does selling outright, or wholesaling. To succeed in wholesaling, a craftsperson must be able to produce in quantity, which is why this kind of selling is out of the question for so many people. Pricing problems eliminate many others. Are your prices high enough that you can take a 50 percent discount and still make money? If so, and you can produce in quantity, maybe wholesaling is right for you. If and when you decide to try it, you'll need some guidelines. It takes courage to walk into that first big shop or store, see the buyer, and give your sales pitch, so let's get into the nitty-gritty of what you should know before you venture into this realm.

While craft shop owners are often warm and friendly and eager to see the work of any new craftsperson, gift shop and department store buyers will need to be *sold* on what you have to offer. They prefer to see sellers by appointment, often on certain days of the week only. Good timing is always important, so don't walk into a store at its busiest time of day and expect the buyer to give you much attention. Don't expect a store to give you a big Christmas order in November, either. Seasonal items are of interest to buyers months in advance of the season itself.

While some buyers are still thinking in terms of ordering a dozen gross of one item, others now more enlightened about handcrafts and craftspeople are realizing that only so much can be produced. The department store buyer who is looking for new products, concepts, and finishes may be interested in talking to any craftsperson who can deliver them, even in small quantities or one-of-a-kind editions.

Ordinarily, however, it would be wise to think in terms of a buyer ordering at least two dozen of anything you offer, perhaps more. If a store should surprise you by offering to buy much more than you had expected to sell, and you are doubtful about when you can deliver the order, be honest with them and explain that you need to recalculate the time required to fill the order. Then go home, figure it out, and come back later to write the actual order that will specify a shipping date you feel confident can be met.

Note that I am speaking here about making calls in person to meet with a buyer. While many craftspeople successfully wholesale to shops and stores by mail, it often pays to get in the car and drive to the nearest large city and spend a couple of days scouting for new shops and stores, setting up appointments to speak to buyers in person.

When offering your crafts in this manner, it is especially important to display them attractively for a buyer's consideration. You might make a special display case for this purpose, or at least carry an appropriate backdrop with you to make sure your products stand out from the clutter on a buyer's desk. Naturally, your samples should be the best you can produce. Never show work that requires an apology.

Each sample should bear a label or tag indicating its wholesale price (retail would normally be twice this amount), whether it comes in different colors or sizes, and what your minimum or maximum order quantity is for that item. If your work is too large or too heavy to carry around with you, you may have to prepare a special photographic presentation of your work. (Amateur snapshots are not recommended here.) Or, take slides and a viewer with you. In fact, this might be helpful even when you have samples to show. Also include any press clippings or publicity your work has received, since this may give the buyer an indication of the interest your work will arouse in the shop or store.

You should have a printed price list, of course, with the retail prices on one sheet and the wholesale prices on another. (Shops report that their customers occasionally like to look at a craft seller's price list, but they can't show it if the retail and wholesale prices appear on the same sheet.) If you can include some simple line drawings to illustrate the items on your price list, so much the

better. A brief description of each item should be given, including size and color. Items should also be numbered with some kind of coding system that works best for you. This will make it easier for the store to reorder in future.

Your price list should also state your conditions for new customers, such as "Check with first order," or "New accounts must provide three credit references." (The craftsperson who asks for references, *checks them*, and perhaps requires prepayment of the first order should have little trouble with non-payment of bills.)

You might be embarrassed to ask a major department store for credit references, since their credit is surely good, but it is often the larger stores that are slowest in paying. For that reason, you might want to include in your conditions statement that interest (at the going rate) will be charged on all accounts not paid within 30 days, then add this note to your original invoice.

Also include on your price list your guarantee, if one is offered. Example: "Work that is unsuitable for any reason will be taken back," or "Items shipped are guaranteed to be of same quality as samples," etc. Your policy regarding shipping charges should be included as well. Instead of charging the actual postage or shipping costs incurred, you may prefer instead to work on a percentage basis, such as ten percent of the total order, and make that a standard shipping charge for all orders. This amount will probably give you more than the actual cost involved, and help reimburse you for the time you spend in packing. Few shops or stores would question this amount, especially if you ship by United Parcel Service (UPS), which is prompt and dependable.

Business Terms and Definitions

In order to converse intelligently with a buyer, you will need to understand certain business terms and be familiar with standard business forms. Here is an explanation of the ones you will most likely encounter:

MARKUP: This is the percentage or amount a retail outlet adds to the price it pays for any item. For example, if you wholesale an item for $5, the store will probably mark it up 100 percent to arrive at a retail price of $10. (Although, as you have already noted elsewhere, some stores may mark up items 150 percent or more, depending on what they think their customers will pay.)

DISCOUNT: You will be mainly concerned with two kinds of discounts. First, there is the cash discount, which is the percentage or amount that is

INVOICE

BUSINESS

ADDRESS

TELEPHONE

Nº. 1234

To _____

DATE	
PURCHASE ORDER #	
SHIPPED VIA:	

TERMS: _____

QUANTITY	DESCRIPTION	PRICE	AMOUNT

ORIGINAL   *Thank You!*

68

Simple three-part invoices like this can be purchased in stationery stores or ordered by mail from office supply companies. Imprinting can be ordered if desired.

subtracted from a retail price to get the price a store will pay for merchandise -- the wholesale price. If you give a 50 percent discount off your retail price, it simply means that your wholesale price is half that amount. A $10 item would wholesale for $5. Thus you can see that a 50 percent discount relates to a 100 percent markup, and it all means the same to you in terms of actual dollars received.

Then there is the quantity discount, or the percentage that applies to the price if a purchase exceeds a certain amount. When you buy raw materials, you may get a discount by ordering more than a specified amount, and when you sell your crafts, you may wish to give your buyers a special discount for ordering your work in substantial quantity.

PRO FORMA: If you're dealing with a shop you feel might have financial problems, or one that has no credit credentials to offer you, it may be wise to ask for your money in advance, before you ship or deliver the work they have ordered. This is known as selling on a pro forma basis.

2/10/30 or 2% 10 DAYS, NET 30: You must decide whether you want cash with order, full payment within 30 days from date of invoice ("Net 30 days"), or if you will give a 2 percent discount when payment is made within 10 days ("2/10/30" or "2% 10 Days, Net 30"). Craftspeople generally request full payment within 30 days, but some do offer the 2 percent discount in order to get their money in hand as soon as possible. Unfortunately, some buyers pay the invoice a month later and still take the discount, in which case the store should be invoiced for the difference. After 10 days, the full amount is due.

F.O.B.: This means "Freight, or free, on board." These initials, and the name of a place immediately after them, indicate the point to which the seller will pay the freight. If the buyer is to pay all shipping charges, on your invoice you would indicate, "F.O.B. (*your town or city*). If you have to pay the freight, however, this notation would read F.O.B. and the name of your *customer's* town or city.

NOTE: This F.O.B. notation could be very important in the event goods are damaged in transit because, legally, title of the goods changes hands at the F.O.B. point. So, when you ship F.O.B. from your town or city and the UPS driver, mailman, truck driver, etc. takes the box or carton, the buyer is then responsible for the merchandise from that point on -- even if he never receives the goods.

ORDER FORM: When a buyer places an order, you will prepare an order form. An all-purpose sales form can be obtained from a business supplies store, or you can simply write the order on a piece of your stationery, making a carbon copy. A smaller shop may sign the original copy in your presence, to make it official, while a larger shop or store may ask you to send a typed version of the order after you get home. Others will use your order form to prepare their own purchase order, a copy of which you will receive later. Your order form should specify the date on which you have agreed to ship, and it is important to meet this date. Future orders could depend upon it. If you do not plan to deliver your order in person, your order form should specify the method of shipping -- parcel post, UPS, truck, etc.

PACKING LIST: Once you have prepared your order and are ready to deliver or ship it to your customer, you will need to prepare a packing list. Make two copies of it, one for you, one for your customer. It should agree in description and number with the information shown on your invoice, and be a complete record of what you have packed in each box or carton being shipped. Describe all items, grouping them under headings such as: "Contents of Box No. 1" (then list all items in that box); "Contents of Box No. 2" (list the items); etc. You need not show prices on your packing list. Include a copy of the completed packing list in one of the boxes or cartons being shipped, placing it on top where it can easily be found. (Or use the handy stick-on packing-slip envelopes which are designed for attachment to shipping cartons. They're readily available in office supply catalogs.)

When shipping more than one box or carton, be sure to mark the cartons themselves by writing "Box #1 of 4 boxes shipped," "Box #2 of 4 boxes shipped," etc., so your customer will know when all have been received.

THE INVOICE: You can buy simple, three-part invoices from a business supplies store, or order them from one of the sources in the Resource Chapter. (See illustration, left.) The last copy of the invoice is for your files while the first two are for your customer, who should return one of them to you with payment. Mail the invoice by first class mail, separately from the shipment, and send it the same day you ship the order so it will arrive before the order and alert your customer to its arrival.

Here's what your invoice should contain in the way of information:

1. Your name and address, your customer's name and address, and the ship-to address (if it is different from the sold-to address.)

2. The date of the invoice, and the date merchandise is being shipped.

3. Method of shipment (parcel post, UPS, truck or bus line, etc.)

4. Invoice number. Use any four-digit number (1001 is a good place to start) and thereafter number all your invoices accordingly.

5. Customer's purchase order number. Smaller shops and stores may not require a P. O. number, but larger stores will need it for identification purposes.

6. Terms of payment. (Net 30 days or 2% 10 days, net 30, as you prefer.)

7. Quantity and description of items, their unit price, and total amount. Refer to your packing list in preparing your invoice, to make sure the information on both forms is in agreement. List the wholesale price of each item in the "price" column, then calculate the figure for the "amount" column by multiplying the number of items shipped by the wholesale price. Then total the amount column.

8. Shipping costs. Generally, the buyer is expected to pay shipping costs, but this should be confirmed at the time you take the order. If the buyer is paying it, simply add the actual amount of postage to the total of the amount column, or charge your usual percentage for shipping costs. Then indicate the proper F.O.B. notation somewhere on your invoice.

A STATEMENT: Contrary to popular belief, a statement is not a request for payment, like an invoice, but merely a summary of a financial account showing the balance due. Unless you are making several shipments to a major account each month, a monthly statement should not be necessary. If a customer doesn't pay your invoice when it's due, simply send a duplicate invoice, only this time, write the words, "SECOND NOTICE" at the top. Usually this will be enough to get action. (There are standard invoice forms available that have extra carbons with gentle reminders like this already printed on them.)

If you run into the situation where an account does not pay you, even after a polite "second notice," send another notice and start charging interest. They are using your money at this point and should be paying for the privilege. If this doesn't work, telephone them, and continue to call regularly until they pay. Let them know you mean business (but no threats, as this is illegal). When all else fails, consider the use of a collection agency,

which is less expensive than suing the debtor on your own behalf.

Once you have established a few wholesale accounts, it will be necessary to follow up on them later since they probably won't call you when they run out of your stock. If your shops are local, call on them regularly, taking any new products you may have developed since your last visit. Leave your price list and brochure with them if they do not wish to re-order, since this may prompt an order later on.

If you have several wholesale accounts you have dealt with by mail in the past, or a number of outlets you're still trying to sell, take the initiative and send them copies of your new price list, brochure, or catalog. For just the cost of postage and printing, you may gain some repeat orders from old customers or bring in two or three new accounts.

When you do receive an order, immediately send back a copy, confirming when you will ship, or any problems you have in filling the order due to stock shortages, etc. The craftsperson who deals with retail outlets in a businesslike manner is most likely to receive new orders in the future.

Sales Representatives -- Working With Them or Becoming One Yourself

Craft sellers often discover that only about a third of their time is actually being spent in production. The other two-thirds may be tied up in less satisfying jobs such as selling, advertising, doing paperwork, making deliveries, etc. Although craftspeople often assume that a sales representative is out of the question for them, a careful evaluation of the situation might prove otherwise. If an additional one-third, or more, of your time could suddenly be freed for additional production, perhaps it would more than compensate you for the commission a sales representative would charge.

Generally, a sales representative, commonly called a rep, will take about 10 percent of the wholesale price as a commission, although some take as much as 30 percent. As the link between manufacturer and retailer, it is the sales rep's job to get the order for the manufacturer, who must then ship and bill the customer. Normally, the sales rep receives the commission only after the manufacturer has been paid. (Not all reps will accept this arrangement, however -- some will expect commission payments monthly, whether the manufacturer has been paid or not. Since few reps are concerned about the credit worthiness of the accounts they sell to, a craft seller can easily get stuck for the commission on accounts that do not pay. (I'll never orders. It's not my job to be a bill collector.")

"Working with sales reps can be a good situation or a disaster," says one wholesaler. "My best experiences have been with reps who had a permanent showroom in a market. They did not charge a fee for showroom space, and only expected a commission after I received payment for the order."

There are several ways to find representatives, beginning with trade magazines that carry notices placed by sales reps who are looking for new gift or handcraft lines. The telephone books of many major cities have a category, "Expositions, Trade Shows, and Fairs," which will guide you to some appropriate wholesale centers. Call them and explain that you are a manufacturer looking for a sales rep. You might also ask a few shop owners in your area for the names of sales reps they like to deal with.

In selecting a rep, it's important to find one who's interested in you and your work. Naturally, reps will be interested only in products that are compatible with their existing lines and accounts. To sell your line, a sales rep should have background information about you and the processes involved in the making of your products. Also needed are price lists, order forms, and samples of the items to be sold. (If you cease a relationship with a sales rep, count yourself fortunate if you get your samples back. Some reps simply keep samples for their own use or disposal.)

You should have a written agreement with your sales rep, or rep organization, that clearly defines their sales territory and commission, plus your terms of sale, credit policy, delivery dates, discounts, and shipping and packaging policies. There should also be a clause that stipulates how either party can break the relationship should it prove unsatisfactory for any reason. Example: You may not be able to make as much as a rep can sell, or a rep may not be able to sell as much as you make. Either way, the arrangement would be mutually unprofitable. A problem often reported to me through the years is lack of communication, where disinterested sales reps simply ignore the calls and letters of the manufacturer.

Depending on the sales territory, a rep may be able to introduce your product line in areas you cannot easily reach -- either a particular city or state, or a particular type of retail market. Sales reps often take their line to trade shows that cater exclusively to wholesale buyers in many different fields. Some have their own showrooms and others simply stay on the road most of the time, visiting countless department stores, gift shops, mail-order houses, and other retail outlets. The small manufacturer who needs new accounts but can't afford a sales staff (or just doesn't want one) will therefore find the sales representative a valuable addi-

tion to the business.

Although the average craftsperson cannot produce in a quantity sufficient to interest most reps, some crafts professionals have found reps to be the perfect way to expand their crafts business. As your business grows, you will instinctively know when the time is right to pursue this type of marketing.

Maybe you are not a producing craftsman at all, but merely one who is interested in selling the work of others. When a craft shop is desired, but there is simply no capital with which to launch such a venture, you might consider becoming a sales representative for some of the craftspeople you know. Craft know-how and selling expertise could be put to work for you on a schedule of your own making, in a sales territory as limited or extensive as you care to make it. It is the concept here that is important. There will always be craftspeople who love to produce, but hate to sell. You might represent several craftsmen who live in isolated, rural areas and need additional retail outlets, or you might start a party-plan marketing operation or take the work of several producing craft sellers to a major gift show. Corporate executives are often looking for unusual Christmas gifts, shops might be delighted to stock the line of handcrafts you represent, and your own ingenuity will no doubt turn up other buying markets.

If this idea interests you, keep the following suggestions in mind, noting that they are also applicable to craft wholesaling in general:

1. Handcrafts are unique and special, and so are the buyers of these items. Make them feel that way. Give them individual stories or selling points or histories on each item that catches their eye. The added extras make each item a treasure, and something that the buyer, in turn, can pass on to customers. (This, of course, implies knowing your products inside out -- processes involved in their making, histories of the people who make them, personal anecdotes, etc.)

2. Use all available resources for leads -- trade journals, yellow pages, magazines -- and know your competition. Most wholesale shows compile a buyers list (show attendees) that's available to exhibitors. If you're not exhibiting at these shows, at least go to see what's happening, and try to get hold of this buyer's list for use as leads.

3. Buyers are always concerned with their space limitations and display problems, so any help you can give on how to display products will make sales easier.

71

4. Organize your time. Keep accurate records of all leads and follow-ups. Call and follow up on customers on a regular basis. Leave literature even at places that don't place an order. They may later have a change of mind.

5. Be thoroughly prepared and competent before walking in to see a buyer. That way you can concentrate on a buyer's moods and attention spans, speeding up when you're losing him, slowing down when interest is indicated. If you have to spend most of your energy looking at your own samples or familiarizing yourself with your products, you'll miss out on the subtle ways of judging and getting to know your buyer.

Finally, says one sales rep I interviewed, "Don't let buyers tell you when they're through buying. If you still have more to show or sell, let them know that. Often it's easy to change their minds with 'just one more' special item."

How to Find Good Craft Shop Outlets

If you exhibit at craft fairs, you will surely learn about good shops and galleries by talking to other craftspeople. If you don't sell at shows, perhaps you know a few shops nearby that might be interested in your work. If so, visit them in person and take samples of your best work with you to show the owner or manager. If there are no shops near you, however, you will have to establish your retail outlets by mail, and many craftspeople do this simply by sending a letter to a shop and enclosing a brochure or photographs of their work and a price list describing all items available. Once you have a list of craft shops and some knowledge about what they might want in the way of merchandise, you can begin to find new outlets too.

As with craft fairs, there are special publications that list shops and galleries interested in buying crafts outright or handling them on consignment. See the Resource Chapter for subscription information to these periodicals, which include *The Crafts Report*, without question the most important periodical for crafts professionals today. Each issue of this "newsmonthly" includes an extensive listing of shops who want to buy, as well as ads placed by craftspeople looking for new markets.

Another periodical that will be helpful to you is *Craft Marketing News*. Publisher Adele Patti also issues (since 1982) the annual *Directory of Craft Shops & Galleries*. The only notable directory of its kind, it lists the names, addresses and merchandise needs of some 600 shops across the country who might welcome contact from you.

(Most of these listings also include the date the shop opened, so you have some measure of its stability.)

Although it may seem pointless to say, it's a waste of time to try to sell your work to a shop unless you know it is carrying merchandise similar in nature to yours. Some shops will have no interest in your work, not because it isn't good, but simply because it isn't compatible with the rest of their stock. While cornhusk dolls might be extremely good sellers in dozens of shops around the country, they would be of little interest to the shop that sells only contemporary crafts. That's why you need to study shop listings carefully before contacting them by mail, and look at the merchandise in local shops before going in to make your presentation. All shops are different, each with a personality of its own. One shop can sell what another cannot, and your goal as a supplier is to give the right product to the right shop.

It will be easier to do this if you understand what shops mean when they ask for specific kinds of craft merchandise. For example, "contemporary crafts" means work that is new, modern, and innovative in design or technique, while "traditional crafts" refers to objects made in proven patterns and forms from older design concepts. "Ethnic or folk crafts" are those that are characteristic of a people or region. Everyone has seen examples of folk or traditional crafts such as apple dolls, quilts, mountain woodcarvings, and tole painting, but not everyone has had exposure to fine contemporary crafts. A better understanding of them can be gained by reading contemporary craft magazines such as *American Craft* and *Handmade Accents*.

Shops often indicate an interest in work that is "utilitarian" or "decorative," categories that are self-explanatory and applicable to all kinds of merchandise. You will also note that there is a continuing demand in fine shops for work that is "unique" and "one-of-a-kind," and I only wish that someone would come up with a couple of new adjectives that aren't as overworked as these.

If you are serious about selling your crafts, you need to subscribe to one or two craft periodicals, not only to stay abreast of the latest marketing information, but to have a continuing source of new outlets and other important marketing leads. Shop openings (and closings) usually receive attention in such publications, which also offer news and information that could be vital to your success. I would also like to direct your attention to my own newsletter, *National Home Business Report,* in publication since 1981. Published quarterly, it offers a continuing supply of money-saving business tips and low-cost marketing methods applicable to all kinds of homebased businesses, including

SOME RETAIL OUTLETS TO EXPLORE

CRAFT SHOPS & GALLERIES
in your area or
listed in directories

GIFT SHOPS
in hospitals & nursing homes
boutiques • bridal shops
card & stationery stores

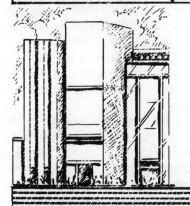

DEPARTMENT STORES
bridal or baby departments
decorative accessories
needlework departments
housewares • giftwares • "notions"

OTHER RETAIL STORES
hardware stores • restaurants
shoe shops • office supply stores
clothing shops • specialty shops
sports stores • florists

crafts. In addition, there is a tremendous amount of information passed along by readers who have learned things the hard way, and want to help others avoid the pitfalls they've encountered.

Other Retail Outlets To Explore

In addition to craft shops, there are many other places to consider when seeking reliable retail outlets, and some of them may be right under your nose. Craft shops are an obvious possibility, but don't overlook the shops normally found in hospitals and nursing homes, or the bridal, baby and gift areas of department stores.

For some time now, crafts have been selling well in large department stores across the country. Getting your work into this market is not easy, and even when you succeed, you may encounter problems you never thought about. In one article I read, a woman reported an unusual experience she had with a big department store. They liked her work but didn't want to buy it. Instead, they wanted it on consignment, which is quite unusual. (Obviously, they weren't sure her work would sell.) Eager to have her work in this prestigious store, the woman gave them more than $500 worth of merchandise that she had priced for retail. They said they would take 50 percent of that amount (not 40 percent, as is the custom elsewhere for consigned merchandise), and she agreed to this. When she returned a month later with a second delivery, she was surprised to find that the store had marked up her prices on some items as much as 150 percent, making them, in her opinion, too high to sell. But there was nothing she could do about it because she did not have a formal consignment agreement with the store.

As you can see, the above arrangement was quite advantageous for the store, which was obviously experimenting to see if crafts would sell, and completely disadvantageous for the craftswoman, who had a major portion of her crafts inventory tied up in a store that had priced most items too high to sell.

This is just one story, of course, not an indication of the experience of most craft sellers who market to department stores. I don't pretend to be an expert when it comes to selling to department stores, but perhaps the following tips, gleaned from crafts marketing periodicals, will provide some insight on how to approach this market.

If you plan to visit the department store buyer in person, be sure to call first for an appointment, since many have pre-arranged days and times for looking at craft lines. If you are mailing your presentation, this may be one of the few times that it is advisable to send a sample of your work, even when it has not been requested. "This just might tip the scales in your favor with a buyer who 'just has to see to believe'," says one crafts marketing expert.

Be sure to include wholesale prices and the maximum quantity for which you are prepared to accept orders. Clearly specify time required for completion of orders, as well. You should also specify a cancellation date, beyond which point a buyer would not have the right to cancel the order for a particular item. (Ideally, this date should be before the date you would normally order materials and start production of the item; realistically, however, this date is often included merely to protect the buyer from late deliveries.)

Even after you receive an order from a department store, don't consider this a firm order until you receive a confirmation on the store's own order form. If you don't receive it, double check with the buyer to see when it's forthcoming, and don't start production without it.

If department stores seem an unlikely market for you, perhaps you'd be more comfortable selling to retail shops. Consider garden or floral shops, for example, which might be interested in any art or craft related to flowers. Hardware stores might add handcrafted kitchenware and unusual gifts to their giftwares section. Home furnishing stores might be interested in wall hangings or decorative accessories, and restaurants might appreciate special floral arrangements, centerpieces, macrame planters, stained glass lamps, or sculpture. Shoe stores might buy a line of originally designed handbags, and specialty dress shops might be interested in carrying items you have knitted, crocheted, or sewed. Or perhaps you could offer to do decorative stitching or embroidery on their line of sweaters, or provide other custom design services their customers would appreciate.

Handcrafted gifts for men are always in demand, so check men's clothing and specialty shops to see if they can use craft wearables and accessories. Office supply stores might like to see handcrafted desk accessories, lamps, or office sculpture. Game and leisure-interest shops may be interested in handcrafted game boards and adult toys. Sport shops sell items for participants and spectators alike...and don't overlook boating and yachting shops, where high prices may not be a problem. (As any boat-owner's wife will confirm, nothing is ever too expensive for her husband's boat!)

Any store that concentrates on a concept of selling, rather than quantity of merchandise, is a possible market for craftspeople these days, and selling them on your products may require little more than just letting them know you are there, ready to supply them with fine handcrafts.

Being a Good Supplier

Without dependable suppliers, it is difficult to stock any kind of shop, so if you want to rate high with your retail outlets, simply become a supplier they can rely on. Once you have made a sale to a retailer, call back in a month or so and try to get a re-order. When merchants realize that you are going to be available to provide goods and service on a regular basis, they will begin to develop confidence in you and be more interested in working with you. Retailers are simply not interested in dealing with craftspeople on a one-shot basis.

Most craftspeople are unreliable suppliers. If you don't believe me, ask any craft shop owner. "Working with individuals is both trying and enjoyable," says one of the shop owners interviewed for this book. "We find a source we think is great, and the next thing you know the craftsman is doing something else and we are left to find a replacement. Even though we certainly have no objection to children, we find that when one of our sources has a child, her production of crafts is cut severely or completely -- often for as long as three years. Also, as craftspeople grow in their craft, their product changes, sometimes for the good of both parties, sometimes not. Again we must search for a replacement. Sometimes the product must increase in price and we feel it is then too high for good turnover, and we are out searching once again."

Most craftspeople do not realize how hard shop owners work to find them. In fact, many spend a great deal of time and money trying to find good suppliers, and some become quite frustrated in the process, as evidenced by one letter I received from the owner of a consignment shop:

"Why should shop owners travel all over the place looking for good people to deal with?" she wrote. "And why are we treated like some passive animal sitting in a lair waiting to be found by some enterprising innocent looking to be fleeced? I'd love to contact good craftspeople directly by phone or mail, and would, if I could find them."

After about a year and a half in business, the owner of a crafts gallery in New York City gave me an interesting picture of three kinds of craftsmen who were then represented in his store. His comments, as timely now as when first written, should help you understand how shop owners everywhere view their craft suppliers:

"Over the past year I find I am dealing with three categories of craftsmen -- the hobby-craftsman, the artist-craftsman, and the professional craftsman.

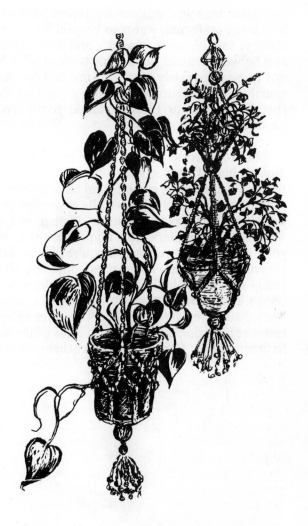

"The hobby-craftsman is the person who makes something at his leisure, maybe has fantasies of leaving everything and just 'doing his thing,' but in reality has many other priorities before producing his craft. These people are nice to have in the store, but they're not a reliable source of income.

"The artist-craftsman produces beautiful one-of-a-kind work, and his pieces add a lot of quality and uniqueness to my store, but do not turn over much because of the price.

"Finally, there is the professional craftsman. He is into a product line. The professional craftsman has developed a group of items that seem to have a consistent appeal to the public after being marketed through a retail outlet. The professional craftsman has come to terms with the reality value of his product, independent of his labors. It is this craftsman that supports our store and contributes to making it a viable operation."

It is unfortunate that so few craftspeople can separate the art from the marketability of the objects they create. As this gallery owner explains, "The hobby-craftsman is more interested in selling

75

the object than in the monetary return he receives. The artist-craftsman wants to be paid for both his concept and his time (research and development), and he would rather not sell his work at all if he is not to be adequately rewarded for it. The professional craftsman usually creates a product for a specific market, or finds a market for a specific product."

So, to increase your sales, try creating a coordinated line of products. Just one or two of something in a shop does not offer much of a selection, so shop owners will be especially interested in the seller who offers at least four to six items in a line.

To create a line, simply think in terms of what goes together. For example, if you're offering fabric covered books and accessories, think of all the things that might logically be covered, from scrapbooks and photo albums to checkbooks, address books, and eyeglass cases. If you're offering decorative accessories, concentrate on areas of the home to create a line. For example, a kitchenware wood craft line might include canisters, salt and pepper shakers, recipe box and napkin holder, while a ceramics bath ensemble line might include an unusual soap dish, tissue box, powder canister, or other containers for personal items, from vitamins to cotton balls.

If you're into clothing, such as appliqued sweatshirts, one line might be for joggers or other sports enthusiasts, while another might be for children. As a consumer, you know what interests you, and this is always a good indication of what others might buy as well.

Although most craftspeople seem to prefer making one-of-a-kind pieces, these are not the items that turn over easily in the average retail store. One-of-a-kind pieces may provide the cream for your table, but if you need bread and butter, do what the professionals do: Concentrate on the development of one or more lines of merchandise that are competively priced to quickly sell.

- 8 -

Selling By Mail

Mail order. The great American dream.

All kinds of people are fascinated by mail order because it is a business that can be started with a small investment and operated on a part-time basis out of one's home. But few people who get involved in it have the necessary requirements for success. What does it take to succeed, and do you have it?

The most important qualities for success in mail order are: organizational abilities, an enjoyment of detail, and a willingness to work hard. The ability to do many different jobs, from writing advertisements to packing products for shipment, is also important. Having the right product is the most important thing of all.

The first part of this chapter is devoted to general information about the mail order business, followed by a discussion of three types of mail order marketing: (1) selling through magazine or newspaper advertisements; (2) direct mail; and (3) selling through a catalog. As the chapter unfolds, you will meet some interesting men and women who have developed successful mail order businesses, and much will be learned from a study of their techniques.

The Best Mail Order Products

What type of craft item sells best by mail? Kits, patterns, designs, supplies, instructions, books and services are easier sold through the mail than finished handcrafts, whose sale so often depends on eye appeal and buyer impulse. But handcrafts will sell when they meet certain requirements, and the following guidelines will help you determine if you have a good mail order item or not.

Products should be unusual in that they are not readily available elsewhere, but not so unfamiliar that people would hesitate to buy them. A good rule to remember is that you should offer the same type of product that others are selling, since a really new and innovative item probably will not sell well. (People won't buy something if they don't understand what it is, or why they should have it.)

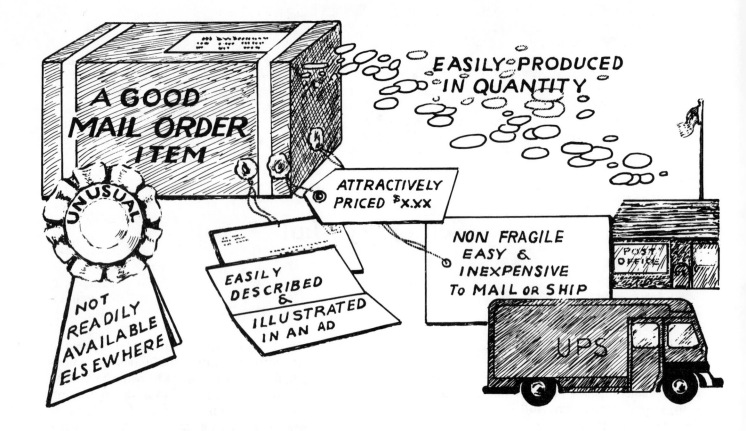

A product offered by mail must be one that can be easily described and illustrated in an ad. Study the mail order sections of various magazines to find out how others do this. At the same time you will discover certain categories of merchandise that are obviously good mail order sellers, such as food items, clothing, garden-related products, kitchenware, unique seasonal items, gifts and personalized handmade items, needlework kits, books, plans, patterns, and various other objects designed to meet specific needs.

Mail order items must be attractively priced, and by that I mean they must give the impression of being a good buy. In days gone by, the best-selling mail order items were usually priced under $10 because people were more skeptical then of buying by mail from companies they didn't know. These days, with everything costing so much more, price is not as critical, and people have come to see mail order shopping as a great convenience. Note, however, that many mail order items today are still priced at the popular $10-level.

Incidentally, the price of a mail order item should be at least five times what it cost in materials and labor to produce, according to experts. This high markup is necessary in order to compensate for increased overhead costs. In addition to advertising and regular postage and shipping costs, you must also consider the cost of packaging supplies and the time spent in packing, shipping, and corresponding with customers about lost shipments, damaged goods, or complaints. And don't forget that your first big ad just might pull in more orders than you anticipate. You might have to hire someone to help you fill them, and if your price isn't high enough to begin with, you could lose all your profit as a result.

You realize, I hope, that a mail order item has to be produced in quantity. If you can't do this, or don't want to do it, then you should forget about selling handcrafts by mail, and concentrate on items that can be produced more easily, such as patterns, designs, books and kits.

As you well know, the best items to sell by mail are those that are nonfragile and easy and inexpensive to pack and ship. The more fragile the item, the higher your shipping costs will be since you will need special packing materials for it. Keep in mind that anything that can be easily damaged in shipment will probably result in your having to replace merchandise from time to time.

Good Advice for Beginners

Marian Mumby, who makes and sells ceramic beads and accessories, shares the following tips gained from experience in her own mail order business.

"It's important to get reliable advice when starting any new business venture," she says. "People who start a business are apt to take the advice of friends, fellow craftsmen, or anyone who happens to sound as if they know what they are talking about. But are these people really qualified? Are they, or have they been, successful in a similar situation or business? Do they know enough about your actual situation or problem?"

Marian also warns about carrying too large an inventory. In the beginning she offered too many types of beads. In order to be able to ship immediately upon receipt of an order, it was necessary to keep a tremendous inventory on hand. "This is a drain financially as your money is tied up too long in an inventory that may or may not move," Marian told me. "We had too many different kinds of beads for the size of our business, so we streamlined the number of kinds of beads, and things began to run more smoothly as a result."

Beginners in mail order would be wise to heed Marian's advice. If you are selling handcrafts or kits, begin with a small line of perhaps half a dozen items. Then you won't have to invest too much in inventory right at the beginning. Run a few test ads to gauge order response, then build your inventory accordingly and prepare for more ads and promotional mailings in the future.

Does it pay to sell the products of others? Sure. Many mail order marketers today are dealers for large manufacturers and publishers. Greater profits can be realized, however, when you create your own products and become the "prime source" for products *other* mail order dealers can help you sell.

Don't worry about starting small. Contrary to popular belief, you can start with just one item, and build a line from there. That's exactly what I did back in 1981 when I began to sell this very book by mail. Then I added a newsletter, some special reports, and finally began to produce other books.

Specialty mail order businesses started by average individuals are likely to thrive whenever they zero in on one particular audience of buyers -- often an audience considered too small by major catalog marketers. If you can identify from 20,000 to 30,000 people anywhere in the U.S. who have a unique area of interest you can serve, this is a sufficient base for starting a specialty mail order business.

Once you've identified your audience and found the right media for your ads, you must zero in on the benefits of your product or service, and write the kind of ad that sounds interesting to prospective customers. There's a trick to this, and you'll find some tips on this topic in Chapter 12.

Packaging and Shipping Tips

Good packaging is important. If you need a special presentation package to house your product -- such as a piece of jewelry, needlework kit, set of printed patterns, etc. -- you might consider the vinyl zipper bag, an item easily found in supply catalogs. Such bags come in sizes ranging from tiny to large, and can be imprinted with your business name, logo, or content instructions. (To get wholesale prices, you may have to order in minimum quantities of at least 500-1000 bags.) Other companies can supply gift boxes suitable for packaging all kinds of items, from jewelry to greeting cards. (I've included a couple of these companies in the Resource Chapter. Read trade magazines and supplier directories to find more of them.)

Shipping cartons may be a problem because, as you will learn when you approach a box manufacturing company, minimum orders (of 500-1000) are often too high for the small business to meet. If you can't afford to buy boxes directly from a manufacturer, write to them and ask for the names of a distributor in your area who may be able to sell to you in smaller quantities. You could get started, of course, by purchasing these items at retail from one of the many office supply catalogs available these days.

Once you've decided how you're going to package your mail order product, you should make a test package, wrapping it exactly as you plan to do when shipping it to your customer. Be sure to calculate the cost of all wrapping supplies, and try to determine an accurate wrapping cost per package. Then have the package weighed at the post office (your scale may not be accurate), and decide how you're going to ship it. Will you use the mail or United Parcel Service? Will you insure your package or run the risk of its being lost or damaged en route? How much will this cost?

Keep in mind that UPS service is readily available to everyone. Drivers will pick up packages at any home, even in isolated rural areas, for a modest, weekly pick-up charge. And they will come as many times during the week as necessary. It is not necessary to pay for this service on a 52-week basis, either; simply call UPS when you need them. They will deliver anywhere, even to a post office box number or rural route. (With a box number address, or someone they cannot locate in the country, they will send the recipient a notice through the mail requesting additional delivery instructions.) Packages do need to be weighed before pickup, and you will be given a chart to calculate shipping charges, which are payable at the time the package is picked up by UPS. For additional information, call your nearest United Parcel Service office.

You Can Bank On A Package When It's Wrapped Like This!

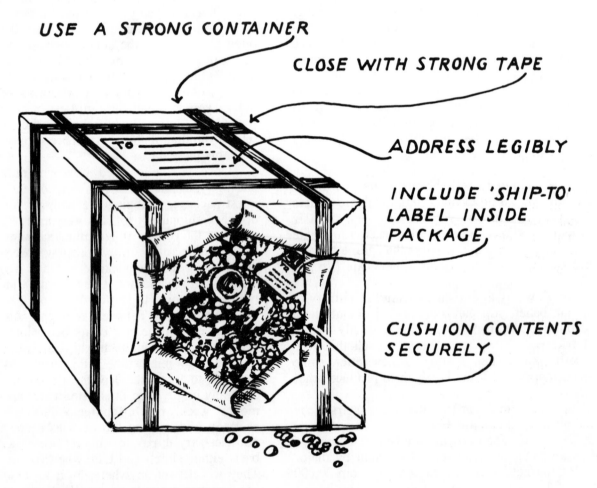

USE A STRONG CONTAINER

CLOSE WITH STRONG TAPE

ADDRESS LEGIBLY

INCLUDE 'SHIP-TO' LABEL INSIDE PACKAGE

CUSHION CONTENTS SECURELY

TO

Illustration idea courtesy of U.S. Postal Service.

There are many different kinds of packaging materials that can be used to ship crafts by mail.
Ideally, a shipping container will be both sturdy and light in weight.

If you happen to be shipping books, note that it is less expensive to ship them by mail at the special bookrate prices offered by the postal service. I have been shipping books this way since 1981, and have rarely encountered delivery or lost-mail problems.

In pricing your mail order product, you will need to carefully calculate your shipping and handling charge. Keep in mind that both UPS and postal rates are constantly increasing, and it's difficult to change all your prices every time the rates change. Sometimes your "handling charge" can absorb the small rate increases for awhile. Now you may be tempted to not charge for handling, but that's a mistake. You may be able to do all the fulfillment of your orders in the beginning, but as time goes on, you may have to hire someone to do this job for you. Plan accordingly.

Should shipping charges be listed separately, or included in the price of the item as a single postage-paid price? That's up to you, but many mail order sellers find less buyer resistance if there is a single postage-paid price that does not place emphasis on the higher postal rates we're all having to pay these days to get anything by mail.

By the way, packages tied with string are no longer acceptable, so plan to use sturdy packaging tape, and be sure to get one of those handy "tape guns" to speed up your wrapping process.

If you elect to ship packages by parcel post, I urge you to insure everything you mail, and test your mailing package thoroughly. Try throwing it out the upstairs window a few times, or kick it downstairs with gusto and see how it holds up.

This in no way duplicates the type of handling usually given to fourth-class packages as they are dumped from trucks to conveyor belts and tossed from one bin to another, but it will give you an idea of whether your product is going to reach your customer intact and undamaged. If you need more padding for the inside of your shipping carton, try plastic "popcorn" or consider air cushion bags or foam padding, available in rolls. Crumpled newspaper may also do the trick, and it's a lot cheaper. (The newest packaging being used these days is nothing more than air-popped popcorn. Try it!)

Mail Order Rules and Regulations

The law is especially important in mail order. Above all, you cannot in any way misrepresent your product or your business, use deceptive prices, or imitate the trademarks or trade names of others. Every word and picture in your advertisements must be true, says mail order expert Julian L. Simon, author of *How to Start and Operate a Mail Order Business* (a classic in its field).

In his book he emphasizes that an advertisement must not fool even gullible or ordinarily trusting people. "If you fool any substantial portion of your public," he warns, "you are in the wrong. And what counts is not your actual words, but what people believe after they have read your ad." In short, customers must get exactly what they *expect* to receive, and must not feel they have been gypped. (Note, however, that a customer can feel dissatisfied without feeling gypped. Being unhappy isn't the same as feeling cheated.)

What you do about unhappy customers depends on what you have *promised* to do. If, like most successful mail order companies, you offer a guarantee of satisfaction or money back, you have little choice but to issue a refund when a customer returns your product -- even when the item is returned in unsalable condition. In my own business, I have offered a money-back guarantee since I began, and I rarely receive more than one or two refund requests a year. I'm convinced that my personal guarantee of satisfaction has often been the determining factor in whether a new customer will order from me or not.

In addition to truth in advertising, you must also be aware of Federal Trade Commission (FTC) laws that pertain to consumer safety and the labeling of certain products, most notably textile wearing apparel, wool products, and items with concealed fillings. The FTC offers several free booklets that explain trade practice rules for various industries, and you should order those that pertain to you. (See address in Resource Chapter, and also see Chapter 14.)

Another FTC ruling states that all mail orders must be shipped within 30 days of receipt, or the customer is entitled to a refund. If for some reason an order cannot be shipped within this period, the seller must advise the customer accordingly and give him the opportunity to cancel the order or indicate a date beyond which he will not wait for shipment.

Finally, you will have to register the name of your business with the county clerk if you are using any name but your own. This simple matter is discussed further in the legal chapter.

Selling Through Advertisements

Craftspeople who currently sell at fairs or through shops have an important edge on mail order selling because they already manufacture products themselves and are in complete control of their source of supply and prices, unlike the mail order entrepreneur who buys merchandise for resale.

If you're going to launch a mail order business selling the products of others, you may need as much as $2,500 to get started on the right foot. But you can literally start on a shoestring if you make your own products, and want to expand your business through mail order marketing. You see, "mail order" is not really a type of business after all -- it's simply another way sellers can market a variety of products and service.

Many people who begin selling at craft fairs naturally expand to mail order marketing when they take a look at the mailing list they've developed from recent shows. (If you're not already doing this, start now to capture the names of buyers and prospects interested in your work. Place a tablet and pen on your table with a notice to "Sign here to get on our mailing list" for announcements of new items, your new brochure, catalog, or whatever.)

To expand your customer prospect base, you'll need to learn how to get publicity (see Chapter 12), and place some ads as well. A few inexpensive classified ads will get you started, and when you feel more comfortable about writing ads, you might want to try your first small display ad. (There is no rule that says you must begin with a $600 display ad in a major consumer magazine. In fact, if you *do* begin like this, you're likely to lose your shirt because there's much more to writing ad copy than beginners understand.)

Where to advertise? Avoid your daily newspaper, which is generally a poor medium for mail order items. Certain magazines are not likely to be profitable media either, which is why it is important to study the mail order sections of many magazines to find the ones right for your products and pocketbook. Wherever you advertise, be prepared to advertise regularly once you start, since repetition of your ad will build customer confidence. Instead of beginning with ads in the major women's magazines, first try the craft and needlework magazines. Their rates are more affordable, and you can be sure that *all* readers have a special interest in craft and needlework products, publications and services.

Although you can start out in mail order with just one item, you will want to add other items to your line as soon as possible. Otherwise you won't be able to benefit from repeat business. When you send that new customer the first product ordered, you will need to include information about something else you offer, to encourage what is known as a "bounceback" sale. (The most important thing to remember about mail order marketing is that *repeat business is the name of the game.*)

If you already offer a line of products, you might venture into mail order the same way major companies do. They select one item -- usually the most unusual product, the best seller, or the one most likely to grab a reader's attention. A photograph of this product is then featured in a display ad, along with the postage-paid price to order it by mail. Since not everyone will order the product, such ads do double duty by also offering the company's free (or inexpensive) brochure or catalog.

When an order is received for the advertised item, the seller will fill it promptly, being sure to include appropriate advertising literature. The quality of the advertised product, and the manner in which the initial order is handled, will have a great deal to do with whether a customer will order from this company again. Once a seller has a mailing list of satisfied customers, a new marketing option presents itself: direct mail advertising, discussed below.

Direct Mail Marketing

Direct mail is exactly what it sounds like: One approaches prospective customers directly, using a letter, brochure, or catalog. In mail order jargon, this is known as "mailing cold" because the addressees have not requested information at this time, and may have no interest in it once they receive it. Of course, the level of interest will be much higher when you mail to prospects on your in-house mailing list, as opposed to renting an outside list or even using a list you've traded with a mail order business friend.

Whether your mailing yields orders depends on many things, from the quality of the names being mailed and how clean the list is (when were addresses last updated?), to the quality and content of your mail piece, the uniqueness of your product(s), the time of year the mailing is being made, and other variables.

Large direct-mail advertisers send several thousand pieces of mail each year and, upon buying a special postal permit and paying an annual fee, they are entitled to special bulk-mail rates. The small business owner who is thinking in terms of sending out only 100 flyers once or twice a year will have to mail at first class rates, since bulk mailings must be made in quantities of 200 pieces or more.

If you have developed a good mailing list of satisfied customers and other people who have expressed an interest in your work in the past, perhaps a small mailing would work well for you. But, before conducting even a small direct-mail campaign, be sure to calculate all your printing and postage costs, then weigh this total against the number of orders (and dollars) you could reasonably expect to receive. The answer will tell you if direct mail is something you should try.

What kind of response can you expect to receive? Let's suppose you have a new illustrated price list or catalog you'd like to get into the hands of about 300 people, as a follow-up to some ad you've placed recently. If all of them are satisfied customers, you might realize an order response of as much as 20% -- which translates to 60 orders.

More than likely, however, you will be fortunate to receive a 4-5% response, which will give you 12-15 orders. (The only certain thing about direct-mail advertising is that you can't be certain about anything.) It's a bit risky for beginners, so don't try it unless you can afford to lose the cost of your printing and postage. I might add, however, that the more mailings you make, the more confident you will become about the profitability of any given mailing. In fact, after years of putting out mailings, I can generally predict the number of orders I'm likely to receive from any given mail list. Since I also know the size of my average order, I can then calculate the dollars likely to be generated by a particular mailing.

I have used direct mail with great success through the years, and my rule of thumb in deciding whether a mailing is profitable or not is simply this: If I get back the entire cost of my mailing with some profit left over, I'm satisfied because, in the process, I've just sold new products to some old customers, acquired several new customers who are likely to order from me again, and also acquired some new subscribers for my newsletter. Many times, too, people who do not order are kind enough to pass my mailer on to friends.

Some people make a mailing to a list of names, and never mail them again. What a mistake! After years of selling by mail, I now have thousands of buyer and prospect names on computer, and I regularly remail these name over and over again until a mailing to a particular list is no longer profitable. Then I simply put those names on hold for awhile until I have something new to offer these people.

The most important thing to remember here is that mail lists go out of date very quickly. In fact, a mail list that's over a year old is likely to be 20-30% out of date. Don't waste your money trying to salvage any list that's over two years old because it will probably cost you less to acquire new customer prospects than it will to clean your list. (Address returns from the post office presently cost 25-30 cents each, depending on whether the post office returns your actual mail piece, or a photocopy of the address portion. So if you mail a thousand names and 300 of them aren't deliverable, that's $75-$90 down the drain -- plus the cost of the printing and postage to mail them in the first place.)

That's why you should make it a practice to mail all your prospects and buyers at least twice a year, including a notation on your mail piece that reads "Address Correction Requested." Then you'll not only know how many pieces are delivered, but will be able to update your mail list accordingly.

Some people have told me they just mail by first class mail because it's always forwarded. True, such mail is forwardable for a limited time, but it does you no good to lose the names of valued customers when they move, and the only way you can get those new addresses is with the "Address Correction" notation on your mail. (This can be included on first class as well as bulk mail.)

Two Mail Order Success Stories

In order to uncover some specific techniques and ideas you can use in your own business, let's take a look at how a couple of craftspeople started in mail order.

A study of the history of Timbers Woodworking (formerly known as Love-Built Toys & Crafts) illustrates how a business can be launched with just one product and a small classified ad. Starting with one set of wood toy plans in December 1972, Dale C. Prohaska, Jr. quickly developed an impressive catalog of supplies for the wooden toy maker, including plans, wooden wheels, books and toy-making supplies. Eight years later, Dale incorporated his company because it was then grossing nearly half a million a year. His story is an inspiration to us all!

Timbers Woodworking has always been a retail-wholesale business, doing 99.5 percent of its business by mail. New customers are obtained through magazine advertisements, and when they order, they naturally receive the company's catalog and usually order from it as well. Originally, Dale's goal was to provide ideas and supplies to parents so they could make imaginative and safe toys for their children, but he soon discovered that many of his customers were professional toymakers looking

for a good source of supply. He therefore established special bulk prices for quantity purchases, and offered schools and Scout groups a discount as well.

Dale's first ad, a $16 classified in *Workbench* magazine, read: "Ten Wooden Toy Plans, $1." That ad yielded 55 orders. The following year Dale put out a small 4-page mimeographed catalog showing about 25 designs and again advertised in the classified section of *Workbench*. The next year, a 12-page brochure was printed with photographs showing plans, wheels and doll patterns. A problem developed at this point, however. "After advertising in nine magazines to send out a free catalog," says Dale, "we nearly went broke paying for the postage. Eventually we had to find a new printer for the catalogs."

Two years after Dale began the business, he took what was a giant step for him: He placed a display ad in *Workbench*. "It was only one inch high and 2-1/2 inches wide," Dale recalls, "but it tripled our business. By early 1975 we were experimenting with several other magazines, and in August we began printing our catalog in newspaper format. This reduced the price of our catalog to about one-sixth of what it was before."

At this point, Dale also changed the format of his woodworking plans to a large folded sheet. Since then, many new plans and supplies have been added to his line. (Pay special attention to Dale's remarks about the expense of mailing free catalogs, and note how a different format lowered his costs.)

Mail order is a great way to sell all kinds of patterns and designs, but few people realize the work that's involved in getting such products into a customer's hands. Colette Wolff, a successful New York designer-craftsman, gave me a brief education on this process, and her frank comments paint a vivid picture of what you're letting yourself in for when you start any kind of mail order business.

Colette designs fabric toys for other people to make from patterns that she publishes and sells through the mail. Her company is called Platypus. Here's how she gets her product from the drawing board into the customer's hands.

"First," she explains, "I have to have an idea for a toy that can be interpreted in stuffed fabric. Then I have to design the toy -- make the patterns and work out all the details of execution. Then I convert the process of making the toy into step-by-step instructions. I leave the sewing machine for the typewriter. Then I proceed to design and lay out -- arranging those instructions into a certain size and number of pages. I illustrate the steps in the instructions, working with a light box, Radiographs, photographs, and other artists' materials, plus

FUNNY PEOPLE
Pattern
Booklet
- $4.00 -

© by Colette Wolff

85

An illustration taken from Colette Wolff's catalog, which includes numerous toy and doll patterns to stitch and stuff. Among them is a pattern for a basic doll body that can be turned into the nine personable characters shown here -- characters Colette calls her "Funny People." Good drawings like this would add considerable interest to any crafts catalog.

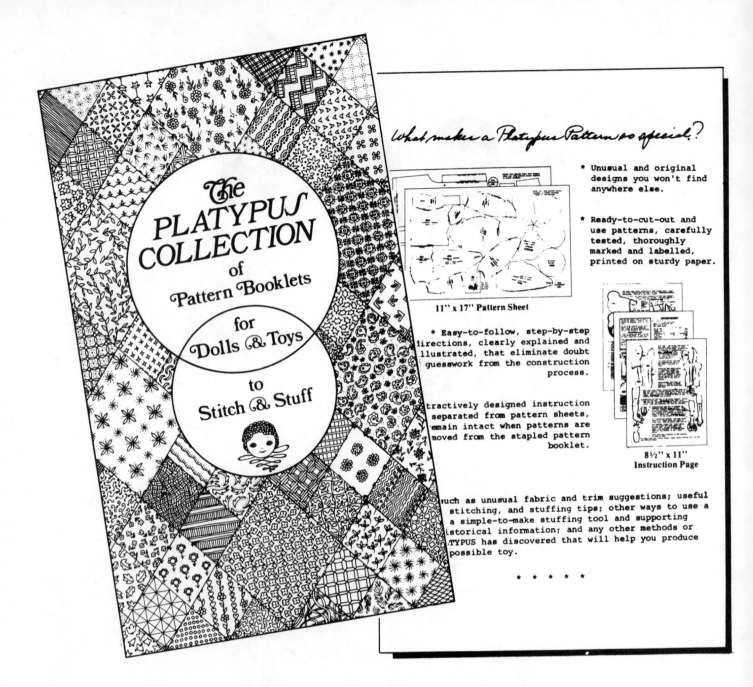

What makes a Platypus Pattern so special?

11" x 17" Pattern Sheet

* Unusual and original
  designs you won't find
  anywhere else.

* Ready-to-cut-out and
  use patterns, carefully
  tested, thoroughly
  marked and labelled,
  printed on sturdy paper.

* Easy-to-follow, step-by-step
  directions, clearly explained and
  illustrated, that eliminate doubt
  guesswork from the construction
  process.

...tractively designed instruction
...separated from pattern sheets,
...emain intact when patterns are
...moved from the stapled pattern
booklet.

8½" x 11"
Instruction Page

...uch as unusual fabric and trim suggestions; useful
...stitching, and stuffing tips; other ways to use a
...a simple-to-make stuffing tool and supporting
...istorical information; and any other methods or
...TYPUS has discovered that will help you produce
...possible toy.

* * * * *

86

Note the front cover of Colette Wolff's well-designed mail order catalog, which creates a warm first impression, then "makes its pitch" on the inside front cover by answering the question, "What makes a Platypus Pattern so special?" Colette takes this opportunity to list the important selling points of her product, such as (1) unusual and original designs; (2) ready-to-cut-out-and-use patterns; (3) easy-to-follow, step-by-step directions; and so on.

On the inside back cover (not shown here) Colette explains how her pattern booklets may be ordered, and the outside back cover has her return address and her Platypus logo, plus space for the mailing address and a special bonus: instructions on how to make a quick-and-easy stocking doll, illustrated with drawings.

oceans of rubber cement. After the copy is prepared for the printer, I must find/choose a printer to do the actual printing.

"Then," Colette continues, "I sell the product, or pattern booklet as I call it. That involves becoming a copywriter; placing ads in magazines; and writing, designing, and illustrating a catalog and flyers. When orders come in I become an office worker and record them, stuff envelopes, type labels, and deal with the U. S. Post Office. It's a one-person operation at the beginning, and perhaps for a long time afterward."

Mail order is a business with a peculiar nature that Colette describes like this: "It runs you, I think, as much as you run it. If someone just wants to make toys to sell, that's an activity that can be controlled, more or less, by the toymaker; and if the toymaker gets sick, wants to go into another activity, take a vacation -- whatever -- the toymaker, after dealing with outstanding orders, just stops. Not so with a catalog mail order business. It goes on every day the mail is delivered. Orders come in from catalogs that were mailed out years before. It requires constant attention. And if you get bored with it, or want to 'close up shop,' a mail order business dies a very slow death, and can dribble on for years."

Colette began Platypus with a $7 ad and a borrowed mimeograph, much like Dale Prohaska. Through the years, her business has stayed at the level generated by the kind of advertising she does. (Mostly, she places classified ads in small needlework and hobby publications because this brings all the business she can handle by herself.) "In order to get to the next level," she says, "I would need a much higher advertising budget for display ads, more space to store all my pattern booklets, files and materials, and machinery to help process the daily mail."

A note in Colette's advertising material offers a tip for mail-order sellers. She is not equipped to send out extensive mailings whenever her catalog expands, but she does maintain a file of large, stamped, self-addressed envelopes from customers who want to be informed about new publications as soon as they are in print. Perhaps this idea would work for you, too.

"One of the nice things about what I do," concludes Colette, "is that when I finally have a design in print, in booklet form, the returns on that title are endless until I decide to take it out of circulation or not to reprint it. My kind of approach to the craft business builds the longer you stay in it."

Creating Your Own Catalog

In Chapter 12, under the subhead "Promotional Materials," you will find information on how to create your own letterhead, business cards, brochures, etc. A catalog can be created in much the same way, and it can be something as simple as one sheet of paper or as complex as the 42-page catalog offered by Alfred Atkins.

Al is a specialist in miniature wrought iron and unquestionably the interesting craftsman/catalog designer I have ever encountered. I asked him to give me some sage advice that could be passed on to others who are interested in creating their own catalogs, and while he was at it, would he also tell me more about his mail-order business.

"Yeah," he replied. "It started like this. Caye MacLaren wrote an article about me in *Nutshell News* after I made some clumsy trinkets for her. Did I ever get mail? A rhetorical question, the answer to which is yes, I ever got mail. It wasn't that I was so great; there just was nobody into metal minis, so I was in the position of one who had invented booze or baseball. Soon I was writing the same kind of letter to many people explaining, 'Yes, I can make a spiral staircase for you. It will cost by the inch of vertical rise, and I do mean COST, etc.' Finally I realized I was writing letters all the time and getting no work done. Had to get out a catalog."

If you are writing letters all the time, explaining what you can and cannot make for your customers, perhaps you need a catalog, too. Whether it's one or two sheets of paper or a nice booklet, make sure it represents you and your work. If you have the money to spend on layout and design (hiring a professional to do the job), it will be well spent on the creation of a professional catalog, but if not, you can create your own. (You can get excellent results with the electronic typewriters on the market today, and if you have a computer, many design and graphic options are open to you. More about this in Chapter 12.)

Many craftspeople begin with charming, handwritten, hand-drawn catalogs and brochures that are real attention-getters. If you can do simple line drawings, or have a friend who will do them for you, that's a good start. Photographs are better than drawings, but they do add to your printing costs.

The content of your catalog should be clear enough for anyone to understand, and items for sale should be accurately described. Do *not* show prices in the catalog itself, but print loose sheets (and order forms) that can be inserted. Then, when it becomes necessary to change a price (and it will), you can simply have the price sheet reprinted. New

87

THE VILLAGE SMITHY

Miniature Catalogue

R.D. 5 ✳ Hemlock Trail
Carmel, New York ✳ 10512

$3⁰⁰

*a paltry figure when you
consider that this is positively
the last catalogue by*

A. Atkins
Blacksmith &
Designer

**SPECIALIST IN
MINIATURE
WROUGHT IRON**

...a surprise...to see all
this mini stuff coming
off my anvil.

a. Atkins

88

items can be added to your catalog by printing additional loose pages until such time as you can afford to reprint the entire catalog.

When describing your products, give color, size, texture, and materials used. If space allows, include additional information as well -- perhaps something about the history of your craft, the origin of your materials, or anything that makes you or your products unusual and interesting. This kind of information will give your catalog a special personality all its own.

Perhaps that's why I like Alfred Atkins' catalog so much. Not because it has 42 pages, but because it has lots of personality. So much, in fact, that it is always getting free publicity. (Everyone who sees it wants to share it with others.) It is not just a catalog of "metal minis," but the personal statement of an artist who obviously has a zest for life and a love of people. (Even if he doesn't trust anyone over 6½ inches tall.) After a lifetime spent in occupations far removed from the world of miniatures, Al, at age 61, is now doing the kind of work he loves best and wants to do from here on in. His unique catalog reflects his humorous approach to life and the great pleasure he receives from his work. A study of it is something of an education in itself. How did he produce it, I wondered.

"I was a commercial artist," he explained, "so had no trouble on illustrations, layout, typography, and production know-how. Always wanted to write a book but never had any message or viewpoint on anything before, so I was all set for copy. For anyone without that precise background, however, I scarce know how to advise that person to go about making up a catalog. Pathetic ones are made by many who rush in where copywriting artists shuffle in sideways. Yet, if you put the making of a catalog into the hands of a professional, you are into, like, MONEY. The work I put into my catalog (and it isn't all apparent) I wouldn't have done for $25,000 for anyone else. I designed and wrote it all with help from any artist whose work was no longer in copyright. I admired the Caswell-Massey compendium, the Dixie Gunworks catalog, and Mark Twain (Sam Clemens), Kipling, Shakespeare, and Dr. David Emanuel Jack, and I decided my catalog would be a compendium of these and would stand or fall or crawl in that form because I had done my best and didn't know how to do any better."

And there you have the best advice anyone can give you. Do your best with what you've got to work with. You don't have to be an artist, illustrator, or layout technician to put out your own catalog, but you do have to have some common sense and good judgment. It will also help to study the techniques of preparing camera-ready copy (see Chapter 12), and you should also study the catalogs of other craftspeople for ideas. It's all right to emulate the style of catalogs that strike your fancy, but please don't copy another person's ideas or artwork. Finally, it's a good idea to get the response of a couple of objective friends once you have planned your catalog. As the person creating both the handcrafts and the catalog they're featured in, it will be very difficult for you to play the role of a would-be customer trying to order from that catalog. What you can understand, another may not. The criticism of an objective friend could be invaluable to you.

Although a good catalog can be expensive to produce and print, please note that it does not have to be given away. Few catalogs are offered free these days. If your catalog price seems a bit high to you, consider the practice followed by Al and many other mail order sellers: offer a refund of the catalog's price on a customer's first order (usually given in the form of a credit on the order.) In advertisements, simply show your catalog's price with the word "refundable" after it.

Another strategy you might try is this: Offer an information sheet or report (priced at $1-$3) that's designed to bring you the kind of prospect names you want for your mailing list. The idea here is that the money you receive will then cover the print and postage costs related to getting your catalog into the hands of these prospects. Part of the problem, you see, is that there will always be "curiosity seekers" (or those individuals who are simply doing a little market research, trying to find out what other sellers are up to), and with increasing postage costs, we all have to find creative ways of offsetting this expense.

What kind of report or information sheet should you offer? If you sell doll patterns, for example, you might offer a little tip sheet for a dollar that includes some of the special tricks and techniques you've discovered through years of making dolls. If you sell books, you might offer a short report on a topic discussed in one of the books, perhaps including new information or updates. If you offer a variety of handcrafted gifts, you could offer a little report that tells people how to use handcrafts to decorate their home, brighten their lives, or answer special gift-giving problems. If you work in a particular medium, such as glass, clay, metal, fiber or wood, you could offer an informative report on how to care for objects made of this material. You should have the idea by now; the options here are as limitless as your imagination. The basic idea, of course, is that whatever you offer as "bait" to get your catalog into the hands of prospects must be interesting enough for them to send a couple dollars for it.

89

If you decide to create your own catalog, remember that it will take you some time. Al had so much fun doing his first catalog that it took him a year to complete it. "Got behind in my work," he says. "Actually, the catalog was out of date by the time it was printed. So I announced my second one at $3 (tired of losing money on each catalog mailed at $1). It took me about 2½ years to get this one out. It got so a day's mail would average three catalog requests and one refund demand. Trouble was, every time I read over a page for final approval I got an irresistible idea for a change or addition. Fun, but you never finish. Had to force myself to reform."

Frankly, I don't think Al will ever reform, and I hope he never loses his sense of humor either. On the cover of his catalog it says: "$3 -- a paltry figure when you consider that this is positively the last catalog by A. Atkins, Blacksmith & Designer." But is it? Not long afterwards, Al told me his next catalog would probably cost $5 and take at least three years to complete. Meanwhile, he continues to wrought his miniature iron wonders for customers who are willing to wait months for them to come off the anvil. Al always has more orders than he can fill and wonders if he ought to raise his prices. "I know I am not overcharging," he says with a wink, "because I remain poor."

A woman once wrote Al saying she couldn't believe he made a living from miniatures. His reply? "It's a *miniature* living!"

90

Left.

Colette Wolff's order form occupies a whole page in her catalog, which is printed to size 5½ x 8½ in. The back of this page has been left blank. Although this form has been prepared in a style different from the one at right, it contains the same basic information. Together, these samples will provide clues on how to design an order form that will suit your own special needs.

Right.

A sample order form from Al Atkins' catalog. Because it is printed to size 8½ x 11 in., two order forms can be placed on one page. (Note: The back of this page is a continuation of the two forms, for customers who wish to order more than eight items.)

THE VILLAGE SMITHY **ORDER FORM** DATE _____

204 Hulbert Hollow Road
Spencer, NY 14883   FROM: NAME _____

                      STREET _____

(607) 589-6166   CITY _____ STATE _____ ZIP _____

QUANTITY	CATALOGUE NO.	Description	Price Each	Total

MINIMUM ORDER $5.00
NOTES:

	Price	Total
Add Shipping & Handling	1	50
N.Y.S. - add tax		
Total Enclosed with Order		

continue on other side

THE VILLAGE SMITHY **ORDER FORM** DATE _____

204 Hulbert Hollow Road
Spencer, NY 14883   FROM: NAME _____

                      STREET _____

(607) 589-6166   CITY _____ STATE _____ ZIP _____

QUANTITY	CATALOGUE NO.	Description	Price Each	Total

MINIMUM ORDER $5.00
NOTES:

	Price	Total
Add Shipping & Handling	1	50
N.Y.S. - add tax		
Total Enclosed with Order		

continue on other side

Special Catalog Markets

In previous years, a number of handcraft catalogs have come and gone. Many well-meaning people, in a sincere attempt to help craft sellers move more merchandise, have launched such catalogs without fully understanding the nature of direct mail marketing or the problems inherent in a catalog business.

Selling through someone else's catalog is the perfect answer for the craftsperson who wants to sell by mail without the bother and expense of creating a catalog or worrying about finding buyers. But those who produce such catalogs often run into a fistful of problems, not the least of which is the high cost of photography, printing and mailing, to say nothing of mail list problems. In the past, I've seen several handcraft catalogs launched by individual entrepreneurs, and none lasted for long. It is not within the scope of this book to discuss the ins and outs of launching such a catalog, except to say I do *not* recommend this type of business to the average individual.

Catalogs more likely to survive are those produced by economic development agencies, craft organizations, or state-funded programs. For example, the states of Missouri, Oklahoma, Arkansas and Illinois have published catalogs, giving selected craftspeople in those states an exciting new marketing outlet. If you happen to live in a state that supports handcrafts in this way, count yourself lucky. (Generally, you would learn about such catalogs through membership in the sponsoring organization, or through articles in craft periodicals.)

That leaves you, then, with two basic catalog options (besides creating your own, of course): Gift catalogs of the kind you often receive in your mailbox, and a few "catalog-magazines" currently in publication.

Gift Catalogs. No catalog can be successful if there is difficulty with its suppliers and, as a seller, you should not try to sell through any type of catalog unless you are prepared to handle all orders received. I recall the letter I received from a publisher who had reluctantly discontinued publication of his handcrafts catalog. "Although it was well received," he said, "we had some difficulty obtaining the quantities of craft items as quickly as they were needed."

If you are the rare craftsperson who can produce in quantity, you may wish to contact mail order firms such as Miles Kimball, Hanover House, Harriet Carter Gifts, Lillian Vernon and others which have been in publication for years.

When I asked the Miles Kimball Company in Oshkosh, Wisconsin what a craftsperson had to do

to sell through their catalog, I received the following response from the company's vice president of merchandising:

> *"Because of the fact that most individuals are not able to produce handmade items in sufficient quantity, I hesitate to encourage you to mention us in your book since, in all probability, the individuals your book will appeal to will not be in a position to supply the demand created by our catalog. It is extremely important that anybody who writes us concerning their idea or their product have facilities for producing the article in quantity. Federal Trade Commission rulings require that merchandise be shipped promptly and, therefore, it is impossible to hold a customer's order for an extended period of time waiting for the production of the merchandise."*

There are literally *thousands* of mail order catalogs being published annually, offering every type product imaginable. To find them, check your library for *The National Directory of Catalogs*, published by Oxbridge Communications, Inc. (It costs close to a hundred dollars, so it's not something you'll want to buy.) If you can't locate this directory, I suggest you order the affordable booklet, *Selling to Catalog Houses*, which provides an overall education on what's involved in this type of marketing -- from finding catalog houses and making a sales presentation, to pricing and invoicing. (See Resource Chapter.) You can also locate catalog houses merely by reading a variety of business and trade magazines.

"Catalog-Magazines." I'm not going to recommend any of these publications by name, but if you read crafts magazines long enough, you'll find them advertised, and perhaps you will consider them to be a viable advertising alternative for your particular products. These publications look like magazines, but are actually catalogs in that they are filled with beautiful pictures of handcrafts and gifts that can be ordered directly by mail from individual advertisers. It's possible that your ad in one of these catalogs, distributed to consumers, would do well for you, but like any advertising, there are no guarantees here, and certainly there are a few pitfalls to watch for.

Ann Lang, who owns Annie Things Possible and is also part of a highly-successful crafts co-op in Holly, Michigan, told me of her experience with one of these publications.

"These catalog-magazines are a risky business," she wrote. "Those with no previous experience in mail order should be warned not to expect immediate results. A lot of time elapses between the creation of an ad and seeing it in print in the periodical. Then it takes even longer to get it into the hands of consumers who may set it aside to 'think about' before they place orders. Most crafters also don't realize that many of the catalog-magazines are purchased by craftspeople like myself who use them as a guide for trends in the market."

Knowing these things, Ann placed an ad for four kinds of nostalgic signs and patterns for those who wanted to make their own. (In essence, she was covering two markets with one ad: crafters and handcraft buyers.) The ad cost $300, compared to $750 for the same size in similar magazines.

Because of financial problems, the magazine did not appear on newsstands until November, instead of August when it was originally scheduled for publication. This wasn't a great problem for Ann, but it affected two of her friends who placed Christmas ads in the same issue. (After complaining about the delay, they all received free ads in the next issue.)

Ann was fortunate to recover her ad costs, and she's satisfied with the overall response to her ad, but wishes her friends had done better. (She was still receiving orders well into January.) In light of this experience, she drew some conclusions and sent me the following tips to pass on to others who may be considering this type of ad:

■ If you are not pleased with an ad due to a mistake because of a publication's error, demand reasonable compensation.

■ Schedule your ads for publication at a time when you will be able to keep up with demand, and deliver merchandise as promised.

■ Include postage and handling costs with the listed price, and remember that breakage can be costly if you do not properly ship fragile items.

■ Magazine ad prices vary considerably, and it may be more beneficial in the long run to go with a higher-priced ad in a well-distributed publication that has proven results.

■ Consumers tend to keep back issues of catalog-magazines, so keep this in mind when you advertise anything. Advertise holiday items in September or October, since few consumers will order later than this due to time needed for delivery.

■ Stay away from items that are repetitive in these catalogs. Country crocks and milk bottles may do well at a crafts shop, but a friend's ad for similar merchandise did not pull well at all.

■ When you send craft items to the publisher to be photographed, include display ideas to avoid having your item pictured all by itself without a proper background setting. (For example, the country crock might have sold better if it had been shown filled with dried flowers.)

Note: For more about Ann Lang and the successful crafts cooperative she helped start in Holly, Michigan, see "Cooperative Ventures" in Chapter 15.

See the next page for an interesting update on how some of the businesses mentioned in this chapter have changed between 1978 (when first interviewed for this book) and now.

Update on Businesses Mentioned in This Chapter

• A note from **Colette Wolff** a few years after I interviewed her for this book indicated that she was moving to a new level in her business. "I'm currently engaged in a major Platypus expansion effort, geared toward making Platypus a million-dollar business in the next five years," she said, adding, "Why not think big?"

By 1990, however, Colette reported that she had dropped all plans for a major expansion. "It's difficult to operate my kind of business in the heart of New York City," she said. "It's hard to find affordable space and good help is also a problem." Although she still operates Platypus to date, Colette hasn't designed any new patterns for some time, preferring instead to concentrate on writing books. The demand for her patterns continues, however, and she still offers a catalog ($1.50). Just as she predicted so many years ago, "...a mail-order business dies a very slow death, and can dribble on for years."

• **Dale Prohaska** of Love Built Toys computerized his business in 1982 so he could control inventory, invoicing, and his ever-growing customer and prospect list, which at that time numbered 160,000 names. He gradually shifted his advertising efforts from magazine ads to direct mail promotions, using his in-house mail list or lists traded with other businesses.

At one time, Dale had 15 employees, but as the years passed and the toy industry grew and changed, he and his wife, Carol, came to the conclusion that big is not necessarily better in terms of a happy lifestyle. For that reason, the Prohaskas left California in 1990 to relocate in Oregon on 38 acres of land, where they now live at a pace more satisfying to them.

Changing conditions in the toymaking industry gradually prompted Dale to diversify into woodworking patterns of all kinds, which in turn prompted a change of business name, to Timbers Woodworking. At this point, Dale was still selling toy-making supplies but now they were limited to specialty parts. These days, the business is merely a part-time endeavor.

I asked Dale if he had any advice to give to mail-order pattern sellers who might like to follow in his footsteps. "Just tell them," he said, "that those stories about getting rich overnight in mail order aren't true. It takes years of hard work to build a successful mail order business."

• Four years after this book was published, I spotted a feature article about **Al Atkins** in a crafts magazine. He was as busy as ever, and since a catalog was mentioned in the article, I presumed he had finally finished the one he said would take three years to complete. At that time, a special project of his was the reproduction of Sherlock Holmes' apartment with all its belongings. He laughingly suggested in the article that he might one day write an original script for a miniature fiction series.

In 1991, I was saddened to learn from Al's daughter that he had suffered several strokes in 1989 that left him partially paralyzed and unable to work. When I spoke to Al at the Reconstruction Home where he had been for some time, he said he was getting better, and would soon be released. "I'm not ready for a rocking chair just yet," he said.

Because he has lost some of the use of his left hand, Al can no longer make his "metal minis," but when I last spoke to him, he was making plans to market a weather-vane kit he had designed, and he had already been to some trade shows to "get the lay of the land." A friend will make the metal parts for him, and Al will put the kits together himself.

Which just proves the old saying, "You can't keep a good man down." Way to go, Al!

- 9 -

Needlework and Design Markets

A survey by a leading craft consumer magazine once indicated that almost 40 percent of the women in the United States do some sort of needlework -- including needlepoint, embroidery, knitting, crocheting and quilting. It's anybody's guess as to how many of these women are trying to sell the products of their nimble fingers.

In Erica Wilson's newspaper column, a reader once asked where she could sell her crewel work and needlepoint, to which Erica replied, "Have you ever thought about giving needlework lessons?" That says a lot about the market for finished needlework.

One woman wrote to me saying, "I have sold very few made-up embroideries. It's terribly difficult to price if you count your labor at any fair rate to yourself. Besides, most people prefer to do their own." This particular woman eventually solved her problem by creating a line of needlework kits that she wholesales to stitchery shops across the country.

Markets for Needleworkers

Selling kits and giving lessons are certainly two options open to needleworkers who want to make money, but they aren't the only ones to be explored. For example, if you can chart needlework patterns, this talent may be of special interest to shops. Perhaps a customer will bring in a design she wants translated to chart form, in order that she might work it herself. Or, if you are a designer, a shop might buy the charted patterns you have published (printed) yourself. Hand-painted canvases are always in demand -- the more original and unique, the better. Read needlework journals to stay abreast of new development in this area.

In an earlier chapter, Connie Stano remarked that a woman can, indeed, make a career from needlework, but it takes great motivation, experience, and creative ability. She believes that a woman working by herself in her own community can be very busy today merely by running an ad in

her local paper offering to finish kits, frame, or design custom pieces. I asked Connie to elaborate on this topic a bit.

"There really is a market for embroidering kits for money," she told me. "Not just for people who are too lazy or inept, but more often for people who are just too busy, or not interested in doing it themselves. There is no law saying these people cannot enjoy embroidery enough to want to buy it. It is a unique operation and word-of-mouth advertising works well on a local level. Some of your best customers will be women who started a kit and lost interest, or found they couldn't do it. Others will be people who bought a kit and then never had time to start it."

Why not take your lead from Connie Stano to sell some of your needlework? Place an ad in your local paper offering to do custom designed needlework, blocking, or framing, depending on where your talents and interests lie. Or, approach a needlework shop and find out if they can use your services as a custom designer. Not all shop owners have the time, talent, or inclination to do custom designing themselves, and they may be delighted to learn your services are available to them. When I checked a new needlework shop in my area shortly after it opened and asked if there really was a demand for custom work, they gave me an enthusiastic yes! In fact, the first week they were open, three women requested custom jobs. One asked to have an antique footstool refurbished with fresh needlepoint, another wanted a humorous sign made for her kitchen, and a third needed a small clutch bag to complement a new evening gown.

Check with needlework shops, too, about the possibility of stitching samples for them. Any shop that offers a variety of needlework kits must also have finished samples to display, as these, more than anything, will encourage the sale of a kit.

Don't forget about small items, such as jewelry, Christmas ornaments, eyeglass cases, and trim items that might be added to dresses or suits. Collars, pockets and belts might be of interest to a custom-made dress shop, to say nothing of special items such as evening jackets, vests, and handbags. Once you enter the fashion field, you can command prices more in line with the hours actually spent on a piece of needlework.

Finally, since needlework of any kind is so time consuming and so hard to market profitably, perhaps you ought to consider the ever-growing miniatures market and doll-house collectors who are willing to pay large sums for miniature masterpieces. The needlepoint picture or rug you cannot afford to sell as a full-size item might be very profitable indeed when done in miniature, to dollhouse scale. (Read magazines such as *Nutshell News* to learn more about the miniatures market.)

Embroiderers should explore the possibility of doing stitchery for specialty shops. For example, you might offer a line of designs from which customers could select a motif to be added to items purchased in the shop, such as sweaters. Depending on the quality of the shop and the price of its merchandise, you might receive a surprising sum of money for a small amount of handwork.

Connie also emphasizes that professional blocking and framing of needlework -- all kinds -- can bring in money, too. This is a skill you can learn by studying needlework instruction books and from simple trial-and-error experience. (Practice on your own work first, of course.)

If there is an interior decorator in your area, find out if he or she is interested in a good source of supply for custom-made pillow covers to complement special room decors. Or maybe you have created some other item that makes a good decorator accent. Home decorating magazines will provide many ideas that can be adapted for needlework items.

Special Tips for Quilters

Quilting falls into the same category as other forms of needlework in that one never receives in dollars and cents what is put out in time and talent. Yet women continue to make and sell quilts, not just for the money, but mostly because they love to make quilts. Since they can't keep all the quilts they make, they simply sell them for the best price they can get.

In 1977 when I was doing research for this book, I met and interviewed Lassie Bradshaw of Georgia Mountain Arts Products, a Cooperative then exhibiting quilts at the Appalachiana Festival in Cincinnati.

"How are quilt sales?" I inquired, and she replied, "Great! The week before we came up here, we sold twelve in one day." The average price of the quilts was $100, depending on the size and pattern. Lassie explained that quilts in the co-op's shop were priced even lower than this. "Some quilts we can get cheaper," she said. "Like, a craftsman comes in and the quality's not really good, but it's good enough that you can sell it, so we price it at $50."

When I said that, at $100, the maker of a quilt was not being well paid, Lassie agreed, but made an important point about quilters in the Appalachian region. "When our cooperative first started," she said, "you could go out and buy a quilt for $7 or $10. After we started the co-op and realized there was a good market for the quilts, we raised the prices. These ladies are now getting a price that is double or triple what they used to get. They've learned the value of their work, which they didn't know before. They used to work for nothing, practically."

Even though they are still not receiving full value for the time spent in quilting, Lassie made me realize that it means so much more to them now because it's more than they had before.

Understandably, urban quilters and more sophisticated sellers can command higher prices for their work than women who live in rural or economically depressed parts of the country. Quilting enjoyed a countrywide revival in 1976 as young and old alike made Bicentennial quilts in uncounted thousands. With the passage of time, quilt prices have escalated, and classic "art quilts" (one-of-a-kind designs by well-known designers) may command up to $5,000 or more in New York galleries. In the average quilt shop, however, fine quilts are more likely to be priced in the $500-$1000 range.

"There are probably 3,000 quilt shops in the U.S. today," says Jeannie Spears, editor and publisher of *The Professional Quilter.* "These shops sell a lot of quilts purchased from individuals who are content to receive half the retail price for their efforts -- usually between $250 - $500 per quilt."

How about just taking your quilts to a fair, where you can keep the whole amount? "A lot of women do that, of course," says Jeannie, "but at a fair you don't have the number of serious quilt lovers you're likely to find in one of the shops, so your chances of selling here are less. And buyers in a fair atmosphere will also expect quilts to be priced lower than they would be in a shop."

In a conversation with Evelyn Mendes, a quilt shop owner in my area, I learned that she often pays between $175-$300 for a hand-stitched quilt. (The lower amount is for patchwork or applique quilts; the higher figure for more difficult patterns such as Lone Star or Cathedral Window.) Says Evelyn, "We are paying our quilters more now than ever before because we know we will lose them otherwise. We appreciate the fact that they are artists, and believe they should be paid for their artistry. Many of our quilters have great color sense, and this is especially important to buyers.

Does machine quilting reduce the value of a quilt in a buyer's eyes? "Most definitely," says Evelyn. "Quilting by hand really makes a quilt come alive. While machine-stitched quilts have a good market, especially for use in children's rooms and college dorms, there is a greater demand for quilts that have been entirely patched and quilted by hand."

Some quilt shops accept quilts on consignment while others buy them outright, taking a 100 percent markup. Some shops may take as much as 300 percent, however, so it might pay you to shop

around when trying to establish a good outlet for your quilts.

I must inject something here. I know one quilt-maker who consigns her quilts to a local shop that retails them for about $300. She also takes similar quilts to craft fairs and sells them for about half that amount. I can see her point. She wants to sell her quilts and feels the $300 price the shop puts on them is too high. She may be right. But she is certainly wrong when she undercuts the shop's retail price when both she and the shop are selling the *same quilt.* This is very unprofessional and, if the shop finds out, they will probably refuse to accept additional quilts from her. Think how aggravated their customers would be if they paid $300 for a quilt, then went to a crafts fair the following week and saw the same quilt for half that amount.

If you find yourself in a similar position, I urge you either to raise your retail prices to match those of the shop you are dealing with, or don't sell the same kind of quilted items in both places. There are specialty quilt shops who are interested in developing relationships with quilters who can supply them with quality merchandise on a regular basis, and when you are fortunate enough to find them, you should work cooperatively with them. "When we find good quiltmakers," says Evelyn, "we treat them as the valued suppliers they are, and pay them accordingly."

Jeannie Spears emphasizes that while it's extremely difficult for a quilter to make a living selling quilts, many women have built successful

97

businesses around quiltmaking talents. "Most of the professionals do sideline things related to quilting," she explains. "They teach, lecture, design for needlework magazines or pattern companies, judge contests, or manage their own quilt shops." Or, if they're like Jeannie, they also write and perhaps publish their own magazine and information booklets. One thing is certain: to earn a substantial income from your quilting knowledge and skills, somewhere along the line you will have to make some compromises. If designing is your primary interest, perhaps you will prefer to concentrate on the creation of one or two fabulous pieces of art a year, marketing them through art galleries. If you're more production-oriented and plan to make multiples of certain items, then you'll have to learn how to cut your production time, Jeannie says. "Or you might concentrate on taking custom-design orders only," she adds. "That's probably the best way to sell at fairs."

Here, you might offer to design children's quilts, heirloom quilts for special occasions, or unique garments of one kind or another. "The only trouble with custom designing," says Jeannie, "is that it eventually gets to some people. They may grow tired of dealing with demanding customers or having to work with colors they don't like."

Here's one more marketing idea you might check out: some quilt shops are going to be interested in hearing from people who can make sample quilts for display in the shop -- perhaps to sell a quilting kit, for example. They would provide the material and either pay a fee for your labor, or perhaps let you have the quilt after it had been on display for a few months, or even sell it in time, splitting the profits of the sale with you. Of course, your quilting skills must be top-notch, and you'll have to meet the shop's deadlines.

A Little-Known Market
For Knitters/Crocheters

There is, unfortunately, little demand for knitted or crocheted garments. Too many women knit and crochet today to be interested in buying this kind of work. Yet I continue to see ads for crocheted and knitted items in the classified sections of women's magazines, and have often wondered just how much of this work actually sells. I contacted the editor of a magazine that frequently runs such ads, and asked if she had any indication of the amount of money women were making from the sale of such handmades. "I have no actual figures on the profit made from selling handmades," she wrote. "From the letters I receive, I would conclude that while there is enough financial gain to make

98

an ad worthwhile, nobody is going to get rich that way. Most of our ladies are either supplementing Social Security, or are mothers of small children using extra time for a bit of fun and profit."

My correspondence with another magazine editor led me to the discovery that there is at least one good market for needlework that is generally overlooked. "There is a great need for anyone who can write the how-to instructions for knitted and crocheted garments," I was told. "The older women now doing this sort of thing are quickly disappearing, and younger ones are not taking their jobs. The pay is good for this type of work."

Sometimes a person will create an original knitted or crocheted piece "off the top of her head" and is unable to write the instructions. A magazine editor may buy the finished piece, but then she has to find someone who can duplicate it and write the instructions for use in the magazine. "Anyone who can look at a finished garment and figure out how it was made -- and put those details down on paper -- has got a great, salable service to offer all craft and needlework magazine editors," my editor friend told me. "Further, once those instructions have been written, the magazine editor must have someone else double-check them, and the pay is also good for this -- perhaps $45-$50 for doing a sweater." One would simply have to make the sweater, exactly following the instructions given, indicating any corrections, errors, etc., as well as verifying the amount of yarn required. Someone always double-checks every pattern published in a magazine, and you might be that someone.

Here are three ways a design for a sweater might get into a magazine, and they will suggest how you can approach magazine editors and yarn companies:

1. A yarn company has come to the magazine editor with an original design it has purchased from a designer. The company would like publicity for its yarn and may give, or sell, this design to the magazine in return for the publicity it would receive by having its yarn mentioned in the instructions.

2. The magazine has purchased the design, pattern, or instructions from someone, and it goes to the yarn company and asks if it has a designer who could make it up for the magazine.

3. A person goes directly to the magazine editor offering any or all of the above.

If any of the foregoing suggests an idea that might work for you, by all means follow up on it by contacting some editors and leading manufacturers of yarns and threads. In other words, don't hide your talents in your needlework basket; bring them out into the open and see what unravels.

Note: Any presentation concerning your talents should be backed up with good photographs of your work and information about your background and experience.

Getting Designs and Ideas Published

Because there are so many needlework and craft magazines being published today, there is naturally a good market for designs and ideas. Yours may be good. . . but are they truly *original?*

A design is not original if it is merely an adaptation of something you have seen at a craft fair, in a shop, in someone's home, etc. Making changes in color, size, or decoration does not constitute originality, either. To take someone else's idea or design and have it published as your own is to invite legal trouble for both you and the magazine.

Many craftspeople are copyrighting their designs these days and fighting back in court when people "lift" them for commercial use.

"There are subtle distinctions between that which is original and that which is adapted from, inspired by, or just plain stolen from something else," says Barbara Hall Pedersen in an editorial in *Stitch 'n Sew* magazine. Barbara gave me permission to quote from her editorial to help my readers understand the problem so often encountered by craft editors everywhere:

"In a magazine like *Stitch 'n Sew* where reader participation is encouraged, we have an altogether different situation. Many of our contributors are not professionals; they are simply talented and experienced needlewomen who enjoy exercising their own creativity to turn out something unique. They will often start with a basic commercial pattern and modify it or improve it each time they make it up until they feel that the resulting product is truly their own creation.

"Sometimes it is hard to tell whether a design qualifies as an original. We suggest that if you have done any borrowing at all from another source, it

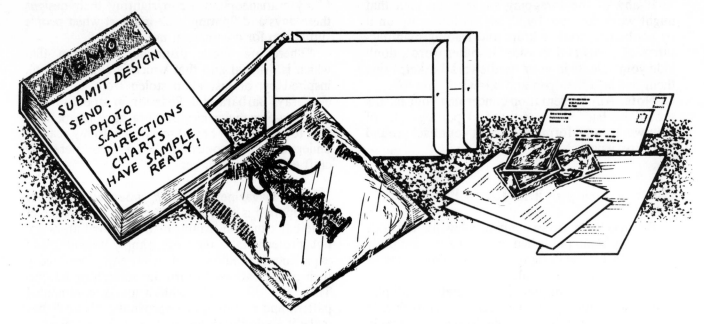

Good craft designers must be organized, as well as creative. A neat, professional presentation will improve the chances of a sale.

would be best to mention it when submitting your idea, and let us decide."*

This is good advice, and I'm sure all craft and needlework magazine editors would appreciate the same consideration from their contributors.

Most editors have some kind of standard release form they send to people whose ideas are of interest to them. Commonly, the magazine would ask the person signing the release to certify that the material submitted is of her own design -- not previously published nor utilizing any part of previously published material. Crafts editor Joyce Bennett emphasizes that too many people do not understand how magazines of this type operate.

"We are not out to rip anyone off or swipe a good idea, so we require a release. We are just as likely to get stuck in the middle because so many people add to or adjust things that often no one knows who is the originator of an item. I'm for everyone being protected."

100 Some craft magazines operate informally, working with contributors on a simple correspondence basis. Says one editor, "We have a limited free-lance budge for ideas, and no standard release form is sent because it would cost just as much for us to copy a person's design as it would to buy it. We really get some very good things from our readers, and we like people to send in their ideas from different parts of the country."

Most of the editors I corresponded with said that the best way to make an initial presentation of an idea is to send a couple of photographs and a brief letter explaining it. This will give the editor the knowledge necessary to make a decision as to whether your idea is one the publication can use. If so, you will be contacted for further information.

TIP: It would be wise to send a self-addressed stamped envelope with your initial inquiry if you want your photographs returned. And, if an editor requests samples of your work, be sure to finish things properly. In particular, needlework should be properly blocked. A great design that isn't properly executed and finished will turn off any editor.

How much money can you expect to make from the sale of a design? This may vary from $25 to $350, depending on the design, your reputation, and the magazine's budget. You can get a good idea of what editors are paying by studying the "Designer's Guidelines" sheet that most magazine editors will send you on request. Don't be afraid to submit an idea, because craft editors do buy from beginners who are professional in their approach and offer original designs and projects of the right type.

Assuming that one of your ideas is accepted by an editor, what then? Says Nancy Tosh, editor of *Crafts 'N Things,* "Once we have accepted an idea for publication, we will need the actual item for photographing, which will later be returned to the designer. We do reserve the right to edit instructions, and rate of payment depends upon the length and complexity of each given article."

Other Tips From Editors:

■ Before sending your ideas to a magazine, study the contents of several issues to be certain your work is comparable in quality and design *and* is the same type of work generally featured.

■ Initially, what magazines want to see are some good photos and a description of the design or craft how-to project you are suggesting.

■ Submissions of work must be accompanied by complete, clear, specific directions that are legibly written. Made-up items must be carefully constructed and spotlessly clean.

■ When wrapping merchandise for shipment, make sure it is properly packed. (Many items have to be rejected simply because they are poorly packed and damaged in shipment.)

Adds Judy Brossart, editor of *Crafts*: "The best advice *Crafts Magazine* has to offer to any designer is to submit an excellent original design -- one that fits our readership and publication -- which uses readily available materials. A well-written manuscript is definitely a plus."

Once you have sold a few designs to craft and needlework publications, you might try one or more of the major women's magazines, such as *Good Housekeeping*. Of course, it is more difficult to be published in these magazines because here, editors often work with in-house designers or manufacturers who furnish project ideas and even color separations in return for advertising considerations. Still, Cecelia K. Toth, director of needlework and sewing at *Good Housekeeping*, indicates professional designers can "break in" from time to time: She explains:

"Most of the designers whose work you see in our magazine are individuals well known in our field. We do, however, sometimes find new and good designers by having individuals send photographs of their work. Frankly, 90 percent is awful, but the 10 percent that is beautiful makes it worthwhile. Initially, photographs are probably the best way of giving us an idea. Payment can be for photograph rights or for the purchase of the item. Rates differ and are individually negotiated."

The Society of Craft Designers. Let me take a moment here to bring your attention to a unique organization that could make all the difference in your ability to earn serious income from your design talents. The most successful designers in the crafts industry are members of this Society -- and it's important to remember that they were all amateurs at one time. Society members receive an informative newsletter, but their greatest opportunity for learning comes at the annual educational seminar which is held in a hotel conference center in a different city each year. For many designers and craft editors, this five-day seminar is the highlight of their year. Here, beginners and professionals alike find business doors opening to them as they meet leading editors, publishers, and manufacturers who explain their needs. Experienced designers take beginners in hand, sharing trade secrets unavailable anywhere else. After an intense day of workshops, everyone gets together in groups for informal evening networking sessions. Here specific problems are discussed and everyone has a chance to contribute "off the cuff" advice and ideas.

I have attended several conferences, both as a speaker and interested "watcher." I've seen the wonder in a beginning craft designer's eyes as she realizes *this* is exactly what she needs. Through the years I've encouraged creative women to join this organization, just as I now encourage you. "This group has opened up a whole new world to me," says Ginger Kean Berk. "I can't believe the contacts I've made. Everyone I've met is so generous in giving information." Adds Carol Krob, "Joining SCD was certainly one of the most important steps in advancing my design career." Not so long ago, both of these women were insecure beginners. Now they own successful homebased design businesses, and have had their projects published in many of the best craft and needlework magazines.

Can Craftspeople Sell To Manufacturers?

"I have completed a project using felt, beads, and sequins that can be made into a kit," one woman wrote. "I found the address of one company, which I wrote, but never received an answer. Could you tell me how to find the names and addresses of companies that would be interested in my project? I would like to sell my idea to them."

I'm sorry to say that the above idea is not marketable, at least not to a craft supply manufacturer. What the average craftsperson does not realize is that craft manufacturers have designers of their own, either full-time employees or freelancers who work on special assignment. Very few craftspeople have the required background and experience to design for the craft industry, and even those who do are not likely to get the time of day from manufacturers, who want not just ideas, but complete marketing programs.

While I was originally researching this topic, an authority in the craft industry told me that individuals who try to sell to manufacturers are more likely to have their designs and ideas pirated than purchased and, often, the larger the company, the greater the chance of this happening. A manufacturer may say "Yes, I'm interested" when a brief explanation of an idea is submitted, and "Sorry, not interested" once all details have been provided. A year later that same idea may be on the market, only the designer won't get anything for it. It will have been cleverly adapted or subtly changed or, in other words, stolen.

This is not to say that all manufacturers operate this way, nor that individuals cannot sell a good idea to a reputable company, but unknown designers have always had difficulty in cracking this market -- at least until the Society of Craft Designers began to grow and gain power as an organization. If you're looking for reputable manufacturers in the industry, you'll be able to find them once you're a member of this Society, and you'll also be able to network with other individuals who have actually sold designs or project ideas to some of these companies.

I once confronted several manufacturers in the craft industry with the rumor I'd heard; namely, that manufacturers often pirate designs and ideas from unsuspecting individuals who believe the whole world to be honest. I also asked them to tell me how a person could protect designs and ideas during the submission process. I received two frank replies (as timely now as when first written) that I've quoted below to give you perspective on this matter and to help you in any negotiations you might have with craft manufacturers.

Writes the art director of Open Door Enterprises, a craft kit manufacturing company:

"You may tell your readers that, though lengthy and somewhat unwieldy, some type of nondisclosure agreement is advantageous if they have what they feel is a good, marketable concept. Rarely have I received in the mail, unsolicited, a usable product for inclusion in any of our lines. Unfortunately, most designers have an inflated idea of their design's worth as a marketable item, and have little, if any, idea about the expense and effort in turning this concept into a profitable seller. A manufacturer incurs the major burden when undertaking research and development on a new product category; that is, cost-time components, merchandising strategy, packaging, advertising, ad infinitum. Your readers should be made aware of this especially since it is the main reason the ideas that the designer has such high hopes for may not be accepted by a manufacturer for promotion (in addition to the fact that few ideas are really new)."

102

Adds the merchandise manager for Bucilla:

"We are constantly on the lookout for fresh, new ideas. For some years now, we have been able to work most successfully with a great many freelance designers who are responsible for successful designs in our stitchery, needlepoint, and latchet rug lines. Practically all of the designers still work with us today and I would venture to say that they are all most satisfied with their arrangement with our company.

"As I am sure you understand, an arrangement with a freelance designer has to be one of mutual trust by both parties. We have never, nor will we ever, 'pirate' a design from a freelancer, and by the same token, if we include something from a freelance designer in our line, we certainly would not expect her to sell a first cousin of that design to another company.

"I receive many inquiries from aspiring needlepoint designers from all over the country. From time to time we do find designs or ideas that can be utilized in our product line. However, these are few and far between since 99 percent of the material that is sent in to us is not what we consider marketable. Therefore, under the circumstances, we would not want you to direct all would-be beginners to our attention."

If all this sounds discouraging, that's the point I'm trying to make. Few readers of this book are apt to be qualified to design for manufacturers, but if you happen to be the exception to the rule and really do have a great product or idea, here are some guidelines that may be helpful when dealing with a manufacturer:

1. Do not send an unsolicited idea to any company, since this constitutes "public exposure" of the idea, according to both the Patent and Copyright Laws, and automatically gives a company the right to steal it from you.

2. Be certain the people you are offering your idea to are reputable and currently showing an interest in the type of product you offer. This will save a lot of time.

3. Your initial letter to a manufacturer should describe your idea in general terms only and should include some information about your background and experience. In this letter you should predetermine the company's interest in the possibility of looking at your idea, and ask it to sign an agreement that says, in essence, that it will receive your idea in confidence, and will protect your rights to it.

4. If you approach a manufacturer and receive a special submission agreement or waiver to be signed, be sure to read it carefully. All rights should remain your property unless otherwise agreed upon by all parties concerned. Think twice if a company offers you a small flat fee and asks you to relinquish all rights because it is not always wise to trust a company about the worth of your design. In truth, they may believe your idea to be quite valuable, but figure that, as a beginner, you'll probably be thrilled to receive a small check.

5. Never send samples of anything until you have a satisfactory contract, and never send original copies of designs or informational materials since they might be lost in the mail.

6. Copyright all designs and written instructions before submitting them to anyone. (See next section.) Safeguard other ideas by keeping records of how and when they were conceived. Include sketches, notes, and other things which give a full understanding of the subject matter. Sign and date them. Show this material to a trusted witness and ask him or her to also sign and date the papers. This will help prove (should it ever be necessary) the idea originated with you on a particular date. Some people put such information in a registered letter to themselves, then retain the unopened letter in a safe place until such time as it might be needed.

Finally, heed these words of advice from a woman who designed and manufactured two craft kits: "The most logical thing to do when you have a good idea is to sit down and THINK. Don't believe everything anyone tells you. WHY are people telling you thus and so? Always look for their motivation, and use logic to reach a sound conclusion."

SPECIAL TIP: Manufacturers in the crafts industry often use one-page idea sheets (or project sheets) to help move their products in retail craft supply stores. Perhaps you've gone into a shop to buy something and received one of these free "idea sheets" yourself. Such sheets are either offered free to shop owners, or provided at low cost.

After you've used a particular supply item for awhile (ribbon, glue, beads, yarn, what-have-you), you tend to accidentally stumble over interesting new uses for the material. Or, perhaps you've simply created an original project that depends on this particular supply item. If so, then you've got the basis for a salable idea.

Designers with good ideas on how to use certain supplies and materials should contact the manufacturers of those products and ask if they purchase project sheets for their dealers. Also ask for samples to serve as a guideline for the sheet you want to send. Payment for such ideas is usually on an outright basis and may range from $25 to $200, depending on the size of the project and the company's budget for such purchases.

You should also be aware of the fact that some manufacturers pay designers a small fee (from $25-$50) whenever they sell a design project to a magazine and mention the manufacturer's product by its brand (trade) name. This, of course, is the kind of valuable publicity that sends consumers into stores to buy the material.

Working With Publishers

If you would like to have your designs published in booklet or leaflet form, approach publishers in this industry. (You'll find them listed in the annual directory published by *Profitable Craft Merchandising* magazine, listed in the Resource Chapter.) Such publishers buy designs in one of two ways: outright purchase or royalty arrangement. You can approach publishers just as you would approach magazine editors. Begin by requesting their Guidelines sheet for writers/designers. This will inform you of their current needs, rate of pay, and submission instructions. Payment rates will vary, depending on many factors. Some designers in my network have told me they've received royalties ranging from 5-15% of the wholesale price of a book or design leaflet, while others have received outright payments of from $250 for a single design to around $2,000 for a booklet of perhaps a dozen designs. I cannot overemphasize the fact that prices vary and are usually negotiable. Your reputation as a designer in the industry, coupled with the size of the company you're working with, will have much to do with the payment you might expect to receive.

I also suggest, before you attempt to sell anything to anyone, *that you do your homework*. This means studying current craft or needlework magazines, looking at the pattern booklets and kits in local shops (a good place to get the names of publishers and manufacturers, of course), and spending time at the library, where you'll find more research material as well as the directories needed to get current addresses for any company you're trying to locate. Please -- *please* -- do not expect other people to do this kind of work for you. And if you're still hen-scratching letters on your child's note paper, forget the whole thing. You simply *must* have a typewriter (at least) to compete with the other professionals in this field.

If you can't type or don't have a typewriter, remember that you *do* have the option of learning. Many people get along quite well with their own hunt-and-peck systems, and today's inexpensive electronic typewriters are easy to use and affordable. Businesses don't have time to deal with amateurs these days, so handwritten letters may be perceived as unprofessional and automatically discarded on receipt.

In conclusion, let me remind you that few designers in the crafts industry can survive on their design income alone -- any more than quilters can make a living sewing quilts. But many designers generate substantial incomes because they've learned how to successfully combine several design-related activities into a complete business package that includes writing, publishing, kit manufacturing or teaching -- topics discussed in later chapters of this book.

Design Copying and the Copyright Law

As already stressed, people who sell their creations should use only original or copyright-free designs. To use a copyrighted design can mean legal trouble, yet craftspeople everywhere continue to reproduce for sale such well-known designs as the Walt Disney cartoon characters, Snoopy, Winnie the Pooh, Raggedy Ann and Andy, and others. All of these designs are copyrighted, and lawsuits have often been brought against craftspeople who use them illegally -- including homemakers who were only selling reproductions of them in church bazaars.

You might make a copy of some design thinking no one will ever know about it, but don't be too sure. Anyone can inform on you, and might, so it's best not to take chances. Making minor changes in someone else's design doesn't protect you either. *In the eyes of the law you can be held liable for copying if your design so much as resembles a copyrighted design.* Remember: the fact that you purchase a pattern or design does not give you a right to sell it in any way, any more than your purchase of a piece of artwork gives you the right to recreate it for sale in some other form, such as notepaper or calendars. Only the original creator has such rights. You have simply purchased the *physical property* for private use.

If you must copy, be sure to use designs currently in public domain. Such designs are available to everyone for use without payment or permission. Although (under current copyright law) copyright protection exists from the moment a work is created, such protection does not last forever. And once a work has fallen into public domain, copyright is lost permanently. How long does copyright protection last? Originally, it lasted 28 years and could be renewed for another term of 28 years if desired. The copyright law that took effect on January 1, 1978, changed that, however, and now provides an extension of the second 28-year term to 47 years instead. Copyrights in their first term must be renewed in order to receive the full new maximum term of 75 years.

Generally speaking, fairy-tale characters and other designs found in old books are likely to be in public domain, and I have already discussed the thousands of copyright-free designs available to you in the *Dover Pictorial Archives.*

For writers, the new law provides a term lasting for the author's life, plus an additional 50 years after the author's death. (Interestingly, Mark Twain asked Congress to do this 70 years ago. "I think that would satisfy any reasonable author because it would take care of his children," he said, adding that the grandchildren could take care of themselves.)

Speaking of authors, many people mistakenly believe that copyright protection extends only to printed works, but that is not true. The purpose of the copyright law is to protect *any creator* from anyone who would use his creative work for his own profit. Under current copyright law, claims are now registered in seven classes:

- literary works
- musical works, and accompanying words
- dramatic works, and accompanying music
- pantomimes and choreographic works
- pictorial, graphic, and sculptural works
- motion pictures and other audiovisual works
- sound recordings

Each of these "classes" requires a different registration form, and you can obtain free forms from the Copyright Office, along with a host of free booklets that describe copyright law in much greater detail than space allows here.

If you've written words that need to be protected by copyright, you should request a Form TX, which is used for books, directories, and how-to instructions for a crafts project, among other things. (Actually, you could copyright a letter to your mother if you wanted to; or your best display ad copy, or any other written words that represent income potential.)

If you were to create an audio or video tape, it could be protected with a Form SR (sound recordings).

Works of the visual arts (Form VA) applies to pictorial, graphic, or sculptural works and covers a

104

lot of ground. Quoting from a Copyright Office booklet, this category includes the following:

"...two-dimensional and three-dimensional works of fine, graphic, and applied art, photographs, prints and art reproductions, maps, globes, charts, technical drawings, diagrams, and models. Such works shall include works of artistic craftsmanship insofar as their form but not their mechanical or utilitarian aspects are concerned; the design of a useful article, as defined in this section, shall be considered a pictorial, graphic, or sculptural work only if, and only to the extent that, such design incorporates pictorial, graphic, or sculptural features that can be identified separately from, and are capable of existing independently of, the utilitarian aspects of the article."

The language of the Copyright Office is not exactly easy to understand, but I interpret the above to mean that most original designs and art/craft objects can be copyrighted. (As you will note a little later on in this section, it is not necessary to send two actual copies of three-dimensional objects with a copyright claim -- photographs or drawings are sufficient.)

Prior to March 1, 1989 -- the date of the last major change to copyright law -- it was necessary to place a copyright notice on your work. Now, however, one's failure to place said notice will no longer result in the loss of copyright.

BUT. . .since the notice is no longer required, those who use material created by others will now be unable to tell whether something is protected (without an expensive, legal copyright search), and they may attempt to use such work and claim "innocent infringement." Because the remedies against innocent infringers are limited, *the Copyright Office still strongly recommends the use of a copyright note.*

That notice should look like one of the two examples below:

Copyright 1993 by Mary Jones, or:
© 1993 by Mary Jones

Copyright notices serve as an announcement to the world that you have laid claim to a particular piece of work. Therefore, such notices should be in a place where they can easily be seen. You can stamp them, cast them, engrave them, paint them, print them, or simply write the notice by hand. In the case of fiber crafts, you can attach an inexpensive label with your logo and copyright notice.

As before, copyright owners cannot sue for infringement unless or until they have registered a work with the Copyright Office. And, for works first published without a copyright notice in the period between January 1, 1978 and February 28, 1989, it is still necessary that they be registered before or within five years after publication and have the notice added to copies distributed in the U.S. after discovery of the omission.

Registering Your Claim. One thing about the copyright law that has many craftspeople confused is the fact that you do not have to *officially* register a copyright claim and pay the $10 fee currently required for such registration. But it *is* mandatory to deposit two copies of all "published" works for the collections of the Library of Congress within three months after publication. Failure to make the deposit may subject the copyright owner to fines and other monetary liabilities, but it does not affect copyright protection. No special form is required for this mandatory deposit. (Additional information about this is in Circular R7d from the Copyright Office.)

Only the "best edition" of a published work is to be deposited with the Library of Congress. In printed matter, the best edition would be a hardcover book instead of the paperback edition; for other graphic matter, the best edition would be that which is in color, rather than black and white; that which is larger, and so on. (When in doubt as to what you should submit, request additional information from the Copyright Registrar. The office has booklets explaining all facets of the Copyright Law. Circular 93, by the way, includes information about all the latest changes to the law.)

Ordinarily, two actual copies of copyrighted items must be deposited, but certain items are exempt from deposit requirements, including all three-dimensional sculptural works, and any works published only as reproduced in or on jewelry, dolls, toys, games, plaques, floor coverings, textile and other fabrics, packaging materials, or any useful article. Also exempt are greeting cards, picture postcards, and stationery.

About now, you're probably wondering why you should ever bother to file an "official claim" and pay the $20 copyright fee. Good question! The answer is simple: If you don't file the form and pay the fee, you'll never be able to take anyone to court for stealing your work. Therefore, in each instance where copyright protection is considered, you need to decide how important your work is to you in terms of dollars and cents, and ask yourself whether you (1) value it enough to pay to protect it, and (2) would actually be willing to pay court costs to defend your copyright, should someone steal it from you. If you never intend to go to court, there's little use in registering copyright claims officially.

But, as indicated earlier, since it costs you nothing to add the copyright notice to your work, you are foolish not to do this.

What *cannot* be copyrighted? Names, titles and short phrases or expressions are not copyrightable, but brand names, trade names, slogans, and phrases may be entitled to protection under the provisions of the Trademark Laws, discussed next.

Inventions are subject matter for patents, not copyrights, and no copyright protection is available for ideas or procedures for doing, making, or building things. (Although ideas themselves cannot be copyrighted, the *expression* of an idea, fixed in a tangible medium, may be copyrightable -- such as a book explaining a new system or technique.)

Finally, the Copyright Office does not compare deposit copies to determine whether works submitted for registration are similar to any material already copyrighted. It is the sender's responsibility to determine the originality of what's being copyrighted. In addition, the Copyright Office is primarily an office of public record, and regulations prohibit it from giving legal advice or opinions concerning the rights of persons in connection with cases of alleged copyright infringement.

If you need advice beyond what is offered here or available from the Copyright Office, you should hire not just a lawyer, but an attorney who specializes in copyright law. There are also firms who specialize in doing copyright searches, but note that they may charge you as much as a hundred dollars to fill out that little $20 copyright form you can so easily do yourself. You don't need this kind of "expensive hand-holding."

Trademarks

A trademark "includes any word, name, symbol or device, or any combination thereof adopted and used by a manufacturer or merchant to identify his goods and distinguish them from those manufactured or sold by others," to quote the Trademark Act of 1946. The primary function of a trademark is to indicate origin, but in some cases it also serves as a guarantee of quality.

A trademark may be owned by any individual, firm, partnership, corporation, association, or other collective group, and one may apply for the registration of a trademark by making application to the Commissioner of Patents. (See the Resource Chapter.)

Trademarks were established to prevent one company from trading on the good name and reputation of another. Therefore, you cannot adopt any trademark that is so similar to another that it is likely to confuse buyers, nor can you trademark generic or descriptive names in the public domain.

The trademark law changed on November 16, 1989. Under the old law, a trademark could not be registered until it was used in commerce, a requirement that has heretofore given a competitive edge to foreign companies who could obtain a U.S. registration without first using a mark in commerce.

Under the new law, a business can apply for a trademark and protect it for up to three years before actually using it. Renewals are now necessary every ten years, instead of every twenty.

It is difficult for the average individual to file a trademark without some outside assistance. The new law has compounded things, too, in that many companies are now building a library of trademarks for products that won't hit the market for two or three years -- which means no one has seen such marks in commerce, and only a search of trademark applications would reveal this information. This is not something the average individual can do.

Like copyrights, trademarks have their own symbol, which looks like this: ®. Small businesses (myself included) often use the initials "TM" with a mark to indicate they've claimed a logo or some other mark. Curiously, after you've used such a mark for some time, you do gain a certain amount of common-law protection for the mark. For example, I have always used the TM mark after the name of my newsletter, *National Home Business Report* (see below), and an attorney specializing in this field told me that, even without federal registration of this mark, I could probably stop someone else from using it, simply because I have been using this mark for several years, and it has come to be associated with my name.

I have included additional information about copyrights, trademarks and patents in my other books, particularly *Homemade Money.* And, of course, a visit to any library will yield a wealth of additional information on the topic.

Also see Chapter 10 for some perspective on patents as they relate to craftspeople.

106

- 10 -

Marketing Kits and Related Products

Kits continue to fill an important need as thousands of hobbyists look for new and interesting ways to spend their leisure hours, and smart craftspeople have been capitalizing on this fact for several years. Even professional craftsmen who feel kits are beneath their abilities (or dignity) agree they can often be good money-makers. If you have created an unusual craft or needlework kit, you do not need to rely on a big manufacturer to get it to market. In fact, you will probably be money ahead if you manufacture and market it yourself.

In designing a kit, there are certain things you should keep in mind. Commercial kit manufacturers figure that a kit should cost no more in materials than one-fifth its retail price; that is, a $5 kit should have no more than one dollar's worth of materials in it. Most craft kits are designed to appeal to beginners and inexperienced handicrafters, and they require a minimum amount of time and skill to complete. All necessary materials, instructions, or tools are included.

Needlework kits, as most women know, are a bit different and come in two basic types: quick, easy, and inexpensive, and time-consuming, challenging, and costly, The kind of craft or needlework kit you design is entirely up to you, of course, but remember that the higher priced and more sophisticated your kit, the smaller your market. Also remember that it's easier to sell a line of several kits than it is to sell just one. Your "line" can be based on one idea, of course, but it should include variations on the theme.

Whether you are trying to reach an art needlework market or the 7-to-97 group of crafters, you are bound to encounter certain stumbling blocks in the beginning, as did the five women you are about to meet. After I've introduced them, I'll let each of them tell you about the packaging and marketing problems she encountered and eventually solved.

Five Kit Manufacturers

Margaret Thompson. Margaret has designed a variety of counted thread cross stitch sampler kits and graphs called "Maggie's Mini Mottos." She discovered counted thread cross stitch at a gift show where she bought some sampler kits for the shop she and her husband owned at the time. Later, when she decided they weren't going to sell unless they were made up, she worked them herself. "Then I was totally hooked," she wrote. "One thing led to another and I started tentatively designing a few on my own. With the encouragement of friends and family, I had the graphs printed, designed a package, found sources for supplies, and was on my way."

Connie A. Stano. You met Connie in an earlier chapter. She and her sister, Mary Lou Nowak, are The Greenfield Needlewomen, and together they have designed and marketed several crewel embroidery kits. "I was doing commissioned designs for a long time," Connie says, "and eventually an idea began to grow. When I presented a small line of my own needlework kits to The Stitchery catalog in Boston, three of the designs were accepted and included in their catalog. The Greenfield Needlewomen thus became a kit manufacturer. My sister and I do the designing and my husband, a lawyer, keeps the books and me out of all sorts of business trouble."

For awhile, the kits were manufactured in Connie's basement with the help of part-time employees, but then the business was moved to a small factory, the made-over first floor of an old house.

Betty Christy. Betty owns Tree Toys, Inc. a national manufacturing company that produces quilling supplies, kits, and instruction booklets. The mother of four grown children, Betty has a background in crafts that goes back to 1946 when she started selling wooden Christmas ornaments called "Tree Toys." Later, she and another woman opened a retail handicrafts shop that eventually grew to include decoupage classes in the back room.

"This was in the early days of the craft industry," Betty says, "when many of today's now-popular crafts were totally unknown to most people."

When Betty sold out to her then-partner, she began to think about all those wooden items she had been decoupaging, wondering what other crafty uses they might have. When she discovered quilling and realized its tie-in with wood, she began to develop her ideas. Later, when a student in one of her classes asked her why she didn't put up her designs in kit form, the suggestion struck a respon-

108

© Tree Toys, Inc.

sive chord. Betty took a partner at that time, and together they launched a quilling kit business.

Carolyn Klein. Carolyn entered the kit field with a line of expensive needlepoint kits she called "Indian Images." When an interesting job in Italy fell through, Carolyn decided it was time to start moving in a new direction. But what to do? At that time she was living in the Chicagoland area with her older brother who had a collection of American Indian ceremonial masks she admired very much. She couldn't afford to buy them herself, but she could needlepoint them, and did. After doing about three pieces, she looked at them and thought, "This is what I'm going to do -- I'm going into business for myself and sell these things."

Carolyn began with four pieces -- got them framed and photographed and did all the backup work (stationery, brochures, etc.) -- then packed her samples and kit packages and hit the road.

Lois L. Moyer. Remember Lois? You first met her in the pricing chapter when I was emphasizing the importance of including all costs in your pricing formula. At one time, Lois was an average home-maker who did all kinds of decorating, made presents for the family, and sewed all her children's clothes. Today, she is a successful businesswoman whose company, Lo Lo Bags, has grown to such an extent that it can no longer be operated from her basement workshop and office.

Lois's clever line of Stitch 'N Sew Craft Kits includes pincushions, pillows, dolls, nursery items, shoe bags and tennis accessory kits, with new ideas in the works. Her first big order got her into the mail order section of a national magazine, and when it came out Lois was so excited she ran over to her mother-in-law's house whooping, "I've made it! I'm going to be busy for the rest of my life with this one mail order house!" But the volume wasn't as expected and it was at this point that Lois took a realistic look at her business and really got down to work.

Although the women you've just met have many things in common, you will note that each entered the kit field through a different door. There are no set rules here; anyone can become a kit manufacturer. But designing a kit is just the first step. Getting it packaged and sold is quite another.

LEFT: In quilling, thin strips of paper are wound and pressed into various shapes, then glued together to form interesting designs like these, from Tree Toys, Inc.

Packaging Problems and Solutions

"Packaging is important," says Margaret. "My kits have on the 'cover' a picture of the sampler, the contents, size, materials used, and a warning: *'Caution--may be habit forming.'*" Margaret's cross stitch sampler kits are packaged in a zip-lock bag with a hole punched in the top so it can be hung up in shops. Her "header," which shows the contents of the kit, is printed in red and black ink on ivory paper, with a black and white picture of the finished sampler printed in the center. This is an effective kit package that proves expensive color sheets are not always necessary to sell a needlework kit. The fact that the embroidery floss is visible from the back of the package helps. Needleworkers can look at the colors and get a good idea of how the finished kit will look. (See illustration on next page.)

Lois's original kit, a shoebag, was also packaged in a plastic bag with a cardboard header done by a local printer. The sewing instructions were simply typed and printed, and included a drawing Lois had done of her boy-and-girl kit designs. She sold her kit in this form until she made enough money to be able to afford the expensive and impressive color sheets she now uses.

"Printing costs are HIGH," Margaret notes. "I couldn't afford to go to color separations on the package in the beginning, although I would have liked to. Printing and packaging are a large part of the cost of the kit."

Carolyn knows exactly what Margaret means. She really ran into packaging problems when she tried to get her art needlework kit on the market, and eventually had to change all her plans. Her 12 needlepoint designs, each based on authentic American Indian artifacts, are dimensional and incorporate such accessory items as feathers, beads, shells, leather thongs, copper wire, etc. Because Carolyn originally hoped to sell these kits in great quantity, she explored silk screening and heat-transfer methods of getting her designs on canvas. But they proved impractical as well as expensive. When she investigated the cost and minimum quantity requirements of plastic bags with firm handles, she found she couldn't afford them either. The cost of full-color artwork was also staggering, she said. She finally realized her kit package, as originally envisioned, would take thousands of dollars to produce in quantity, and she just could not do it.

Her solution? Instead of a complete kit with yarn, she opted to sell only the hand-painted canvases to shops, as well as to individuals by mail order. With each canvas, she included a small plastic bag of accessory items stapled to one corner, along with a card giving the history of the

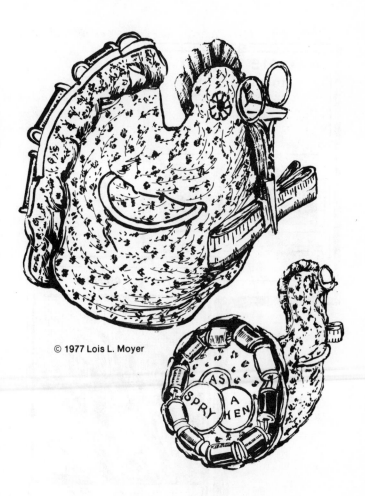

© 1977 Lois L. Moyer

Lois Moyer knows that the right combination of cleverness and practicality in a kit product will make a good money-maker. Shown here is her unusual sewing kit, a long-time best-seller.

piece. In the other corner she stapled a color photograph showing how the finished piece would look. She worked out the yarn requirements for each of her designs, (computed for Paternayan yarn), then gave this information to shop owners so they could direct customers in the purchase of yarn, whether Paternayan or some other brand.

Now listen to the words of a woman who shall remain anonymous -- a kit designer whose product never made it to the marketplace, in spite of the fact that she tried to do everything in a professional manner. Let's call her "Mrs. X."

"Beware of hiring a professional to do your package design," she warns. "I went to a marketing consultant who spent hours talking to me about my kit, at the rate of $50 an hour. He hired a box designer who took three months to produce a simple package I could have done myself. Then he suggested we call a manufacturer's agent into the

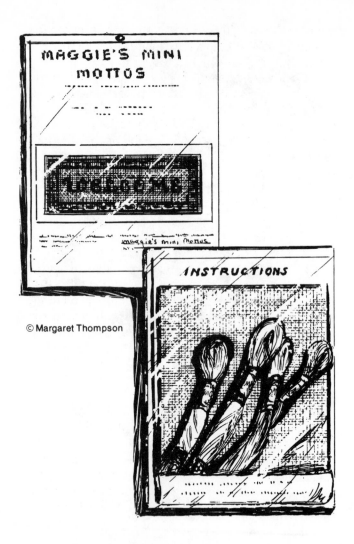

© Margaret Thompson

Margaret Thompson's needlework kits are simply but effectively packaged in clear plastic bags that can be hung up for display.

picture. He wanted to handle my kit, but not in the package that had been designed. Then I signed a contract for a different designer to do the prototype and found that a revision in the original package would cost yet another fee."

At this point, Mrs. X had already spent several months and over a thousand dollars with very little to show for her effort. In the end she decided to do her own manufacturing and created her own package -- just a plastic bag with a printed cardboard header folded over the top and stapled shut. When I tried to reach Mrs. X by phone a few months later to see how her kit business was progressing, her phone had been disconnected. I'm afraid things didn't work out well for her.

Point of story? Your own ideas and simple packaging methods may be just as good as those of a professional, and certainly they are going to be a lot less expensive.

TIP: Before you spend your hard-earned dollars to hire the advice of *any* professional adviser, visit your local library because this same kind of advice is often found in books written by the same kind of experts.

Presenting and Promoting a Line

In a letter Connie Stano sent, she said: "I presented a small line of my own needlework kits to The Stitchery catalog in Boston, and three of these designs were accepted for inclusion in their catalog." I wrote back asking if it was really as simple to sell as line as she made it sound.

"It is just that simple," she replied. "You can just present your line to a customer and wait for acceptance, or more often, rejection. It is also just that complex, as most good things look simple on the surface." Then Connie got to the heart of my question with these remarks:

"Before the line can be presented, months of work on the products must be completed, preceded by almost a year of market research, letter writing, reading, and management decision-making, preceded by years of practice and experience in the field. It must be remembered that the product you submit is the product they expect to order. Availability of supplies, their cost, and a complete plan of the actual production are necessary before the line is submitted. You must be prepared for complete rejection all the way up to being killed by success. In other words, there are literally a million details and bits of knowledge beyond the craft itself that are needed to market a product nationally and professionally."

Connie concluded by saying that the best advice she could give to anyone interested in selling commercially is to "stop thinking like a *crafts-person* and start thinking of yourself as a *business person*."

That remark reminds me of one made by Ray Martell, the jeweler craftsman you met earlier in the book: "An illusion that seems to die hard among craftsmen is that you can run a business without being *in* business. It's a lovely dream, but it's very hard to make enough money with one's eyes half closed. It's often difficult to make enough money with ideals stripped, pragmatism wide open, and nothing between you and the goal post."

When looking for catalog houses that might carry your kits, don't forget to check the listings in *The National Directory of Catalogs* published by Oxbridge Communications.

Lois Moyer's marketing approach was quite different from Connie's. She didn't do a lot of market research or planning, and never read any how-to books like this one. Instead, she just dived into the pool figuring she'd either sink or swim. Sure, she made mistakes in the beginning, but she corrected them as time went on and learned from each new experience. The success she has enjoyed almost from the beginning attests to just how well and how quickly she *applied* what she learned. (There's a big difference between acquiring knowledge and actually putting into practice what you've just learned.)

Lois sold finished items in craft shops for awhile but eventually got tired of hearing people say they could "do it themselves." That's when she decided to let them do just that, and worked up some kits. They sold, bringing in $30-$40 a month, "which didn't excite me," Lois recalls. "I wanted to see bigger figures." She finally decided she was either going to do something big with her kits or forget them, and she entered the field with the attitude of "I'll never know unless I try."

She began her marketing campaign by contacting a couple of catalog houses. At this point she had a line of boy-and-girl shoebag kits. She picked up the phone, asked to talk to a buyer, and came on strong: "This is Lois Moyer of Lo Lo Bags, and I have a line of shoebag kits I think you should see."

"Well," replied the interested buyer, "we're just closing a catalog. Why don't you send me some samples."

She sent them. The buyer called back right away saying he was interested. "We're gonna run it," he told Lois. "What's your pricing?"

SILENCE. Then, "What do you mean, '*what's my pricing?*'" When the buyer heard that, he suddenly knew he was dealing not with a professional, but with "a little lady in her house," to use Lois's words. But the buyer was kind. He told Lois to sit down and think about it, figure it out, and get back to him.

At that time Lois was still buying her fabric from the local store she had always dealt with, doing all the work in putting the kits together, and sewing all the necessary samples herself. Because she didn't know what her actual costs were, she could only guess at a suggested retail price. So she got on the phone and started calling suppliers saying she had a large order to fill. (Fortunately, she had filed for a resale tax number earlier, which entitled her to buy at wholesale prices.)

Lois recalls her feelings at the time. "All of a sudden I had to react quickly and come up with what I thought was a decent price, and what I thought I could make money on." She finally called the buyer, gave him her price, and got an order for 120 kits. "WOW!" she thought, and then, "How am I ever going to do it?"

The buyer featured Lois's kits in an ad in the *Ladies' Home Journal* craft catalog, and like so many other beginners in mail order, Lois figured she was going to get rich from this one ad. But the volume wasn't as great as expected. (She had forgotten to consider the percentage of people likely to respond to an ad.) Later, she realized she wasn't going to make it on one account and began to call other buyers. She also began to expand her line of kits at that time.

She found her first sales representative quite accidentally in a buyer's office. He saw her work and asked to carry it. At his suggestion, Lois got a price list printed and made up some samples for him to use. Soon the representative was presenting her line in several states. For the first year Lois worked with only one representative, and he offered a lot of guidance. He called on some New York magazines and got her items in *Good Housekeeping*. But that presented problems Lois hadn't counted on.

Good Housekeeping looked at her "Ernie the Engineer" shoebag and decided they would have to have something suitable for either a boy or a girl; so Lois took the same fabric used in the engineer shoebag and created two new shoebags, "Freddie and Franny Farmer," with striped pants. But the magazine had room only for one kit, so Lois had to package a special kit to enable readers to make either one or the other -- boy or girl -- which was a lot of extra work to meet the magazine's particular requirements. Of course, the national exposure for her company justified all the time and effort it took. "It's part of being in business," says Lois.

After she exhibited in her first trade show, her business really picked up and she acquired many new accounts and several more sales representatives as well. At one point she had eleven representative organizations promoting her growing kit line to retail stores, chain distributors, and catalog houses all over the country.

When Carolyn Klein was ready to sell her line of Indian Images needlepoint kits (before she switched over to selling just hand-painted canvases), she entered a needlework exhibition in Des Moines, Iowa that promised to attract some 8,000 people. The idea was that her work (finished pieces of needlepoint) would be exhibited with a sign that said where, in that city, people could buy her work. She bundled up her best pieces, delivered them to the exhibition and asked where to find the best needlework shops in town. Then she visited them, told them about the exhibition, and sold several kits before driving back home to Evanston, Illinois.

111

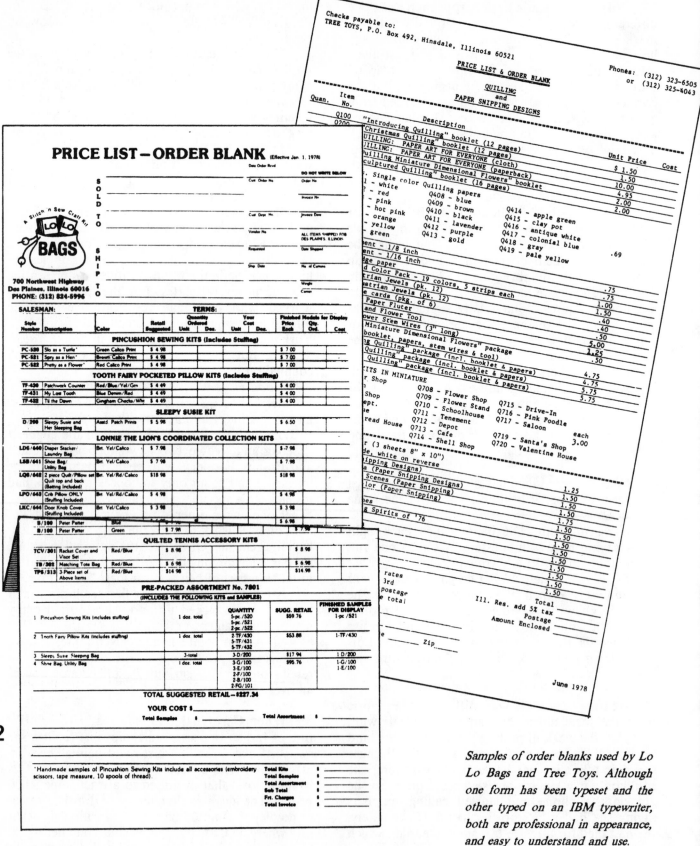

Samples of order blanks used by Lo Lo Bags and Tree Toys. Although one form has been typeset and the other typed on an IBM typewriter, both are professional in appearance, and easy to understand and use.

Results? Interesting. Carolyn got no re-orders from any of the shops, but agrees she didn't prod them for re-orders, either. The exhibition committee wrapped up her work and sent it back air freight, collect, which not only cost $36 to claim, but necessitated a trip to the airport to pick it up. This, added to the gas and other expenses to drive to Iowa meant that Carolyn didn't gain much financially. That was the only time she entered an exhibition. Although this idea didn't work too well for Carolyn, it might work for you, particularly if the exhibition you enter is close to home.

Carolyn's next marketing effort was to call on all the needlework shops in her area, and on one of these calls she met a sales representative who eventually took her line and sold it like crazy. After a while, though, this woman's husband moved and she didn't want to start a new territory, so Carolyn lost the best salesperson she ever had. She found another rep who liked her work, "...but he has a different attitude," says Carolyn. "He keeps asking, 'Can't you do something for $16?' And he takes my authentic Indian sashes -- which come with a history explaining what they are -- and sells them as *bellpulls*. That hurts! My God, I'm so out of touch. First of all, I've never understood why people make bellpulls when they don't pull bells, and you can be sure the Indians never designed or used them."

The above represents a point of view, of course. Carolyn realizes she's out of touch with the craft needlework market, and certainly out of touch with some of the representatives who are currently selling for her. Her line is expensive, more art than craft, and Carolyn has found that once a shop buys one of her designs they will not buy the same design again. They want a new piece to exhibit. Since Carolyn has only 12 designs in her line, her sales are somewhat limited. It takes a lot of time to develop each new item.

It also takes time to create the samples that are necessary to sell any kind of kit. Remember that sales representatives will have to have samples to show to buyers, and even more important, salesmen must have made-up samples to sell to shops who will be carrying the kits. Even if you sell your own line, samples are a must. A shop must be able to show the customer what the finished product will look like. They don't have time to make up kits themselves, so they will want to buy a finished sample at a good price.

When Lois Moyer was faced with the matter of having to have dozens of samples sewed, she found that labor rates in her area were too high, and eventually she had to find sources out of the country to do this work for her. Be sure to include the cost of samples in your overall pricing structure, or you may not realize the profit you expect.

What other advice do these women have to offer budding kit manufacturers? Lois says to plan in advance, but be flexible enough to react quickly when you haven't. "And never accept no for an answer. There is always an alternative. Accept advice, but don't let others make your decisions."

I know Margaret and Betty would second that suggestion, and Margaret also urges beginners to start small and plan wisely. Betty says to grow slowly. "That way you can keep things under control, and that's very important to the overall success of any business.

Exhibiting at Trade Shows

If you have a line of kits that can be wholesaled -- or any kind of product that crafters would use to create finished craft or needlework items -- then you should consider exhibiting at one of the many annual craft and needlework trade shows held across the country. (Such shows are always announced in the various trade magazines serving the crafts and needlecrafts industry. I've included a few of them in the Resource Chapter to get you started.) Exhibiting in such shows would enable you to introduce your products and publications to craft supply retailers and distributors nationwide.

Let's use the HIA (Hobby Industries of America) show as an example. While it's quite expensive to rent a full-sized booth for this show, the largest of its kind, small manufacturers can participate for only a few hundred dollars when they enter the Division Area Display (also called "Tabletop Section"). In this special area apart from the booths occupied by large commercial craft suppliers, exhibitors have six feet of table space in which to display their wares.

Betty Christy's experience with the HIA show will answer some of the questions you may have about this kind of marketing, and remove some of the fear as well. To each show, she takes samples of all her kits, books and supplies, plus a large supply of flyers and price sheets for distribution to interested buyers. Betty suggests that first-time exhibitors take at least 500 copies of printed material for handout, adding that it is probably best not to leave these materials on the table with your samples. "People tend to take anything that's free," she says, "and distributing printed materials in this manner can get expensive. Hand out your literature only to those who stop by and express and interest in your line."

Like other exhibitors in the show, Betty sends a supply of "press kits" to the HIA press room. Various members of the press who attend the show can then take the materials of interest and use them to write their articles and stories. Betty says she usually distributes at least 50 sets of promotional materials, and a great deal of publicity is realized as a result.

I told Betty she made the whole thing sound so simple. "It is easy," she replied, "especially if you like trade shows and like dealing with the public. But I do want to mention one thing. You cannot sell adequately sitting down. We go through the pros and cons of this at every show. People want a chair to sit on. Well, sure, after four days you're tired, and I mean TIRED. Sometimes you're almost sick. But if you're sitting down and you have somebody coming by to look at your products, you're not going to sell to that person. You need to be at eye level with him." (Betty's advice echoes what you read earlier in the craft fair chapter. No one can do a good job selling in a sitting position reading books or "star gazing.")

When I asked Betty what other advice she would give to beginning manufacturers, she brought up the matter of catalogs and price sheets. "Never include the price of an item in your catalog or on your fly sheets," she warned. "We did that the first time and it was a mistake. If you're going to deal on both the retail and wholesale level, and work with distributors, you will need different pricing arrangements for each. Print your prices on separate sheets and include them with your catalog or descriptive fly sheets."

Tree Toys' advertising literature contains printed black and white pictures with complete descriptions of each item. In the beginning, Betty used fly sheets, then went to a catalog, and then back to fly sheets again. "They have proved more practical and less expensive, and they bring in just as many orders as a catalog," she says. "You can eliminate fly sheets, change them easier, and they don't have to be stapled."

Incidentally, color coding also plays an important role in Tree Toys' printed materials. Retail price sheets and order forms are printed in yellow; wholesale, in green. Betty also suggests the use of code numbers for each picture used in your advertising materials, with a different number series for each type of item. For example, Tree Toys' paper snipping designs are numbered P101, P102, etc., while the quilling kits are numbered Q101, Q102, and so on.

Perhaps I should emphasize here that Tree Toys gets all its business from two forms of advertising: exhibition in the annual HIA trade show,

and classified advertisements that run regularly in several craft magazines. A short classified ad ("Quilling--Instruction booklets, kits, and supplies") brings in a steady stream of inquiries that usually lead to orders. Customers who order once generally order again because Tree Toys' products and service are excellent. "We have always stressed quality control rather than quantity control," says Betty, who adds that it is *not* necessary to run expensive display advertisements in this type of business.

This, and the fact that Tree Toys does not have a minimum-order policy probably accounts for a large part of its success. Because Betty once had a retail shop of her own, she realizes better than most how difficult it can sometimes be to meet the minimum quantity requirements of certain manufacturers, so Tree Toys makes it easy for their smaller customers. As a result, they get a lot of business from craft shops who can't meet the requirements of their larger competitors.

Now let me give you a few tips I picked up from talking to two other women who have exhibited in previous HIA shows, both of whom shall remain anonymous. The first one, the same Mrs. X you met earlier, took just one kit to the show and went unprepared at that. She was so eager to get going that she made a fatal mistake: she showed her idea before it was actually ready to be sold, and competitors were no doubt there like vultures, "lifting" her idea as soon as they saw it. It was a good one, too. With their experience and money, it would have been easy to put the product on the market under another name before Mrs. X got her first order. (For all I know, that's exactly what happened. You'll recall I found her phone disconnected when I called to see how things were going.)

The second woman, who went to the show with two good craft kits, said she went for experience and got at least $5,000 worth. Even though she didn't sell much, she discovered that her product was of interest to the mass manufacturers, and thus, the mass market. "I learned that I should concentrate on selling to the mass merchandisers -- Venture, Lee Wards, etc. This is actually cheaper for me as they take only a 10 percent discount, whereas wholesale distributors would need 30-35 percent."

This woman gave me the following advice about exhibiting in a trade show: "Get your act together and when you're ready to go, hit BIG. You've got one year's run before the big manufacturers will steal your idea. If you show an item before you're ready to produce, you've had it."

This woman believes that big manufacturers, who already have all the outlets and contacts and avenues to success, constantly prey on small manufacturers like her. But she doesn't let this bother her. "Already I know that two manufacturers are working on the same kit idea I took to the show, but by the time they get it on the market, I will have had time to make my killing and will be out with yet another new idea. You gotta take your chances; if you hide your product under the bed, no one will ever see it. You must leave yourself vulnerable at times in order to get into the position where you need to be.

Other Tips for Trade Show Exhibitors:

■ Before exhibiting in your first trade show, attend the show as a visitor to get ideas on how to create an effective display, the kind of hand-out literature exhibitors are using, and the kind of products being shown.

■ Don't forget the extra expenses connected with any kind of out-of-town trade show, from travel expenses and freight costs, to fees over and above the regular show registration fee (it costs to get extras like carpeting, electric outlets, and even to get your merchandise carried to your show site).

■ Your main problem at a show that attracts thousands of people is to figure out how to get the attention of maybe five or ten percent of them, and once you do that, how to get them to write orders.

■ There are many kinds of trade shows these days, each featuring certain kinds of products and attracting certain kinds of visitors. Before exhibiting in any trade show, make sure you have a clear understanding of that show's buying audience. This chapter is concentrating only on craft supply shows, since that's the logical marketplace for craft kits. If, however, your kit is related to needlework, knitting, quilting, miniatures, decorative painting, etc., you should explore the trade shows especially for these industries.

On a personal note, I'd like to tell you about the one and only time I exhibited at the HIA show, back in 1979 right after this book was first published.

I went to this show as the representative of the company that published *Creative Cash,* and I went in the naive belief that thousands of craft supply shop owners would jump at the chance to buy this book for resale in their shops. Certainly their customers are my most likely prospects, right? But what no one told me -- and I didn't know to ask in those days -- was that craft supply shop owners did not purchase directly from the manufacturers and publishers exhibiting at this show. In those days, most shop owners ordered supplies from distribu-

tors only. I went to the show with a price list that reflected the typical book publisher's wholesale prices: 40% dealer discount, and 50% distributor discount. But craft supply distributors need a much deeper discount than this, and the pricing formula for *Creative Cash* simply couldn't bend in that fashion and still allow for profit. As a result, I didn't sell a single book at this show, and to my knowledge, none of the publishers of this book has ever been able to offer a discount that's right for this particular market.

But the show wasn't a total loss. I learned a lot about the crafts industry that day, and I also learned something about the art of selling. After two hours of patiently sitting at my table, waiting for craft shop owners to come over and talk to me, I began to see that this just wasn't going to happen. So I got up from behind the table, went out into the aisle, and literally began to "collar" people, handing them one of my lovely color flyers, and telling them what a great money-maker I was offering them. Of course, as soon as I got their attention, I lost them because their next question was always, "Who's your distributor?" When I replied I didn't have one yet, they said to let them know when I did, because they wouldn't be interested in ordering directly from me.

I understand that craft distributors are not as essential to today's small manufacturers as they were several years ago. In fact, most of Betty's sales at trade show (and she now exhibits in several each year) come from "mom-and-pop operations" who don't want to order from distributors because of their high minimum order requirements.

So, the moral of my story is that it will pay you to do your homework. Find out if you need distributors to successfully market your products, and if so, contact them before you get involved in exhibiting to make sure your pricing is right. If it isn't, it hardly matters that you do everything else right. Take it from one who learned the hard way.

Patents and Manufacturing Pitfalls

Many people who get a good idea immediately think, "I'd better get it patented." But what they don't think about is the time and cost involved in the patent process. It can take a couple of years and several thousand dollars to do the job these day, so you'd better be sure your product or idea is worth the effort before you go this route. One designer brought up this good point against patents: You can sit with a patent for 50 years, but what good is it if the idea doesn't sell?

What is a patent, exactly? It's a "grant issued by the United States Government giving an inventor the right to exclude all others from making, using, or selling his invention within the United States and its territories and possessions," according to a booklet issued by the Patent Office.

A patent may be granted to anyone who invents or discovers a new and useful process, machine, manufacture, or composition of matter, or any new and useful improvement thereof. Any new, original, and ornamental design for an article of manufacture can also be patented.

You can get detailed information directly from the Patent Office (see Resource Chapter), but what I want to concentrate on here are the *realities* of getting a patent, and what some of my readers (and some lawyers) have told me about their experiences.

I recall the remark a lawyer made on television: "A patent itself only gives you the right to file an action in court, and it isn't valid until you go to court and prove it. You can't stop an infringer, and if you do go to court, you'll probably lose."

Attorney Mary Helen Sears (who double-checked for accuracy all the patent/trademark/copyright information included in my *Homemade Money* book) told me that it's dangerous to submit a patentable item to a manufacturer before filing a patent application unless the manufacturer, *in advance* of hearing the invention, commits itself that *you* are the owner. "Don't do this without competent legal help," she says, "or you will lose *all*."

Since a patent gotten with the help of a patent attorney can cost as much as $5,000, you might be better off selling your idea to a manufacturer for a flat fee up front, or on a royalty basis if you can get it. A good example of this is the lady I read about several years ago. She designed a crocodile sleeping bag and presented the idea to a reputable manufacturer who liked the idea. She made something like $25,000 for that design and later sold several other ideas as well. The manufacturer who bought her original idea owned the design and name, but she was protected by a contract that said she originated the idea and would receive a 5 percent royalty as a result. (Source: An article in *Family Circle* magazine, November 1970, p. 38.)

Once you go on the market with an unpatented idea or product, no one else can patent a similar idea; however, they can place on the market a product similar to yours. (This is when one begins to understand what competition really is. Just think of all the similar products on the market and you'll know what I mean.)

"Similar" is the key word here. First, you cannot patent anything that would be obvious to anyone skilled in the process or field; second, if your patent is contested by a company with clout, it will be child's play for them to prove that your patent resembles some item already patented, and this will automatically void any patent you may hold.

Most of the feedback I've had from my readers suggests that patents are something the average small business person should avoid. "I found a patent attorney, made an appointment, and came away feeling depressed," one reader told me. "He thought my idea was good and marketable, and he said he'd be willing to help, but it would be costly and time consuming. He said a search would need to be done ($400 or more) and a pamphlet prepared with illustrations and all the legals, to the tune of $1,500-$3,000, and maybe as much as two years' time. His advice? Select a company name, register that; design and trademark a label, and produce the item myself."

The attorney also told my reader that if it was a hot item, it would be only a matter of time before it was stolen, changed a little, and produced in mass quantities. "If you want to make money, you have to do it first, be first, and fight like crazy to STAY first," the attorney concluded.

Actually, the above prices seem low, based on what a patent attorney quoted in a workshop I attended. He said it usually costs between $5,000-$20,000 to obtain a patent, and even when you do have a patent, you can't be sure of keeping it, *or even using it.* Now that was startling news to me, and I asked him to explain. "Conceivably," he said, "you could patent something only to find that a prior patent existed, automatically making yours null and void. Patents are not always in file when a patent search is underway."

Several years ago I met an artist who went the full nine yards with a patent, and her story will give you a good idea of what's really involved here. "If you've really invented something fantastic, your first job is to get it patented," says Linda Markuly Szilvasy, whose favorite canvas is an eggshell. In a letter, she told me about the "complicated, expensive mess" she found herself in when she set out to get her new product patented and marketed.

"This all started when I wanted something, knowing there had to be something to give real strength to my egg shells," she wrote. "I use heavy gold-plated findings and do oil paintings on egg shells, and I wanted them to last and be considered works of art. When I found nothing on the market that would satisfy my needs, I began to experiment and eventually developed my secret process. I was immediately warned by others in the field to find a lawyer or the 'big guys' would steal it."

116

Although Linda's product (which she named Diamond Hardener Finish) was originally created to toughen and beautify egg shells and make them less likely to chip in the cutting process, the product turned out to have other craft uses as well. It's no-odor and china-like qualities make it excellent for use on all craft materials. Linda felt she really had something here, so naturally she wanted to protect it.

"The first thing to do is get a lawyer that specializes in patents. The lawyer's fee is not inexpensive, and is payable whether the patent is granted or not," says Linda. "Sometimes a judge will rule it a thing that does not deserve to be patented. Also, inventors may apply for a patent only to discover someone else has already applied for one on the same thing."

Individuals can make their own patent searches, of course, but lawyers are generally used for the job because there are over three hundred different patent classifications with thousands of subclassifications in each class.

Be wary of organizations that promise to help you patent and market your invention or idea. I had planned to recommend a certain company in this book, a well-known "invention-developer" whose name had been mentioned with great respect in dozens of books and articles. Then I happened to hear on television that this company, and one other as well, had been investigated and convicted by the Federal Trade Commission for misrepresentation of certain facts. It was reported that only three inventors out of 30,000 actually made any money from the inventions patented by these firms, and the newscaster suggested that individuals should avoid these firms and all others like them. Either file a patent application yourself or use a qualified patent attorney, he advised.

Even with an attorney, Linda ran into problems in getting her product patented, but they were small in comparison to the ones she encountered in trying to get her hardner/finish manufactured and packaged. Here's additional advice she asked me to share with you:

"Be very careful if you select someone to be your agent -- someone between the manufacturer and you who is responsible for marketing and advertising your product. This is usually done for a percentage (a large one), but if you do not want to be involved with the actual business and are content to accept a small royalty for your product, it is ideal. Talk to someone who uses the agent and be assured he is reliable. Experience has shown me that if a lousy agent does not hold up his end of the three-way contract, all you can do is sue, and that can cost thousands. A contract, I have learned, almost boils down to nothing more than merely having the right to sue.

"Keep in mind, when setting up such contacts with an agent or company, that you may find they do a shabby job later on, and you may have absolutely nothing to say about it if no control is written into the contract, such as specific amounts to be spent on advertising, etc. It's tough.

"As a woman, the first problem you will run into is getting funding. The Small Business Administration will grant loans if you really have everything down as far as facts and figures and can convince them of your management skills. Going to a bank can be futile, however, unless you have collateral or want to use family assets.

"Put much time into researching prices -- custom-made boxes, bottles, labels, printing, etc. These varied by hundreds of dollars in their estimates (which you must request in writing and with samples when applicable). More times than I like to remember, I took someone's word on the phone only to find the price was much higher when I was ready to buy. When telephoning, always get the name of the person to whom you're speaking, and keep good records of all conversations while researching. Get guarantees of shipment times. How much heartache I have gone through because some essential thing was late! Always have contingency plans."

Linda remarked at this point in her letter that she eventually lost all her trust and naivete in dealing with people, and she no longer takes anyone's word on anything. Check everything twice and get everything in writing, she warns, and this is good advice no matter what you're doing.

Because Linda's product was a chemical one, she realized the importance of having her business incorporated (which protects family assets in the case of a lawsuit). Interestingly, Linda found lawyers' fees for incorporation varied by as much as $200. Because of the nature of her product, liability insurance was also necessary, and this really created a nightmare for her.

"If you are putting out some type of chemical product, you will be lucky to get product liability insurance," she told me. "It can run as much as 10 percent of the retail value of what you have produced or stored in inventory. The forms you have to fill out to get product liability insurance are formidable, and they want to know such things as who does the packaging (they wouldn't be too impressed with a backyard-type operation); how long it has been sold, etc. I have been told that most large chains will not touch a product unless you can furnish them with a certificate of insurance proving that your product is covered.

117

"Do check carefully with a lawyer about your labels," Linda adds. "First remember that no matter how explicit your warnings are, you are still liable for someone getting hurt with your product, no matter how stupid a thing they do with it." (Or, in the words of Helena Rubinstein: "If there is a wrong way to use this product, somebody will find it.")

Linda continues: "I had all my labels printed ($$$) before checking, only to find they were illegal because my complete address was not on each one. More labels had to be printed ($$$). Also, some products must get a special number from the Food and Drug Administration (a lawyer can advise if you have such a product). This number must then be printed on the labels."

As you can see by now, a good legal adviser will be worth his weight in gold and, according to Linda, will charge darn near that much. Marketing experts are also a great help, she says. "They can get your product on the market, serve as adviser (charging an hourly fee, of course), or set up contracts and work for a percentage. If consulted in advance, they can give you much valuable information as to exactly what the market is like, and help you set up pricing formulas for distributor's prices and wholesale and retail."

Linda says she cannot stress enough the importance of doing comprehensive research before you begin, because once you have invested in something like this, you're committed, and the costs can really get out of hand if you haven't done enough beforehand research. Take packaging, for example. A chemist told Linda to use a lid liner that proved to be the wrong kind. It dissolved and she had to pay for double packaging of one element and replace kits already sent out. This cost her over a thousand dollars. "Who can you trust?" she asks, then suggests this rule of thumb for others to follow: "Check with several authorities, then experiment and test everything yourself." Linda has also learned to have all elements checked before having them packaged, since a packaging company is not responsible for checking to see that what they have been sent to package is what you think they have received. "I also learned that little gem the hard way ($$$)," moans Linda.

"As far as instruction sheets go," she adds, "I am beginning to feel they should be written for a third-grade level. You cannot believe how easily people can get confused, or how little they understand. Assume they start with absolutely no knowledge of the type of product you are selling or of techniques involved in its use, and write your instructions accordingly."

Linda has come to the conclusion that there is an awful amount of work and money involved in a venture such as hers, but realizes that other women like her may someday take a similar plunge into the manufacturing business. She says she's glad if her experience and advice help someone in the future, adding, "I now know why executives tend to have ulcers. I also know why I was told it takes a couple of years to 'work out the bugs' and show a profit. Some never do. A very high percentage of new businesses go under in a year. I am fortunate to have a very understanding and considerate husband. That can be as helpful and necessary as a good lawyer."

Update on Businesses Mentioned in This Chapter

• **Linda Szilvasy** sold her unique product for three years before she ran in yet another major problem that could not be overcome.

"The problem was simply that the chemicals became too expensive ($100 a quart) to make it possible to sell the product to more than a limited audience of crafts professionals. I'm now down to my last half-gallon of the product, and hope it will last my lifetime because there won't be any more."

Linda dissolved her corporation after the product left the market and, these days, she's content to market a line of kits for serious "egg artists." And lest you think we're talking kid stuff here, note that the retail price of Linda's kits are over $50. "These are quite profitable," she says, "and very popular with my customers. There are a lot of serious egg artists out there--more than anyone would imagine." In addition to designing kits for her line, Linda also creates original works of art for individual customers and exclusive art galleries. Her work generally sells for around $400-$500, but she has received as much as $1800 for one of her prototype designs.

Linda is the author of *The Jeweled Egg*, which describes her artistic techniques. When the publisher decided to let her book go out of print, she purchased the remaining inventory of some 3,000 copies, and also sells the book by mail, along with her kits. You'll find her address in the Resource Chapter.

"From my patent experience," she says, "I learned to do all kinds of things I never knew I could do. I'm still very busy with my work, and I guess I won't grow old and mentally feeble 'cause I sure don't get a minute to rest. My real love is designing, and I have a lot of ideas I haven't tried yet."

• **Connie Stano** sold her business to T.S.R. Hobbies, Inc. in Lake Geneva, a company that wanted to diversify and open a crafts division. Connie became Executive Vice President of that division, and when I last heard from her, she was in the midst of organizing, hiring, and getting a new line on the market.

• I lost touch with **Carolyn Klein** several years ago, but heard through the grapevine that she suffered a tragic loss shortly after this book was published. She had left all her designs, finished pieces, and complete records of her business with her brother in Chicago while she went to Florida to take care of her mother, ill at the time. Her brother's house caught fire and everything was destroyed, including all the ceremonial masks in his collection which has originally inspired Carolyn to start her business. She never answered my last letter, and I've often wondered if she was able to recover emotionally from such a great loss.

• I laugh when I recall that **Betty Christy** told me she was thinking about retiring when I first interviewed her for this book. But Tree Toys just keeps growing. She eventually dissolved her partnership to continue solo and, at 66, remains one of the busiest grandmothers I know. A leader in her industry, she has developed many new products through the years. "Specialize in one thing," she advises beginners. "Don't spread yourself too thin. Take one item and do variations, working with other materials and trying new combinations of materials."

For example, from quilling kits, Betty moved into the design and publication of paper snipping books (still scissors-related, you'll note), with designs printed not just on black paper (common to this craft), but on pewter and brass foil paper and antique parchment as well. Her newest products are still related to cutting, but now she's diversifed by offering die-cut miniature silhouettes and laser-cut iron-on fabric silhouettes, which automatically takes her business into the fabrics industry. (Betty was planning to exhibit in her first quilting show when I last spoke to her.) Another new product is boxed note cards featuring one of her silouhetted "Ooh-La-La Ladies."

Betty still sells both wholesale and retail, and has an excellent reputation in her industry plus a large mail order following of individual buyers.

How long does Betty plan to work? "I don't know," she says. "Forever. As long as I'm able and have a product to sell. I've got a lot of ideas and I'll never finish everything."

At this point in her busy life, Betty doesn't see business as being stressful, even though she has two warehouses, 14 books in print, 18 cottage-industry people who pack kits for her and help with the mail, nine grandchildren, and the special volunteer work she does for the hospital. where she has 5,000 hours' worth of volunteer service in the emergency room. "I love this work. It's my recreation. Actually, I have the best of three worlds -- my family, Tree Toys, and the hospital. I've really been lucky."

• And **Lois Moyer**? A lot of changes here. To accommodate growth at one point in the past, Lois had to lease factory space for about 1½ years. Then, the unexpected loss of a major account necessitated a move out of the factory. The last time I connected with Lois, she had an office outside her home to handle the design and sales end of her business, and all kit manufacturing was being done by a sub-contractor. She no longer works with sales reps, by the way. "After having worked with so many of them, I believe I still do the best job of presenting my line," she says. "Many of my accounts tell me they prefer to deal directly with me."

Recently, when I tried to reach Lois for an update, I found her address to be too old for forwarding by the post office. I can only assume she's still in business, and operating from a new location. Or perhaps she sold her business so she could move on to something new. Remember: the only thing that's certain in a crafts business is that it's bound to change, and the people running it are bound to change as well.

119

120

Artist's depiction of Lyndall Toothman -- "Granny" to her friends -- and her dog, Flintlock, at work at a country crafts fair. Lyndall's specialty is spinning dog hair, and her services as a demonstrator are in great demand by various tourist attractions in America that feature old-time crafts. She spends a lot of time on the road each year, traveling from job to job in a bright yellow van that symbolizes her sunny outlook on life.

- 11 -

Profit From Specialized Know-How

If you like to talk to the public while demonstrating your art or craft, you may have a promising career as a crafts lecturer or demonstrator, a field that is often overlooked even by professionals. The best thing about lecturing or demonstrating is that you do not necessarily need a product to sell. But, since the primary purpose of a lecture or demonstration is to educate and entertain, you do need some special qualities not found in everyone. To succeed in this field, you must know how to sell yourself and be able to generate enthusiasm among your listeners. You don't have to be a comedian, but a sense of humor is a tremendous asset when trying to keep the attention of a crowd. The element of surprise is also important, and a thorough knowledge of your particular art or craft is essential.

A remarkable woman from West Virginia incorporates all of the above as she demonstrates the craft of hand spinning.

Portrait of a Successful Crafts Demonstrator

Lyndall Toothman has long been a teacher of both hand spinning and weaving. Even in her late 60s, she is a dynamic and ageless woman who has made quite a name for herself as a demonstrating craftswoman. Her services are in great demand by various tourist attractions in America that feature old-time crafts. Why? Because she is by no means an ordinary spinner nor, for that matter, an ordinary woman. In fact, a lot of people have been after Lyndall to write a book about her life and experiences, but she's not too interested in that. The fact that she's lived it is enough, in her estima-

tion, although she admits with a grin that her life has certainly not been boring. (Thrice married, she is now single again and firmly resolved to remain that way for the rest of her life.)

Single, yes; but Lyndall is neither lonely nor alone. When she isn't traveling with her granddaughter, Lee, also a demonstrating spinner, she still has her dog for company, and he's no ordinary dog, either. Flintlock is a fluffy grey Keeshond who accompanies Lyndall as she travels about the country in her bright yellow van, and he also shares the spotlight with her as she demonstrates her skill in spinning dog hair.

Yes, *dog hair*. That's her specialty -- her gimmick -- and it seldom fails to command attention. To date she has spun the fur of more than 90 different breeds of dogs, as well as cats, llamas, bison, camels, horses, wolves, lions, and every other fur-bearing creature she can get hold of (including the beard of an electrician whose auburn hair she admired.) You can imagine how much all this gives her to talk about, and talk she does!

As adept at telling a good story as she is at spinning a fine yarn on her old Saxony wheel, Lyndall delights in answering the many questions asked by a curious crowd, and generally embellishes her answers with lots of country wit and wisdom. She is always a surprise to those who stop to watch her work, and a diamond in the rough to those who are privileged to know her as a friend.

There she sits, gently rocking in her favorite chair, spinning away with all the casualness of a shoplifter about to make her move, looking not at what she's doing, but at the gathering crowd instead. (She's sizing them up, that's what she's doing.) She wears wire-rimmed spectacles and a white crocheted cap atop her head, and no one would suspect that this lovely "old" woman in a pink Colonial dress and white apron -- this cute little granny -- actually prefers blue jeans to dresses, and is a strong and energetic worker who, after the age of 60, designed and built her own log cabin almost singlehandedly. Bystanders are seldom prepared, either, for Lyndall's sharp wit and ready sense of humor, which comes into play the moment anyone speaks to her.

"What's that you're spinning,?" someone in the crowd will ask.

"This is dog hair," she replies firmly, with a strong emphasis on the last two words that make them sound like "dawg hair."

"Nah," another will argue, "you're kidding."

"No I'm not," she says, pointing to her green display board hanging nearby. It's literally covered with photographs of animals, mostly dogs, and stapled to each picture is a small hank of yarn. Lyndall explains that this is yarn she has spun from each animal's fur. She speaks in a high-pitched, crackly voice that's perfectly suited to her character of "Granny," and just as the crowd is really beginning to believe everything she's telling them, she sets them up for a fall with a line like this:

"There's only one kind of dog hair I've been unable to spin so far," she says with great seriousness, and after a slight pause for effect she adds, "and that's the Mexican hairless."

She chuckles pleasantly with the crowd, who now realizes what a delightful entertainer she is. And a good spinner, too. A few people move closer for a better look at her hands, which have never stopped moving for a minute. By this time, of course, she has completely captured the attention of everyone within earshot, and is ready and waiting for the two questions most frequently asked along about now: "Do you kill the dog?" and "Does your foot get tired?"

"No, my foot doesn't get tired," she assures them, "and I don't kill the dog, for heaven's sake! He's sleeping right over there." Then she explains how one simply washes and brushes a dog to get its fur, and several ladies may sigh with relief to learn she doesn't practice cruelty to animals. Soon, someone will inquire about the furry garments hanging on the tree or wall behind her, and she will tell them it's a coat, or a shawl, or a poncho she has made by weaving or knitting the yarn spun from various kinds of dog hair.

"How long did it take to make that coat?" another may ask, and Granny will answer with a twinkle in her eye, "I'm not sure. All I know is, the dog wore it one year and I wore it the next." The crowd roars with laughter -- they love her! When she tells people, "Yes, you can wash and dry the coat in the machine," someone is bound to look at her incredulously and say (as I did years ago) "But

won't it shrink or something?"

"Of course not," Granny answers snappily, "does your dog shrink when you leave him out in the rain?"

Occasionally someone will make a remark that annoys Lyndall, in which case she's apt to spit out a reply that leaves the person at a complete loss for words, like she did to the fellow who came up to her and said, critically, "That's not the way my grandmother used to spin." She looked at him for a moment and then said with subtle sarcasm, "Well, then, your grandmother just wasn't a good spinner."

In an interview with Lyndall, I asked her if she sold her work. "No," she said, "I don't. I give most of it away." Actually, she usually spins dog hair on a 50-50 basis. That is, if you give her a sack of dog brushings, she will spin the yarn and keep half of what she has spun as her payment for spinning. If someone insists on keeping all the handspun yarn, she may charge them about $20 a pound to spin it. And that's poor payment indeed, considering it takes about an hour to spin two ounces. After Lyndall has a good supply of yarn on hand, she will use it to make a weaving, or perhaps crochet or knit a hat, purse, sweater, or poncho. Then, in all probability, she will give it to someone who has done her a favor or been kind to her in some special way. Since she is well paid for demonstrating at fairs and shows, she can spin and weave for the sheer love of it when she gets home, and that's the way she thinks it ought to be.

Lyndall says she has the best of two worlds, for she travels and demonstrates her craft in the summer, then retreats to her quiet mountain hideaway in the winter -- the home she designed herself -- an eight-sided log cabin she calls her "Appalachian Hogan." Here she can watch the morning mist rise from the valley below, enjoy nature at its fullest every day, and spin and weave to her heart's content.

It's true that not everyone has the special ability it takes to be both an engaging entertainer and a skilled artisan or craftsman, but Lyndall's demonstrations are always an inspiration to young and old alike, and a reminder that there are more ways than one to demonstrate a craft and make money from one's special talents.

Lecturing for Pleasure and Profit

If Lyndall's type of demonstrating is not your "cup of tea," perhaps you can identify with designer-craftsman Alice Leeds. She does soft sculpture and is always researching new concepts with the ultimate goal of integrating them into her work. Although she is involved with gallery shows and exhibitions, selling is not her primary motive for working. She sort of "slipped into speaking" from a special interest in cyanotype (blueprint photography). She became so involved in the unlimited range of this process that she naturally began to lecture on the subject at schools, craft seminars, and adult education classes.

How did she get started? "I was invited to show some quilts at a quilter's convention," she told me, "and I volunteered to lecture on the cyanotype process. The talk was a gigantic success and, through word of mouth, I got other speaking engagements." Alice generally charges $35 for her talks, and her primary problem is that, if anything, she is forced to discourage publicity because she just doesn't have the time, what with her craft work and, in her words, "a super-delightful, albeit demanding almost-two-year-old." For now, blueprint photography on fabric is merely a hobby for Alice, and lecturing about it just a sideline interest. But who knows where this will lead her in the future? And who knows where *your* special new interest may already be leading you.

Lecturing about your craft can be profitable in itself, but when lecturing is used as a means to an end (that is, selling the things you make), it can mean even greater dividends for you. Do you remember Ginnie Wise, the farm homemaker I wrote about in Chapter 5? To entice new customers into her homebased shop, she would invite garden clubs, church groups, hobby and craft organizations, and farm women's clubs to hold their regular meetings in her home. At the end of their meeting, Ginnie would present her own program, offer some coffee and cookies, and invite them to browse in the gift shop. Ginnie's program was simply a talk about the historic area along the Sandusky River and a "show-and-sell" session in which she explained her craft.

At first Ginnie made no charge for her program, but eventually she asked that there be at least fifteen people in attendance, or there would be a fee. (That eliminated the smaller clubs that were more interested in a free program than anything else, and also helped the individual clubs to urge better member attendance.) Ginnie said this method of advertising her shop would have been more effective if she weren't situated "so far off the beaten track," but she was always able to create a lot of enthusiasm in people who later came back just to shop. I think Ginnie's original approach to lecturing would also work for the shop you have in your home -- or the one you're just dying to start now that you've read this book!

If you think you'd enjoy lecturing, but don't know what to talk about, consider this suggestion

from Margo Daws Pontius, a cornshuckery artisan who has given over 500 lectures and 80 all-day workshops to date. "Supplement your talk with poems that fit in with the theme, or pleasing stories of the era your craft originated in," says Margo. "Or, add music to create an unusual mood, or try unusual lighting techniques. I have tried all of these with tremendous results. An audience loves someone with imagination, so don't be afraid to give them a chance."

How to Become a Successful Lecturer

It's time now for some specifics on how you can become a successful lecturer-demonstrator, and where better to learn the tricks of the trade than from an expert like Margo? Through lecturing to audiences in three states, ranging from children to "golden-agers," she has shown thousands of people how to make cornshuck dolls and taught them to appreciate our great American heritage in crafts. In her 18 years of researching cornshuckery, she has found the history of this craft as fascinating as the actual making of the dolls, and this has naturally provided her with wonderful material for her lectures.

In turn, Margo has provided me with some wonderful material for this book, but before I share her tips on how to become a terrific lecturer, I must tell you how she has cleverly managed to solve her special source-of-supply problem.

When I first became acquainted with Margo, I never gave a second thought as to where she got her cornshucks, figuring she got them from the corn-

field, like everyone else. But she doesn't. In fact, Margo is a city gal who didn't even know a farmer at the time she began her craft, so she naturally had to resort to using sweet corn from the grocery store. With time and experimentation, she eventually worked out a good method for drying and storing the shucks and has been using Wisconsin sweet corn for her craft ever since.

Now this fact in itself may not be surprising, but the quantity of corn consumed in the Pontius household is a bit startling. In order to keep Margo supplied with sufficient shucks, she, her husband, Alan, and their three teenagers Bob, Jim and Ann, somehow manage to gnaw their way through *eighty dozen ears of corn a year!* That's almost 200 ears apiece, and if that isn't the world's record, it is at least a noteworthy statistic. It was certainly enough in 1976 to capture the attention of the Wisconsin State Committee who asked Margo to represent Wisconsin during the Bicentennial by sending a series of her colonial dolls to the White House. Understandably, Margo is quite proud of the personal letter she received from President Ford as a result, and says it hangs over her ironing board to inspire her to greater things.

Margo's dolls have also been featured on the cover of craft magazines and in the Sunday supplements of leading newspapers, exhibited in various art galleries, and publicized on television -- all because she toots her own horn through the medium of lecturing.

I've emphasized Margo's accomplishments to show you the kinds of things that can happen to people who bring their talents out into the open where everyone can see them. I'm sure you've heard that old expression about hiding your light under a bushel, and Margo is a perfect example of a person who not only turned the basked over, but filled it with corn. In the beginning she says she was neither an authority nor a daring individual, but now she is both, and she thinks the nicest part of lecturing is to inspire someone else to say, "I'd like to try that." Here, then, are her tips on how to become a terrific lecturer:

• **Be an authority.** Know your craft and its background, and all the techniques.

• **Be daring.** Many artistic people do excellent work, but often in established patterns set before them. If you do your craft similarly to someone else, then display it differently, but do be unique.

• **Be on a budget.** Figure the costs of your displays and the continual upkeep. Make sure your lecture fee covers the important extras, such as having your hair done or your suit cleaned, or car mileage.

• **Develop enthusiasm!** If it is not a natural asset, it can be developed. If you truly love your art, just let the "glow" out for others to see.

• **Keep up to date.** Work the latest topics of the day into your lecture and displays, such as ecology, big hats, or patriotism, as the case may be.

• **Inspire your audience.** When they go home, perhaps they will try your art or craft, or perhaps they will want to buy yours, or both. It all depends on you.

Margo thinks the most important key to your success as a lecturer may lie in this one word: *responsibility.* "A dynamic word," she says, "and one that can make or break you." Here are some additional points she emphasizes:

1. **Confirm all details,** such as the date, time, place, and where in the building you are to lecture, audio facilities available, table or space requirements, and the fee for your lecture.

2. **Keep careful records of each lecture.** You'll need them for tax purposes.

3. **Be prompt.** Don't let yourself "get lost." Obtain a map of the area if necessary, and make advance arrangements about the door you are to use to unload your displays.

4. **Keep up your displays,** replacing backdrops and mats when they need it. Always check beforehand to make sure everything you need is still there and in good condition.

5. **Remember the weather.** It's your worst enemy. If the roads are bad, allow extra time to arrive safely. In wet weather, ensure the safe arrival of your displays by placing them inside extra large plastic bags.

6. **Be careful about your appearance.** People will react to you according to how you appear to them. If some disaster strikes you and there is nothing further you can do to improve on your appearance, let the audience know in a humorous way and then proceed from there.

7. **Other responsibilities.** Always be courteous to your program chairman, and stay awhile after your lecture to give people the opportunity to come up and take a closer look and ask questions before you pack things away. If this is a good time for you to sell your art, then by all means do so.

The Elements of a Good Display

You will notice Margo's frequent mention of displays in the forgoing paragraphs. This, to her, is the most important part of any lecture, and I must agree that where crafts are concerned, it is vital for success. "How often have you gone to hear a lecture," Margo points out, "only to come away with an unclear picture of what the person was trying to say? If only a display had been used so one could visualize it as well as listen to the words. So often we can *see* an idea even when we can't understand what we hear."

When you make your display, Margo suggests you keep the following things in mind:

• **Keep it simple.** Eliminate everything unnecessary to the message.

• **Make it interesting and attractive.** Use colored mats and tagboards to create a setting, and then add anything that will contribute to the theme of your program.

• **Give it a definite message or theme.** For example, you might lecture on your art through one or more seasons, a certain era, or a place in history. Or, use folklore, nationality, ecology, nature, or even song titles to provide a theme.

• **Keep the size within reason.** You will naturally be limited on size as to your means of transportation in getting displays to the lecture site (Margo says the 13 x 18 in. mats are excellent when accompanied by a 21 x 28 in. tagboard. These backdrops can also be fastened to cemetery wreath tripods, which are lightweight, collapsible, and readily available.)

• **Don't overdo.** Once you start making displays, the ideas never seem to stop, and if you're not careful you can make too many. Then your lecture becomes too long and you will lose your audience. They can absorb only so much.

• **Use psychology.** Not only must a lecturer understand how to get the attention of listeners, but he or she must design displays with their needs and interests in mind, appealing to the entire audience, whether they are men, women or children.

One of the displays used by Margo Daws Pontius. Simple, yet obviously well planned, it stresses one of the points Margo makes in her lecture: with corn-shuckery, anything is possible.

125

• **Check the finished display** for position, eye level, balance, and originality. To really see it, take a snapshot of it.

• **A final tip**: If you set up your displays ahead of time, your audience will be able to anticipate your lecture. Instead, try setting them up while you talk. This works very well if you keep your displays simple.

Where to Lecture, and Why

Assuming you have worked up a good lecture, how do you get that first, all-important lecturing date? There are literally hundreds of clubs, groups, and associations who need unusual programs to present to their members, to say nothing of elementary or high schools who are looking for something different and interesting to stimulate their students. Contact them and see what happens. Your local Chamber of Commerce or PTA is also a good place to start, and a thorough reading of your newspapers will probably turn up the names of several garden clubs, church groups, or art/craft associations that might make likely prospects for you. As for getting future dates, Margo thinks the trick is to give your first lecture in such a well-prepared way that word of mouth will take it from there. In the beginning she was asked to give one lecture, and within three months was asked to give forty more.

Lecturing or demonstrating one's craft is a craft in itself, and not suited to everyone. But if you have a flair for promoting your own business and have just a touch of "hambone" in your personality, lecturing or demonstrating could prove to be a perfect way for you to increase sales in your shop, gain new students for your craft classes, or help you sell a line of finished crafts, supplies, or books. A good lecture to the right audience could also boost the number of custom-design orders you get each year, promote the new book you've just written, increase the sales of any kit or tool you may have designed, or stimulate interest in a special service you may offer in the community. In cases like this, it may be profitable to give your lectures free of charge, provided, of course, that you are able to advertise or sell your products, publications or services after your talk.

Remember, too, that your lecture could encourage people to visit the local shop or gallery where your work is currently for sale, as well as provide an excellent way to enlarge the size of your mailing list. By providing cards for interested people to fill out with their name and address -- and perhaps a note or two about their special interests -- you can build a good mailing list for

that brochure or catalog you plan to issue in the future.

In short, lectures offer tremendous possibilities for meeting new customers, and perhaps you ought to consider what lecturing might do for you. If the word "lecturing" turns you off because it sounds too formal, the following section on teaching may be more to your liking.

Teaching Techniques and Ideas

If you have an excellent working knowledge of your particular art or craft, and a desire to share that knowledge with others, you may find teaching a rewarding and profitable experience. The topic of teaching crafts in one's home was discussed briefly in Chapter 5, but now I'd like to give you more information about teaching in general, and tell you what you need to know before starting a class or workshop of your own.

Let me begin by emphasizing, in the order of their importance, the five qualities needed to be a good teacher, according to Virginia Harvey, noted textile artist, teacher and author.

1. Organization
2. The ability to clearly explain processes and theories, etc.
3. A good strong voice
4. Patience
5. A sense of humor

Virginia also offers the following suggestions for teaching and making arrangements for a class. "First, the information to be given each day should be planned carefully. Second, good visual aids and large-scale demonstration materials are necessary in teaching manual skills to large classes. Third, since people learn in many different ways, explanations should be repeated several times, each time saying it in a different way.

"Finally, when making arrangements for a class, remember to include a careful explanation of the material to be covered, as well as what will not be covered. This will be useful during your negotiations for the class, and should also be given to the students who sign up for lessons."

Virginia also recommends that a simple contract be signed with the sponsoring group, and says deposit is advisable. This deposit should be nonreturnable after a certain date so schedules can be finalized without fear of cancellation at the last moment. It is also a good idea to exclude from class everyone who is not officially enrolled. (This neatly eliminates children and pets, which occasionally cause embarrassing situations for both students and teacher.)

Information on teaching, such as that offered by Virginia Harvey, is doubly appreciated when one considers there is so little published material for the nonprofessional teacher, yet so many nonprofessionals currently entering the teaching field.

When someone asked me recently, "Who teaches the teacher how to teach?" and "How does the lady next door know the woman up the block can teach?", I found myself on the doorstep of this conclusion: There are basically two kinds of teachers in the crafts field today -- those who are professionally trained, and those who are not. (My husband puts it more simply: Those who are good and those who are bad.) But this doesn't imply that teachers with college degrees are good, and those without them bad. In fact, some of the best teachers in the craft field today have never received any kind of formal training, which leads me to believe that, in the end, the most important thing about teaching is whether a student can learn something from the teacher. Many people believe the best way to judge a teacher is by his or her following. Where crafts teachers are concerned, if the students are producing usable, well-finished products, then the teacher must be getting the message across.

A beginning teacher who has never taught a class before will probably learn more than the students, so perhaps it is the students themselves who are teaching most of today's craft teachers how to teach. And, if the woman up the block can teach the lady next door how to use a particular skill she didn't know she had, so much the better.

Years ago, I got acquainted with a lovely woman across the street who was fascinated by a hand-weaving technique I had learned. (Maori weaving--see page 130.) When she said how much she'd love to learn this craft, I agreed to give her a couple of lessons both on technique and the art of creating her own charted design. Until she showed me her first weaving a few weeks later -- an original design, no less -- I had no idea I was such a good teacher. It was a great feeling to share a craft in this way, so I encourage you to share your knowledge with others, too.

But, a word of caution here: It is one thing to learn something about a new art or craft for your own enjoyment, and quite another to begin teaching others what you know when you are not yet confident of your own ability. It is unprofessional to pass along to students information that is inaccurate or techniques that are improper, so if you really want to be a good teacher, it is best to know your art or craft thoroughly before you take on a class.

Ah, you protest, what if this just isn't possible? What if you live in an isolated area where there are no teachers, and you know a little but not a lot about what you are doing? Or, what if you have rediscovered an old art or craft technique no one else knows about, but wants to learn? Maybe the only way you can become an expert at what you do is start teaching others, so everyone can learn in the process. That's exactly what happened to Pat Virch, now one of the nation's leading rosemalers.

A self-taught teacher and lecturer since 1963, Pat is also largely self-taught in the art of rosemaling, and her success story is both interesting and unusual. Perhaps it will encourage you to share your knowledge with others through the medium of teaching, even though you may feel less than qualified to teach right now. Says Pat, "Be honest and admit you will share only what you know, and that you still have plenty to learn."

How One Teacher Learned to Teach

Pat Virch maintains a studio in her home for classes and workshops, and conducts an annual rosemaling seminar there each summer. She began as a "Sunday painter" and eventually became interested in decorative painting. Her career in rosemaling actually began the day someone passed her a plateful of cookies at a homemaker's meeting. On the plate under the cookies was the first example of Norwegian rosemaling she had ever seen, and she fell in love with it.

Eventually she took a couple of courses in the art, but just as she was getting serious about it she had to move. Although no one in her new area was giving lessons, or even doing rosemaling, Pat continued to study and research the art, particularly in the Norwegian American Museum in Decorah, Iowa, which houses the largest collection of Norwegian rosemaling in America.

One day Pat met a woman who gave her some unusual and practical advice. She said that the only way Pat was going to find other people interested in what she was doing was to start teaching. "But I'm no teacher," Pat protested, "and I'm still learning the art itself." But her friend argued: "If you really want to find someone to paint with, you'll have to teach them how first." This logic worked on Pat, simply because she is the kind of person who needs to show others what she is doing, and enjoys sharing the pleasure she derives from painting.

Even though she felt extremely inadequate as a teacher, she nonetheless found the courage to offer rosemaling lessons. She began by copying down all the notes she had taken as a student, and digging out all the patterns her own teachers had used. She mixed the colors the way she had been shown, told her new students to purchase quality brushes, and proceeded to give them all the good advice she could. Before long, she was not only an excellent rosemaler, but a good teacher as well.

It was at this point that Pat actually began to climb her "ladder of success." She explains: "I guess I would have continued to work in my basement just being a rosemaler and teaching others, and having a few patterns printed for my students, if I hadn't read a certain article in a new crafts magazine.

That magazine was *Creative Crafts*, and it prompted Pat to write the editor and tell her what she was doing, which was developing the Norwegian art of rosemaling. Editor Sybil Harp was delighted to hear from a new craftsperson, and asked Pat to write an article for a future issue. When Pat told Sybil she didn't know how to write a magazine article, Sybil replied with the encouragement and suggestions needed. By emulating other articles in the magazine, and having some pictures taken, Pat was able to write a fine two-part article that was soon published.

Then Pat started getting mail in response to the article. So many people asked for copies of the article that she asked the publisher for permission to reprint it for distribution. This was not possible, however, since the magazine owned the copyright on it. Therefore, in answer to an obvious need for information on rosemaling, Pat decided to write her first how-to book, and ended up publishing and distributing it herself. (Story in Chapter 13.)

One thing naturally led to another until Pat had gained national attention as a rosemaler. By now she was creating her own designs based on traditional patterns and had issued two portfolios of designs with colored prints. Major book dealers in Norway began to carry them. Meanwhile, Pat's husband, Niron, was becoming more and more interested in what she was doing, and since they are both of Norwegian descent and extremely interested in their heritage, the Virchs made trips to Norway in 1970 and 1973 to photograph and research all the old pieces of rosemaling, further deepening their interest in this art form.

Pat started giving workshops in order to promote her book, and before long decided she wanted to travel to other areas. But she did have a husband and four children to think about. Remembering those days, Pat says, "I want to say right now that there is no way any woman can get this involved with a business out of her home unless she's got complete cooperation and support from her husband. So I'm giving this word of advice: to be completely dedicated to something like this, you have to have no personal obligations and ties anyplace else."

Pat asked her husband about doing workshops and he gave his approval, although he did feel she was on an ego trip and wasn't charging enough. After two weeks on the road teaching workshops in several cities out of state, Pat came home feeling like an expert, but decided this sort of thing could not continue. In the end, it was decided that she could make more money advertising and promoting her book in magazines instead of traveling, and she began running national workshops in her studio instead. (Incidentally, Pat's workshops are unusual, as national workshops go. "People bring their whole families," says Pat, "and when the course is finished, we entertain all the families with a pot luck supper, going up to our cabin on the lake. It has been a charming experience not just for me, but for my family too.")

Pat is indeed fortunate to have a husband who understands and appreciates what she is doing. In fact, since learning woodworking, Niron has become interested in making Norwegian style pieces for his wife to decorate. Although his craft began as a hobby, it now appears that, upon retirement, Niron will be doing woodworking on a full-time basis. "Then," says Pat, "the two of us will be traveling together when I have requests to teach. Niron is becoming so skilled in carving the decorative scrolls that in time he'll probably do some teaching himself."

I asked Pat for some guidlines on what a beginning teacher should charge. When she began, she charged only a dollar per session, asking students to pay as they came. Occasionally this didn't work well, however, so she started giving 8 lessons for $10, payable at the first lesson. Then, if someone didn't show up midway through the course, she did not lose as a result.

The above prices are far too low for today's times, of course, but Pat's pricing logic is still sound. A good tip, she says, is this: "Make sure you are worth a lot more than what you charge, and you will never have disappointed people." Actually, Pat says that what she does is not teaching as such, but more like sharing. Her hundreds of students might argue that point, however.

Pat's second rosemaling book received a special Medal of Honor from the Norwegian American Museum in Iowa. (There are only 13 such medal holders in the U.S.) Rosemaling has gained new popularity in the United States and abroad because of the efforts of Pat Virch, once just a busy homemaker with a new hobby. And to think it all started with a plateful of cookies. Don't you agree this story is good food for thought?

How Teachers Can Attract Students

The best way to get students is simply to publicize yourself. Don't wait for students to find you; go out and find them instead. They are eager to be found and ready to learn, and they will be forever grateful to anyone who will teach them what they want to know.

Try to get a write-up in your local paper, join local art or craft organizations, and speak to them (lecture) if given the chance. Plan an exhibit of your work and see if you can display it in a bank or library near your home. If there is an art or crafts gallery or crafts supply store near you, contact the owners and tell them what you can do. If they aren't holding classes already, they may be interested in starting them.

Are craft classes important to the success of a craft supply shop? "Absolutely!" says shop owner Marti Fleischer. "But only if taught by competent teachers under good working conditions, and if

paid for by the students. Teachers are not hard to find. They don't have to have a degree in education to teach crafts. Anyone who has spent several years devoting a good bit of time to a craft is competent providing they have studied the background, read about the subject, and created original designs. It helps, too, if they have taken some classes themselves."

If your local high school or community college offers adult education courses, contact the school's registrar to see if there is any interest in a class such as you offer. Contact the extension center of your state university, nearby recreational centers, and the recreational department of your park district. If your supermarket or laundry has a bulletin board, by all means tack up a clever poster and see what happens. A simple classified ad in the paper or a regional craft magazine or newsletter might bring surprising results. By reading some of the many craft and needlework journals being published today, you will discover other opportunities to obtain free publicity as a teacher.

Let's go back to the library for a moment. One woman I know got started teaching simply by offering the library a special exhibition designed to give the public a better understanding of arts and crafts in general. It drew so much interest that the library eventually hired the woman to give a series of general craft classes, which ran for two hours one day a week for a period of six weeks. The library paid for all the supplies and offered the teacher a flat salary. She was also allowed to sell her line of art/craft supplies in the class, which nicely supplemented her income. Perhaps this idea will work for you, too.

Once you've lined up some likely teaching prospects, give some thought to your presentation. Letters of inquiry to anyone should include your qualifications as a teacher and an outline of the course you are offering. If contacting prospects in person, take along samples of your best work as well.

Each time you present a class, ask your students to complete a "critique sheet" that gives them an opportunity to rate you as a teacher, indicate what they've learned from you, and offer suggestions on how your class could be improved. In every class, there will be people as eager to criticize as to compliment, so don't let the criticism get you down. Instead, use this information to identify problem areas that need improvement. When you receive favorable comments, ask your students if you can use their comments (along with their name) as testimonials in your promotional material. Also ask the person who hired you for the teaching job to give you a letter of recommendation you can use in the same way.

How One Teacher Became an Author

Now I'd like to tell you an interesting story that will give encouragement and ideas to beginning and professional teachers alike. It's about a woman who started her first class by putting a sign in the butcher shop window of a foreign country.

A funny thing happened to Joyce Ronald Smith on the way to New Zealand with her husband one year. In one of the books she had taken with her, she "discovered" the ancient lost craft of Maori handweaving, or *taaniko*, a little-known process devised by the Maori of New Zealand in about the 14th or 15th century. Here was an intriguing craft that required neither tools nor loom. With a simple twisting movement of the hands and wrists, Joyce found she could manipulate fibers into a woven product.

Before the boat docked, she had not only taught herself the basic techniques of this lost art, but had actually created her first project -- a belt that she wore down the gangplank in hopes it would serve as a conversation piece to learn more from the people. It didn't, however, and when she asked a local taxi driver where she could find examples of taaniko, he didn't know what she was talking about. In fact, the only Maori handweavings Joyce could find at first were exhibited in a museum. Later, while traveling with her husband Lane, a painter, she found a small village where the people at least knew something about the craft, even if they no longer practiced it.

Joyce says in the book she later wrote: "This method of weaving so ingeniously devised by the Maori, seemed to be begging me to release it from the past, experiment with it, and realize its vast potential."

Thus inspired, Joyce began to produce weavings with the kind of frenzy that attacks all creative people in the midst of a new discovery. She made rugs, wall hangings, jewelry, lamp shades and belts, and in time more and more people began to drop by the cottage to see Lane's paintings and her weavings. One day someone asked her if she would consider giving lessons, and she thought, "Why not?" That's when she put up that sign in the butcher shop window. And the people came, Maori and non-Maori alike, to practice the ancient lost art of taaniko. And, just like Pat Virch, Joyce learned from her students, each of whom had a new weaving variation to show her.

When the Smiths' visas expired and they had to leave New Zealand, they returned to their home in Rhode Island with Joyce all fired up with the idea of reviving this craft in America. Toward that end she wrote her first book, *Taaniko -- Maori Hand Weaving,* which was published in 1975 by Vineyard Books.

Some people think that when you write a book you achieve instant fame and fortune. Unfortunately that's not true. Joyce's publisher did arrange for an appearance on national television which brought in some fan mail, but no invitations for workshops or classes. This was a disappointment, of course, because Joyce had been a full-time teacher of art and design for many years, and she believed teaching to be the most logical way for her to spread the word about taaniko weaving.

Thus you can see that even professional teachers have to work to find students. In a letter Joyce told me, "None of my workshops came to me as a result of my book or the television interview. I have had to make an effort to solicit all teaching and workshops. My first workshops were conducted by putting posters in congested shopping areas and by running an ad in the newspaper. Later I felt it better to affiliate with the educational programs of established institutions such as museums, colleges, craft organizations, etc. My going rate for private lessons is equal to what the local music teachers charge. For group lessons, the salary is determined by whatever institution I am teaching for. I make an effort to get $25 an hour. For day-long workshops, I charge $100 plus expenses."

Incidentally, Joyce often uses lecturing as a means of attracting students. "I have given many lectures about taaniko and New Zealand using slides," she says. "Many groups have signed up for the lecture first and this produced enough interest for them to request a workshop at a later date."

Thanks to Joyce, Maori handweaving is alive and well, at least in Rhode Island where she has numerous students, and probably in other scattered areas of the country as well because of her book. And I can't help but wonder if Joyce didn't leave behind in New Zealand an enthusiastic person like herself who continued to rekindle interest in this craft among the Maori people themselves. Perhaps someday this type of weaving will attract wide attention among America's fiber craftspeople, but until then Joyce plans to stay busy teaching, exhibiting, and selling taaniko. In the last letter I received from Joyce, she said she was exploring the possibilities of another little-known textile technique native to Peru. Do you suppose she's going to revive yet another lost craft for us? I hope so.

You may never revive a lost art or craft, or write a book about it, or appear on national television . . . but then again, *you just might.* Of all the successful people you've read about so far in this book, few ever imagined where their special interests and know-how would lead them. Teaching is just one more option open to the talented person interested in earning extra money. The fact that it can be pursued in or out of one's home makes it all

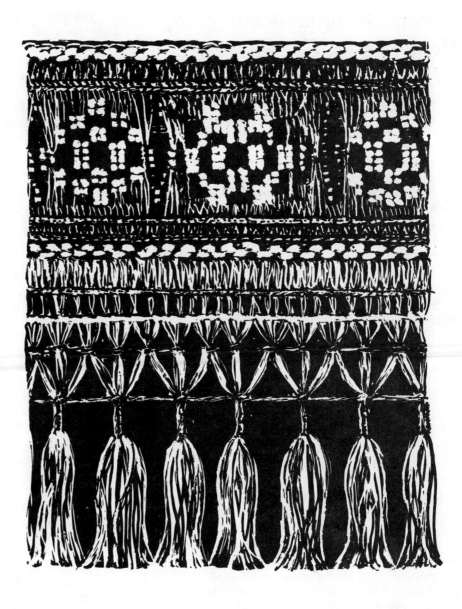

A taaniko weaving design, adapted from a flyer used by Joyce Ronald Smith.

the more appealing to some. While formal training is always helpful, it is seldom required in the field of arts and crafts where craftsmanship and experience are far more important. What is required, however, is the sincere desire to share your knowledge with others, and as a teacher you should certainly strive to carry on the great tradition of teaching that Albert Einstein so neatly summarized with this remark:

"It is the supreme art of the teacher to awaken joy in creative expression and knowledge."

Do that, and you'll be a great teacher.

Author's Endnote: When I wrote this book, the last thing I ever imagined was that I would wind up being a nationally-known speaker. Like most of the women profiled in this chapter I, too, just "slipped into speaking" as a result of years of experience in my field. Because the thought of speaking was uncomfortable to me, I never gave the idea much thought until someone asked me to come to Michigan in 1982 to present a series of crafts marketing workshops. That was the week I suddenly discovered I was good at speaking, loved this kind of "live interaction" with people, and had something special to share with them.

I do encourage you to try teaching or speaking. When you speak about the thing you love most, it enriches not only your own life, but the lives of others.

131

Update on Businesses Mentioned in This Chapter

• **Joyce Ronald Smith's** excellent book went out of print shortly after I interviewed her for *Creative Cash,* and I have since lost touch with her. I'll never forget Joyce, though, for from her book I learned the art of Maori handweaving, which became one of my favorite crafts. (Especially nice for traveling and vacations since it requires only one's hands and some yarn.)

• **Pat Virch's** career continued to bloom after this book was published. She went on to publish several other rosemaling books, folios and pattern sheets, and her continuing studies into the techniques of early American decoration also prompted a book on decorated tinware and a stenciling kit. Her designs are also being used now by companies who are creating folk art kits and plastic ornaments.

Pat spends some 300 hours each year teaching folk arts, both in her studio and throughout the U.S. She has also taught in Canada, Switzerland, Norway and the Netherlands. She and husband Niron organized their first Folk Art Tour to Norway in the summer of 1980, and have repeated this tour in years since.

• In spite of a serious leg injury that gave her trouble for a long time, **Margo Daws Pontius** continued her lectures. From cornshuckery, she expanded to a new topic, International Eggery, and I found myself wondering if her family was now eating as many eggs as ears of corn. One year, as a result of special publicity, Margo received several invitations to speak at state conventions -- yet another new speaking experience for her. I regret that she moved without notifying me of her new address.

• **Lyndall Toothman -- "Granny"** -- is still one of the most interesting women I've ever known. She has kept in touch through the years, and one of my favorite letters from a few years ago said: "I still work four months at Cedar Point and the rest of the time I am here and yon. Spent last winter in Texas and loved it! I don't know how I get myself in so many different situations, but it seems like I am never doing the things people expect a 70-year old to do. P. S. I now have a blue van with a gray turtle top."

When Lyndall turned 80 on May 1, 1990, she was still doing the unexpected for one of her age. To celebrate this birthday, she bought a new red-and-white Pontiac Trans Sport Van. Instead of spending her later years in a senior citizen's home, she's still traveling "here and yon" while also being Artist in Residence at Morehead State University in Kentucky. She can't have a dog here, but she does have a part-time job doing spinning and weaving workshops, and says she's "real happy and hopes to stay there many more years."

Her latest letter had me in stitches. "Four days after I got the van," she wrote, "I went to Georgia to the Foxfire Festival. An *old woman* of 70 asked me if I drove when I told her I had come alone. I told her no, the Lord was doing the driving, I was just holding the wheel." Then she told me she had been invited to do a small festival in Frozen Head State Park in Tennessee, commenting, "The first time I went there three years ago the campground was beautiful but primitive--I mean *wild.* This year Ranger Yeary told me they had put in a bath house with toilets and showers. I said good, now I won't have to go behind a tree."

It's humor like this that has kept reporters on Lyndall's heels through the years. She has been featured in hundreds of articles and made numerous radio and television appearances. She obviously thrives on attention and, in fact, I think this is one of the things that has kept her so young. Lyndall recently realized a secret dream -- being invited to go on the Johnny Carson show -- but in the end had to cancel the appearance because her arthritis had became so painful. Doctors told her nothing could be done about it (except take Aspirin, of course) so she went back to a book she'd used in the past, followed the diet instructions to the letter (raw milk and all), and says, "It worked! This is the second time this book has pulled me out of a wheelchair." (*A Doctor's Proven Hew Home Cure For Arthritis* by B. Franklin, M.D., Parker Pub. Co., West Nyack, NY.)

Lyndall is a great reader. As a child she loved to go to bed early so she could read and then dream about all the places she wanted to see. "I read everything I could get my hands on, but I couldn't have imagined then the interesting life I would have, nor all the wonderful people and places I'd get to know. They say old people don't dream, they have visions," Lyndall adds, "but I still dream, so I must not be old yet."

I'll never forget Lyndall's words when we touched on the topic of dying that summer's evening so long ago. "It don't bother me none," she said. "It's just going to be my next great adventure!"

Meanwhile, she keeps traveling in that new van of hers. In 1990, for example, she worked the Strawberry Festival in Plant City, Florida, an Appalachian Festival in West Virginia and a show in Fort Boonesborough, Kentucky. Then she took a vacation to Grand Caynon, Big Bend National Park and on down the Rio Grand River to Brownsville, Texas, *camping all the time from October to February.*

The following year, Granny worked in Buzzard Bay, Massachusetts for a few days before going on to New Richmond Fort on Staten Island. Believe me, this woman doesn't have the foggiest notion of what the word "retirement" means! "One of these days," she writes, "you may hear Willard Scott announce that Granny Toothman is 100 years old today and still working at MSU!"

It wouldn't surprise me a bit.

- 12 -

Publicity, Advertising, and Promotional Materials

One evening after a long day of writing, I decided to watch television for relaxation and tuned in on that great old classic, *A Star is Born*, with James Mason and Judy Garland. With crafts still on my mind, it wasn't difficult to relate some of the lines in the movie to the crafts business, such as: "Star quality" is the "little something extra" one has; "Talent isn't enough;" and "A career can sometimes rest on a trifle."

"Star quality," as you can imagine, is that elusive "something extra" that makes entertainers like Judy Garland stand out from all the other entertainers in the world. In order for you to stand out from all other craftspeople, you must have a little "star quality" of your own. But having that elusive "something extra" will not insure financial success, or, as James Mason put it so aptly, "Talent isn't enough."

There are many talented craftspeople in America who are creating work that literally sparkles with star quality, but few of them advertise their wares or seek free publicity. It's as though they believe there is some kind of magic telegraph that will transmit their message to the world and bring buyers to their door. These people have not yet learned how far a bit of advertising or free publicity can go. To them, it is merely a trifle not worth bothering about; yet, it could mean the difference between success and failure.

If your success in crafts is going to "rest on a trifle," at least make sure that trifle isn't a lack of publicity because there's plenty to be had. Says Joan P. Acord, former executive secretary of United Maine Craftsmen, "I think that if I could make one point to people beginning to sell their craft (assuming, of course, that they are technically competent), it would be to urge them to take advantage of the many kinds of publicity they can

get free. Only a very small percentage of craftspeople, including many so-called professionals, realize the importance of this."

So where do you find all those golden opportunities for publicity? Let's begin with newspapers.

Getting Newspaper Publicity

Since local newspapers are always in need of good news and feature stories to fill their pages, they can be a gold mine of free publicity for enterprising businesspeople. Study the various sections of the paper to determine which one is most appropriate for your particular news -- the women's pages, travel, arts, entertainment, business, etc. Then send a news release to the editor of that particular section, or perhaps to someone who writes a regular column for that section of the paper.

What kind of information is truly newsworthy? Some of the following topics might be of interest to an editor, and could even lead to a feature article on you if you come up with a well-written letter or press release:

- A special demonstration of your art or craft at an annual festival or fair

- A one-man or one-woman show of work at a local shop or gallery, or a special exhibit in a bank, library or shop window

- New classes you may be starting, or your availability to lecture on a topic of interest to women's clubs or civic organizations, etc.

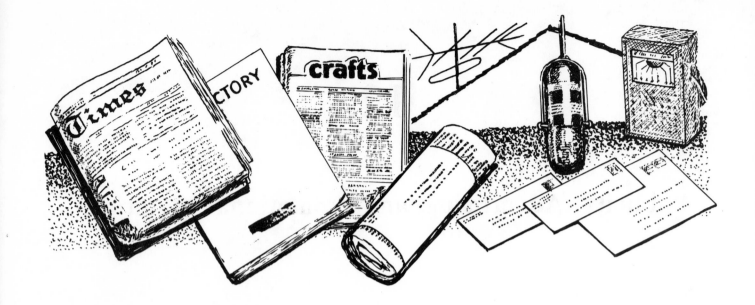

Publicity is available to everyone. Use the media
to your advantage whenever possible.

■ The activities of your local crafts guild, and your involvement with it.

■ The opening of your new shop or home-based business

■ The availability of some special service or unusual catalog or report free to the public

■ An art or craft you do that is so old it's historically interesting, or so new that few people know about it yet

■ A product you've created that is new or of special interest to a particular group of people -- homemakers, sports fans, gardeners, collectors, etc.

134

■ A new book, directory or manual you may have written or published

■ A new craft or hobby kit you've created, a new tool you've invented, or a new use for an old tool and how it relates to the work you do

■ A major prize or award you've received

■ The idea you just thought of that's even better than the above suggestions

Okay. Now you know what you want to publicize. But you can't just say that you are opening a business, giving classes, or exhibiting in a show. You must give the editor a reason for using your publicity, because giving you free advertising is *not* his purpose. There must be something about your news that will compel the editor to pass it along to readers. It might help if you could tie your news into the activities of a charitable organization, a benevolent group, a prominent local citizen, a particular season, or a national holiday. Or perhaps what you are doing is an indication of a new trend, or something no one else has done before. Maybe it reflects favorably on your community or benefits a certain group of people--children, working wives, senior citizens, etc.

These days, the fact that millions of people are working at home, many of them in their own businesses (and many of them craft-related, I might add), is news in itself. In writing your release, then, you might add some insight on what it's like to work at home, since this may have "human interest" appeal to an editor. Perhaps I should mention at this point that I have built my own business through publicity, always emphasizing the home-business trend in my press releases and the fact that I can help others succeed in this field. I generally include some helpful tips to make my "news" truly helpful to readers. (See sample, page 137.)

In writing your release, you must keep asking yourself what there is about your business that might interest others, and then put yourself in the editor's place and ask: "Why should I print this story?"

Preparing a Press Release

A press release, or news release as it is sometimes called, must immediately capture the editor's attention or it will promptly be filed in the wastebasket. Publicity specialist Mike Pavlish emphasizes the importance of including information the editor wants. "That is, facts to back up your statements, plus crisp who, what, when, where and how details." He adds: "Busy editors don't have time to sort through irrelevant copy and cut it down to the main points, so write clear and crisp, using only the important, relevant information."

Remember that your release is an announcement of news, *not* an advertisement. Use simple English. Short sentences. Short paragraphs. Give no sales pitches, but do include all necessary facts and information.

Type your release on plain white paper, size 8½ x 11 in., or design a special "NEWS" letterhead similar to the sample on page 137. Allow wide margins (1-1½ in.) on both sides, and double-space copy to make it easy to edit. Keep your release to one page if at all possible. (If you need two pages to tell your story, print it on two separate pages -- not on the back of the first page.) In the upper left-hand corner of the release, type your name, address and telephone number, or include the name and phone number of the individual to contact for additional information. Down a few lines and over to the right, type (and underline) *one* of the following lines, depending on when you want your release to appear in print:

FOR RELEASE ON (indicate date)
...or...
FOR IMMEDIATE RELEASE
...or...
FOR USE AT WILL

TIP: If the information in your release is going to be good for a year or more, use the last line. My use of this phrase on press releases has brought me publicity as long as two years after the release was mailed. Editors often file "For Use At Will" releases in reference files that are pulled months later when a writer is assigned to do a story on that topic.

Back to writing your press release. Go down a few lines and, in the center of the page, type your press release heading in capital letters. Examples:

NEW CRAFT SHOP OPENS IN OAKDALE

**CRAFTSWOMAN DISCOVERS
NEW USE FOR OLD TOOL**

**NEW CRAFT CLASSES
BENEFIT SENIOR CITIZENS**

**RUG HOOKING TO BE DEMONSTRATED
AT ANNUAL FESTIVAL**

The most important information should come at the beginning of your press release since editors usually cut from the bottom up if it is too long to use. Thus, your opening paragraph might be tailored after the following example, which illustrates the five W's of journalism:

> *A special demonstration of hand spinning (WHAT) will be presented by Sally Jones (WHO) at Ye Old Yarn Shoppe, 13 Oak Lane, Anytown (WHERE) on Saturday, August 24 from 10 a.m. to 6 p.m. (WHEN). The shop, which sells yarn, supplies and equipment for fiber workers, hopes to create renewed interest in the art of spinning (WHY). Classes in both spinning and weaving will be offered this fall.*

If you want as much publicity as possible, send your announcement to several papers. But if you're trying to get a feature article written, send the release and a special cover letter to a particular editor. In your letter, briefly explain why you think the article would interest the paper's readers and give some colorful background information not included in the release. Indicate your willingness to supply additional information should it be of interest, and advise whether you can write the article yourself. Enclose a photograph if you have a good one -- an 8x10 or 5x7 glossy black and white print. (Snapshots are of no use to a newspaper, but could serve to spark an editor's interest and result in a photographer being sent to your place of business.) If you send a photograph, add a cardboard stiffener to your envelope to protect it from being bent in the mail. Enclose a self-addressed, stamped envelope if you want the photograph returned.

How does free newspaper publicity compare to paid advertising in the same publication? When Marti Fleischer opened her new craft shop in Oak Ridge, Tennessee, she placed several ads in the paper announcing her Grand Opening. "A few people came by the first day," she said, "but sales were pitiful."

135

Ye Old Yarn Shoppe
13 Oak Street
Wilmette, IL 60091

(312) 723-4962

FOR IMMEDIATE RELEASE

ART OF HANDSPINNING TO BE DEMONSTRATED LOCALLY

A special demonstration of hand spinning will be presented by Sally Jones at Ye Old Yarn Shoppe, 13 Oak Street, Wilmette, on Saturday, August 6, from 10 to 4.

The shop, which sells yarns, supplies, and equipment for fiber workers, expects the demonstration to create additional interest in the art of spinning, a craft that is now enjoyed by thousands of people throughout the country. Beginning and intermediate classes in both spinning and weaving will be offered by the shop this fall, and reservations for them can be made on Saturday, or by calling the shop prior to August 31.

Sally Jones, a local professional craftswoman, has demonstrated the art of spinning at numerous festivals and shows throughout the country and won several awards for the garments she has created from her handspun yarn. She will be teaching both the beginning and intermediate spinning classes at the shop this fall.

Sample of a typed press release, shown in reduced size. It was prepared on plain white paper, size 8½ x 11 in. A special NEWS head (see right) could also be used.

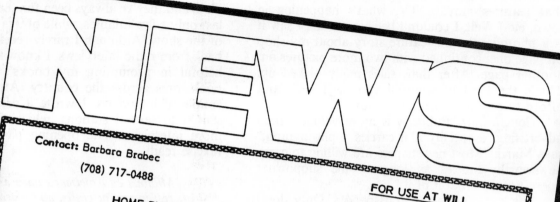

Contact: Barbara Brabec

(708) 717-0488

<u>FOR USE AT WILL</u>

HOME BUSINESS EXPERT WILL HELP YOU SUCCEED

A million new homebased businesses may be launched this year, according to research by organizations in this industry. This will bring the total number of homebased businesses to fourteen million and make such businesses the fastest-growing segment of the American economy.

If you're thinking about dipping your toes into the entrepreneurial waters, make sure you do your homework first, advises Home Business Development Specialist Barbara Brabec. "You could, for hundreds or thousands of dollars, hire a variety of professionals who would answer your business and legal questions, help you write a business plan, devise successful marketing strategies, and create printed materials with pizazz," she says. "Or, for less than you might spend for an evening's entertainment, you can invest in a "success package" of easy-to-understand small business guides that will teach you the how-to's of all these skills and more. Answers to your entrepreneurial questions and small business problems are as near as your bookstore, library, or mailbox."

To get started, send for Brabec's "Proven Guides to Success in a Business at Home" catalog. It describes her books, which include <u>Homemade Money</u>, <u>Creative Cash</u>, and <u>Help For Your Growing Homebased Business</u>. Also featured is <u>National Home Business Report</u>, a unique networking and marketing tool and your connection to everybody who is anybody in the home business industry.

Self-employed for most of her life, Brabec runs a full-time, homebased publishing and mail order business with the assistance of her husband. In recent years, she has emerged as an international authority on homebased businesses, serving not only as an information specialist and educator, but one of the industry's major developmental forces. She is often the featured speaker at major entrepreneurial conferences, and her publications are recommended by the SBA and used as teaching aids in small business courses across the country.

To receive your FREE "Success Catalog," write to: National Home Business Network, P. O. Box 2137, Naperville, IL 60567.

137

*Press release used by author to promote her home-business books
and newsletter. Many newspapers and small business newsletters
have run this release or shortened versions of it.*

"About this time, the local newspaper decided to run a series on arts and crafts and gift shops in the area. (We have a Friday night tabloid section that features movies, TV, what's happening in town, etc.) Well, I couldn't believe it when I saw it -- a photograph and feature story about my shop on page one, continued with two more pictures on another page. After that, sales really picked up. That's the kind of windfall you need and can't afford to pay advertising rates for."

Conclusion? "Publicity is more valuable than advertising, especially if it carries a photograph," says Marti. "Most newspapers are willing to carry newsworthy stories as long as the shopowner doesn't make a habit of it."

The same goes for craftspeople. Only don't wait for a lucky bolt of publicity to streak down from the heavens as Marti did. Make your own luck and generate your own publicity by writing your own newsworthy announcement and sending it to the paper when you need publicity the most -- at the *beginning* of any new endeavor.

Radio and Television Appearances

Although competition for air time is intense, there are opportunities for craftspeople to receive publicity on radio or television shows, particularly local cable shows. Radio "talk" shows might like to interview the author of a new crafts book, or talk with anyone who has information and ideas their listeners could put to use. Children's television shows sometimes feature a craftsman who demonstrates a particular skill, and other morning and afternoon radio and television programs may have a host-guest format that features interesting personalities of one kind or another.

If you think you are doing something that could be discussed or demonstrated on radio or television, write or telephone the program director and explain why your appearance might interest listeners or viewers. Obviously, it is important to study the format of a show before trying to get on the air, and once on the air you would want to be able to speak or demonstrate your craft with confidence. Much of the advice already given in the chapter on lecturing could be applied to any radio or television appearance you might make.

Again, let me add a few notes about my own experience in this area, which came as a direct result of having written this book. I was shaking in my boots the first time I was asked to give a radio interview over the telephone, but was amazed at how easy this was to do. The trick here is to concentrate only on the person you're talking to -- the radio show host -- and don't even *think* about the thousands of people who are listening to what you say.

I've given dozens of telephone interviews since then, and they've always been fun. Some interviews last only a few minutes, while others last the length of the show. Although I rarely receive direct feedback from radio interviews, I know they have been helpful in promoting my books' availability in bookstores across the country. After I'd done a couple of interviews, I wrote a press release and sent it to several stations, which resulted in still more interviews. The opening paragraph of my release read:

> *Millions of Americans have a leisuretime interest in arts or crafts, and a growing number of them are currently wondering if their craft or hobby could be turned into a profitable home business.*
>
> *Barbara Brabec, author of the best-selling book, CREATIVE CASH, has the answer to that question, and she welcomes telephone interviews on this topic.*

If you're an authority on any topic, you will have little difficulty in finding radio stations interested in interviewing you. (Use media directories in your library to build a mailing list for your press release.) There's little benefit in getting radio publicity unless you can direct people to *go somewhere* or *do something* after they've heard you on the air. For example, as a teacher, you might wish to be interviewed in connection with a workshop you're teaching at a crafts conference. If you're the author of a book available in bookstores, by all means encourage your publisher to book some radio interviews for you, or book them yourself if you've published your own book. If you're opening a craft shop or planning a holiday boutique, a few minutes of radio publicity could make a tremendous difference in customer turnout. Give it a try! (But don't forget that radio show hosts also need a good reason for giving you free air time. Emphasize the BENEFITS you can offer listeners.)

Magazine Publicity

People who think of newspapers or radio first when trying to get publicity, especially craftspeople, often tend to overlook the golden opportunities awaiting them in magazines. Prior to 1970 there were only a few magazines being issued for artists, craftspeople and needleworkers. Today there are dozens of them, as a quick check of your local newsstand or library will reveal.

Remember that each of these periodicals has an editor -- an individual who is always on the lookout for interesting articles, photographs, press releases, and informative letters from readers. An editor often passes press releases, reader mail, and article ideas on to individual columnists writing for the magazine, or to other editors who handle the magazine's "Department Pages." (These often feature new products, things worth sending for, people in the news, industry news, and so on. Of course the only way to learn about all the publicity opportunities in magazines is to *read them*. I stress the importance of reading because too many craftspeople have told me they're just too busy making crafts to have time to read. But I say you can always find time to read if you are hungry for information and ideas. If you're serious about making money from your crafts or needlework, or making a name for yourself in your field, you should be reading every publication related to your field of interest, as well as a few trade papers and several consumer and general business magazines. Together, these publications will keep you abreast of what's happening in your world, alert you to new marketing opportunities, business trends and the changing interests of consumers.

If you can't afford to subscribe to everything you should be reading, check your library for copies of some of the publications. Or, if you have several friends with interests similar to yours, perhaps you could each buy one or two subscriptions, then pass issues around. Beg or borrow them, *but by all means read them!* If you are making any money from your crafts, you cannot invest it more wisely than this.

I guarantee that the more you read, the luckier you will become because you will "just happen" to discover interesting opportunities for publicity each time you read a periodical. Here's how to zero in on the different kinds of publicity available to you in both large and small periodicals.

Publicity Through Feature Articles. Self-published craft and needlework publications, unlike consumer magazines, have little money (sometimes none) to pay for articles. Thus it is often difficult for an editor to find feature article material for each issue. As a long-time periodical publisher, I probably appreciate this fact more than most people. During the years I published *Artisan Crafts* magazine (1971-1976), I really worked to dig up stories. Few people ever came to me asking to have a story written about them or their craft and, in corresponding with other editors, I found this was more often the rule than the exception. Perhaps most craftspeople are just too bashful to bring their work to the attention of an editor, or too busy, or perhaps they think that very little good will actual-

ly come of such publicity anyway, particularly in a magazine of limited circulation.

Don't make this mistake yourself. If a publication has only a thousand readers -- or just a hundred -- it is not too small when it means publicity for you or your work. If only one reader responds to your article in a positive way, you could receive immeasurable benefit. For instance, I once did a story on a particular artisan and another editor from a major magazine picked up on the story. She did a color feature on this person, giving her national publicity of a kind she couldn't have purchased at any price. I'm sure this sort of thing happened far more than I know since only a few readers ever took the time to let me know what my publicity did for them.

Which brings me to emphasize a point: When an editor, columnist, or free-lance writer drops your name in print, remember to say thanks. You might need that person again sometime.

If you are capable of writing an article about your craft, telling its history, describing your special technique, or exploring various other angles, you could certainly benefit from writing for one of the larger craft or needlework magazines. Since editors of consumer magazines often read the craft and needlework magazines to get ideas for their own craft and needlework sections, your story could easily catch the eye of someone special and lead to additional exposure for you and your products (to say nothing of additional sales). If you can't write what you believe to be an acceptable magazine article, but do have a craft or technique that you feel would be of interest to an editor, simply write a detailed letter explaining this. Often this is all that's required to get the publicity pendulum swinging your way.

Also note that some of the contemporary craft magazines offer what might be called "spotlight" publicity. For example, *Fiberarts* magazine has a "New Works" section where fiber artists may be able to get their work featured editorially (no charge). *Handmade Accents*, a full-color quarterly that promotes contemporary arts and crafts to appreciative buyers, also features interesting craftspeople in this way. Says editor Steve McCay, "We're always on the lookout for new material and slides of new works to show off to our readership." (Both magazines are listed in the Resource Chapter.)

Now let me give you just two examples of what can happen when you are lucky enough to get publicity in a major magazine like *Woman's Day* or *Family Circle*. Remember Betty Christy (Chapter 10)? In one of the "freebie offers" occasionally used by *Woman's Day* to entice new advertisers,

Betty offered magazine readers a free, die-cut silhouette. She was astounded when she received over 44,000 requests for the offered sample! "It took hours and hours to open and process all the mail," she recalls, "and I had to hire extra help to do it."

About 20% of the people ordered from the catalog Betty enclosed with the sample, making the promotion highly profitable. But because Betty didn't have a computer at the time, she ended up throwing away the balance of her prospect names. (I cringe at the thought of her losing so many wonderful customer prospects, and hope you'll never make this mistake!) Now that Betty has a computer she says she won't let this happen again, adding: "I'll also never offer anything free without charging a dollar for postage and handling." (A word to the wise, folks.)

Let me also share my two *Family Circle* publicity stories. The first came right after this book was published when one of the magazine's columnists gave *Creative Cash* a one-paragraph mention, adding that it could be ordered by mail directly from the publisher. Within three months, 5,000 orders were received, and in time, another 5,000 people asked for the free brochure that was mentioned. Many of these people also ordered.

A few years later, after I had started my business at home, I was fortunate to receive publicity in the same magazine for both my book and newsletter. Result? Almost 9,000 requests for a $1 information package I offered along with my catalog. Almost 20% of those people eventually ordered this book or subscribed to my newsletter, so you can see this "spot of publicity" translated into thousands of dollars worth of business for me. (The funny thing about this experience was the incredulous look on the face of the bank clerk who each day had to count the hundreds of one-dollar bills we were bringing in for deposit. "Where are all these coming from?" she wanted to know.)

Publicity Through "Free Plugs". Study the new products section of various magazines -- craft, consumer, and business alike -- noting the type of items usually given space. Mostly it will be new tools, kits, unusual materials, or hard-to-find craft or needlework supplies. Handmade items are seldom featured unless they come in kit form or illustrate the use of specific materials that are for sale. Occasionally, however, a craftsperson can get free publicity by offering to send a catalog to interested readers. If you believe you have something to offer that is suitable for mention in a particular magazine, simply prepare a press release and send it to the editor. Your release will probably be considerably shorter if and when it appears

in any magazine, but this kind of mention, however small, is worth seeking since it draws a good response from readers.

There's a method to this kind of madness, of course. Editors know that if you receive a good response to your "free plug" (and you only get one of them), you'll be more likely to send a paid advertisement in the future. Note, however, that some consumer magazines never give free plugs. Instead, they offer extra "editorial mentions" to paid advertisers.

Publicity Through Letters To the Editor. Occasionally a letter to an editor will end up being quoted in his or her column, but usually it ends up in the letters section of the magazine. By reading various magazines, large and small alike, you will note that many people manage to get publicity for themselves, their products, or businesses, merely by writing an informative letter. Such letters may provide an answer to a question posed by a reader in an earlier issue, pass along information about a topic previously discussed in the magazine, or merely comment on articles the magazine has published in the past. In publications of limited circulation, the editor may include the sender's address if it is believed that it will benefit the magazine's readers to do so. At the very least, one's city and state is usually mentioned with the sender's name, making it possible for interested readers to get a telephone number through Information.

Publicity in Newsletters. There are literally thousands of newsletters in print today -- so many, in fact, that there are newsletter directories in libraries, just as there are directories which list magazines. There are at least a few hundred newsletters being published for creative people, including artists, craftspeople, designers, writers, self-publishers, graphic artists, desktop publishers, and home-business owners in general. The circulation of such publications is generally small -- from a few hundred readers to a few thousand at best -- but remember what I said about the size of a periodical's readership. It has little to do with the value of publicity received.

When you build your press release mailing list, be sure to include all the small-business newsletters you can find, because they are particularly receptive to press releases from other small business owners. I've included the best business and marketing-oriented newsletters in the Resource Chapter of this book, but you should also send releases to newsletters edited for craft consumers and hobbyists since they're as likely as anyone to buy your products, publications or services.

Other Opportunities for Publicity

Directories. Directories offer a tremendous opportunity for publicity, and the best way to learn about them is through reading a variety of business periodicals which tend to announce the publication of new editions. Several directories offer free listings to authors, book and newsletter publishers, consultants, and small business specialists like myself.

For example, I have my newsletter listed in *Ulrich's International Periodicals Directory*, Oxbridge Communications' *Standard Periodical Directory*, and *Power Media "Selects"* (a listing that positions my newsletter as one of the best in its field). As a book publisher, I'm entitled to free listings in Dustbook's *Small Press Record of Books in Print*, and R. R. Bowker's *Books in Print* (an invaluable library reference). As an author and speaker, I'm also listed in the *Directory of Experts, Authorities & Spokespersons*, as well as *Contemporary Authors*. You get the idea by now. I've tracked down the directories most likely to be helpful to me, and requested a free listing form. With a little effort, you can do the same for yourself.

In checking the Resource Chapter, you will note several smaller directories published especially for craft sellers. For example, if you're a crafts designer, you should register for inclusion in Adele Patti's *Pattern Designer Directory*, which is designed to help craft sellers obtain patterns and designs they can use (without fear of violating someone's copyright) on craftwork they sell.

If you're a craft shop owner in search of handcrafts for resale, a listing in Adele's annual *Directory of Craft Shops* is free and made to order for you.

If you sell craft or needlework supplies of any kind, you can get a free listing in one or more of Teri Hales' three *SourceLetters* and companion directories.

If you're a sales rep in search of new handcraft lines, you can be listed in Sharon Olson's unique *Directory of Wholesale Reps*.

As you can see, opportunities for free directory listings are everywhere. You need only read to find them (and by reading this book you have a head start on a lot of other craft sellers).

Publicity In Books. Hundreds of new craft books have been published in recent years, and thousands of craftspeople have had photographs of their work included in them. It has become common practice for craft writers to send news releases to art and craft editors when they begin a new book because they welcome contact from craft professionals willing to share information and photographs. Watch for such announcements and follow up on them when you are producing the type of work that is needed by an author. Although you will receive no monetary gain from inclusion in such book, it will do wonders for your ego.

I'm a good example of an author who is always on the lookout for interesting and successful craft businesses. When I'm not working on a new book, I'm always interested in receiving informative letters I might quote in my "Selling What You Make" column in *Crafts,* or in my newsletter, *National Home Business Report.* When I give publicity to someone however, I usually attach an address to the mention so readers can find them -- and order whatever it is they may be offering. (The Resource Chapter of this book is but one example. If you happen to offer crafts marketing information that should be listed in a later edition, be sure to send me your press release.)

Following Leads

Time out! I have some advice to pass on concerning the subject of following up on leads once you read about them. Let me illustrate my point with a brief story.

When my husband was coordinating a unique international crafts festival for Busch Gardens back in the 70s, he searched the nation for 20 outstanding folk artists and craftsmen with considerable product for sale and the ability to demonstrate their art or craft. He already knew some of these special people, but to find the rest, he sent a press release to several craft magazines. He clearly stated his needs, then invited interested craftsmen to send complete information about themselves and their craft, including a brochure or photograph of their work.

He received perhaps thirty letters. Most were hastily scribbled notes which simply said, "Send me more information about your show." Instead of sending Harry the information he had *specifically requested in the article they read*, these craftspeople were asking him for more details. He didn't have any printed literature to send, nor the time to give a personal reply. (Or the desire to do so, considering that his needs had been made clear in the press release). Only three people sent exactly what had been requested, and one of them was invited to participate in the show. That craftswoman not only sold thousands of dollars' worth of merchandise, but also received a lot of publicity in major craft magazines as a result.

Moral of story? When you come across an interesting opportunity, follow up on it with every-

141

thing you've got. If an article asks for complete information, send it. If it asks for a resume, be sure to include an account of your background and qualifications. If it says to send photographs, don't send slides, and vice versa. If it says "mail inquiries only," don't telephone. And so on. Although you may sometimes follow through with your best and receive nothing for your effort, at other times your professional approach -- and compliance with instructions -- will bring an opportunity right to your doorstep.

Advertising

If you have a product to advertise and sell by mail, your thoughts may immediately turn to a big, beautiful ad in a prestigious consumer magazine. But unless you are an experienced advertising copywriter, that ad (which will cost you an arm and a leg) may not even pay for itself in orders received.

Before spending a lot of money on a display ad, first explore your market by placing inexpensive classified ads in several magazines that seem best for your product. If you can get a good response from classified ads, this may indicate that an even greater response might be received from display ads in the same publications. But when you're ready to move up to a display ad, buy the smallest one available because it's still going to be a learning experience for you, and one of your goals should be to keep the lesson as painless as possible.

Display Advertising. It isn't easy to write effective advertising copy, but you can learn a lot merely by studying the ads of others. For example, whenever you notice the same ads running in magazines month after month, you can assume the advertiser has received a response good enough to warrant a rerun of that ad. Study the style of such ads carefully, noting in particular the headline of the ad and how easy the advertiser has made it for people to order the advertised product. See if you can identify the key words in the ad that clearly explain the product's benefits, for it is benefits -- and benefits alone -- that sell products. (Remember, customers are always asking, "What's in it for me?")

In preparing a display ad, author Merle Dowd suggests you think of it as a small billboard. "While long-copy ads pull mail orders," he says, "you should aim for quick impact with small display ads. Include a benefit or a big promise in the headline along with your name if you can work it in. A reader must see your ad before he or she can react to your message."

Merle also stresses the use of an eye-catching

142

logo or symbol that will attract attention and build your identification from ad to ad. If you can write the copy for your ad, and plan its general layout, the magazine's advertising department can take it from there and do the necessary typesetting and "paste-up" for you. The charge for this is usually quite reasonable.

Good ad copy is necessary to pull orders, but even perfect ads won't pull if they are placed in the wrong publications, so take your time in analyzing the many magazines out there before deciding which ones are right for you. Request advertising rate cards, then create a little chart that shows the costs of classified and display ads in each magazine. Compare these prices to the guaranteed circulation figures to see which offers the best advertising bargain. (In other words, how many dollars will it take to communicate with a thousand people?)

Placing A Classified Ad. The primary difference between classified and display advertising, besides cost, is its appearance and placement in a magazine. Display ads are scattered throughout the editorial pages of a publication, while classifieds are grouped in the back under various category headings. Often, a classified ad will pull better for you than a display ad for the simple reason that such ads are read by people who are looking for something in particular. If your ad happens to be there when someone happens to be looking for what you offer, you'll get a response from that person.

In writing an ad, it's important to demonstrate with words exactly how your proposition, or product, will benefit the reader. Since you are going to be charged for each word used in your ad (including your address), don't waste them. Be clear and concise. Use a telegraphic style of writing, omitting unnecessary verbs and adjectives. Abbreviations are okay, as are incomplete sentences. Before sending your ad to a magazine, study all the ads in the classified pages to make sure your product fits in with the type of merchandise being advertised by others. Emulate the style of ads you think are best, and remember that magazine ads generally have to be placed two to three months before the month of publication.

Copywriting Mistakes to Avoid. The biggest mistake beginning advertisers make with classified ads is to write ads of 100 words or more, including opinionated phrases such as "You'll really LOVE it" or "It's so beautiful." Instead, try to keep ads to a length of 20-30 words, and stress your product's benefits, such as "Will save TIME" or "Guaranteed to last."

Other advertisers waste money by using too many words to express a simple thought. For example, *"Please enclose your check or money order in the amount of $10, adding $1.50 for postage and handling. Send order to Brownstone Productions, P. O. Box 190,"* could be dramatically shortened to: *"$11.50 ppd. from Brownstone Productions, Box 190."* At 50 cents a word these changes would save you $10; at $3 a word, the savings would be $60.

These days, with shipping costs constantly on the rise, it's probably best not to emphasize what you must charge for shipping and handling. That's why so many advertisers simply include a single postage-paid price that covers everything. (It's best to round off this figure to an amount generally used by mail order sellers, such as $4.50 or $10.95. Don't use prices such as $3.15 or $8.65.(Refer back to the pricing chapter if you don't understand the logic of this.)

Note that the first words in a classified ad usually begin with capital letters, serving as the headline for your ad. These first few words are critical to your ad's pulling power. They must quickly tell the reader if the rest of the ad is of interest to them. If you will study the classified ad pages of several magazines, you'll notice the frequent use of the following words, which are the 12 most persuasive words in the English language, according to ad copywriters:

YOU * SAVE * MONEY * NEW * LOVE
EASY * HEALTH * SAFETY * RESULTS
DISCOVERY * PROVEN * GUARANTEE

When writing ads for a crafts magazine, it is a good idea to "call out" to your intended audience with a word that identifies a group of craftspeople (Quiltmakers, Home Sewers, Dollmakers); or places emphasis on the craft itself (Jewelry Supplies, Quilling Kits, Cake Decorating); or announces the main benefit of your product (Free Pattern, Discover the Secret, Save Money!) and so on.

Keying Your Ads. When advertising in more than one publication at a time, you need to "key" your ads to determine which one is bringing in the most inquiries. What you must do is write your address in a special way so you can tell by the way the envelope is addressed exactly which magazine prompted the response.

EXAMPLES: When using your business name, you might say "Polly's Patterns" in one ad, and "Patterns by Polly" in another. If using your own name, you could say "Mary Smith" in one ad, and "M. Smith" in another. Or, you might use

"Box 281" in one address and "P. O. Box 281" in another. Or add a code, such as "Dept. C-12," which could tell you that the ad was placed in the December issue of *Crafts* magazine. Some advertisers place initials after their name, such as "Crafty Creations/PQ" (the initials being your code for the magazine's name).

NOTE: When changing your name, street address or post office box number in any way, check with the post office beforehand to make certain this will not affect the delivery of your mail.

Selecting Magazines for Your Ads. Which publications should you consider for an ad? Check the newsstand for craft consumer publications that might be right for you, and also give some of the smaller craft publications a try as well. (See the Resource Chapter to sample some of them.) Here, ads may cost as little as 15 cents a word.

To find out whether classified ads for handcrafts and needlework actually bring in many orders for advertisers, I selected half a dozen ads from as many magazines and wrote the advertisers, explaining my purpose. I offered each person a mention in this book in exchange for a little information. Surprisingly, only one person answered my letter, proving once again that most craftspeople do not follow up on opportunities for free publicity. Here's the ad I selected from a popular sewing magazine:

FOR SALE: Beautiful handmade quilts and other things. List, 25 cents.

This ad was placed by Mrs. Elbert Baker of Centerville, Tennessee, and when I wrote to her, I asked these questions:

1. Do you often advertise your quilts for sale and do your ads bring in many orders?
2. Do you have difficulty selling your quilts?
3. Do you consider yourself a beginning, or experienced seller?

Mrs. Baker replied: "I realized not long ago the difference between myself and a beginner (although I'm not a professional), when the beginner thought she would get an order from every price list she mailed. My ads result in my mailing several lists to all parts of the U.S. and some foreign countries. I usually average one order for each eight or ten price lists mailed. Most are for quilts and, except for one baby quilt that was the wrong color, I've never had to take any back. Most people locally make their own quilts, so most of mine are sold by mail. So far, I've never gotten far enough ahead of demand to have any extra for craft shows. I make quilts and all other crafts because I love doing that type of work. For the last few years, I have advertised quilts and other things in several of the Tower Press magazines, and last year I made over $2,000 as a result."

Note that Mrs. Baker says she averages one order for each eight or ten price lists mailed out. An order response of 10 percent is excellent, and few beginners should expect to receive such a high order response from the mailing of a price list. The average mail order seller will be lucky to get a five percent response from individuals who have specifically asked for more information, and as little as a one percent response from a mail list purchased outright or traded with another seller.

As a rule of thumb, nicely printed brochures will always bring more orders than a letter and price list; small catalogs (6-12 pages) will always bring more orders than a brochure, and anything printed in color will bring more orders than black ink on white paper. (If you can afford to print in only one color besides black, go with red. It's a proven "response motivator." For more color with little extra cost, switch from white paper to a colored stock, such as light blue, gray, ivory, or tan.)

Before advertising the availability of a free brochure or catalog, be sure to calculate the cost of each piece you will be mailing and consider whether you can afford to give it away. If a price list or brochure costs you 10 or 15 cents to print, and another 25 cents to mail (and the price of a first class stamp will soon increase), a hundred pieces will cost you $35-$40 to mail. When this cost is measured against the dollar amount of any orders you might expect to receive, you may decide (as Mrs. Baker apparently did) that it is unwise to offer advertising material free of charge. That's why so many craft sellers offer information for 25 or 50 cents, or ask for a self-addressed stamped envelope (always abbreviated in ads as "S.A.S.E." "SASE.")

Those who offer expensive color brochures or catalogs are likely to request as much as a dollar to cover postage and handling. Occasionally they also indicate in their ads that this amount is refundable, meaning it will be applied to one's first order. Instead of money or a SASE, some advertisers ask for one or two first-class stamps.

Although the above methods will automatically cut down the number of responses received from an ad, you may find you have simply eliminated most of the "curiosity-seekers" who wouldn't have ordered in the first place. Some people are natural born catalog collectors and craftspeople, in particular, seem to enjoy sending away for anything that's free since it might give them a good idea they can use. One technique I'm now beginning to use, to help offset the cost of my catalog and increasing first-class postage, is to offer one- or two-page resource lists for a dollar, or special reports for $4 or $5. This enables me to put valuable information into my readers' hands while also including my catalog in case they're ready to learn more.

A Final Tip: Remember that the goal of a classified is NOT to solicit orders directly, but rather to acquire the names of interested prospects who might buy from you AFTER you send them your best printed advertising material. In other words, you "go fishing" with a classified ad and "sink the hook" with your brochure or catalog. And once you've got a mail list going, remember what I said earlier about the importance of remailing those prospect names over and over again. (See pages 82-84.)

The Promotional Materials You Need

In spite of the fact that advertising is an integral part of business, few craftspeople do much of it. Instead, they promote themselves and their work largely through the use of a good letterhead, business card, brochure, or "hang tag" on their work. Since you will need one or more of these things to do business, a discussion of each follows, along with information on how to design them yourself and prepare your own camera-ready artwork for a printer.

Letterheads. A well-designed letterhead is essential to any business and, because it says so much about the sender, should be designed with care. Contrary to popular belief, it is not necessary to spend a small fortune to get quality stationery and matching envelopes printed, nor do these items have to be ordered in great quantity. Copy centers and small print shops are quite common these days, even in smaller towns. The high-tech photocopy equipment in such shops enables you to walk in off the street with something to be printed, and a few minutes later have a hundred copies in hand for as little as five or ten cents a page (depending on the kind of paper you want). If your artwork has a lot of black in it, or a photograph, the printer will probably suggest that you have a plate made (instead of the more common paper masters) to assure a better print job. More time for printing would have to be allowed for this kind of job.

While you can order as few as a hundred sheets of stationery, you'll have to order business envelopes by the box. (Number 10 envelopes, the ones used by most businesses, come 500 to a box. Envelopes in size 9x12 are packaged 250 per box.)

144

Punzel's Primitives
On N. Harpur Lake

Rosemaling
by Audrey

Woodenware
by Roy & Jim

ROUTE 1
WESTBORO, WIS.
54490

PHONE
715-427-3129

ELYSE SOMMER INC. / 962 ALLEN LANE. WOODMERE. NEW YORK 11598/ P.O. BOX E

Author
Representative

TREE TOYS

BETTY CHRISTY
DORIS TRACY

The Mumby Bead Company
MFGS OF FINE CERAMIC BEADS & ART SUPPLIES

TELEPHONE
AREA CODE 714 548 4532
24 HOUR SERVICE

2931 GRACE LANE
SUITE E COSTA MESA
CALIFORNIA 92626

Love-Built Toys & Crafts

Toys, crafts and ideas
for the imaginative child and creative parent

Artist

RUBY TOBEY
2315 W 32nd South
Wichita, Kansas 67217
Phone 447 5656

Oil Paintings
Drawings
Watercolor Sketches
Miniatures
Original Stationery

16-583-1555

145

An originally-designed letterhead speaks well for one's business. Note how, in the above examples, individual craftspeople have designed their letterheads around their particular talent or craft. Elyse Sommer's typewriter design, for example, clearly shows she is a writer; Ruby Tobey's letter gives samples of her style of drawing, which is probably helpful to her in acquiring custom-design orders; the train engine on Love-Built's stationery is based on a product in their line, and so on.

If you don't feel you can design your own stationery, you can order inexpensive business stationery by mail. (To make this job easier for you, I've included in the Resource Chapter a couple of office supply catalogs that offer stationery, envelopes, business cards and other necessary printed materials by mail.)

Business Cards. An important tool for any crafts seller, business cards are readily available from any printer, or they can be ordered by mail. (If you'd like to have your own artwork adapted for a business card, see Vermont Business Forms in the Resource Chapter. They have worked with many craftspeople through the years, and offer a samples package that will give you some ideas.)

Brochures. Like stationery, brochures can be designed by you and printed by any printer. If you keep them simple, print in one color only, and don't have a lot of complicated cuts or folds, cost can be kept to a minimum. But here's a word of advice from rosemaler Audrey Punzel: "Don't put the price of your various items on the brochure itself. Instead, print that information as an insert. Retail shops may want to show customers what you offer, but don't want your prices showing. Also, when you have to change your prices you can save on the expense of a new brochure by just ordering a new price insert." Audrey points out that it doesn't make a customer happy to see old prices crossed out and new ones written in.

Brochures can be as simple or elaborate as you care to make them. Most craftspeople, however, begin with paper to size 8½ x 11 in. which is then folded in thirds to create a simple self-mailer. Or you might try 9 x 16 in. paper, folding it in half, then half again, which gives you a self-mailer measuring 4 x 9 in. Consider the many different ways this kind of simple brochure might look when printed on different colored paper, textured card stock, or in some color other than black.

Decorative Stickers and Labels. While not necessary, these always add a touch of professionalism to craft merchandise and may be ordered in quantity for less than you might think. Check office supply catalogs for gold and silver labels which can be printed to your specification.

Hang Tags. A hang tag not only adds a professional touch to your products, but is a good promotional tool as well since it carries your message home with the buyer. For this reason, many craftspeople consider hang tags an important form of publicity and advertising. They can be designed and printed as easily as stationery and business cards. Once printed, you can punch holes and add ties.

A tag should carry information that indicates who made the item, how and why it was made and, in some cases, how it should be cared for. What you put on your tag will depend on who you are and what you do. The weaver who spins and dyes her own wool would certainly want this fact mentioned on her tag. The potter who digs his own clay would use that as a selling point. The toymaker who sells unfinished wood for safety's sake, the needleworker who uses only the finest yarns, the rosemaler whose designs are completely authentic -- all would use such information to their advantage on a tag. Anything that makes you or your work unique is information that belongs not only on a tag, but on other promotional materials as well. (See sample below.)

Also see Chapter 15 for other tags required by law, particularly on items of clothing.

Roger B. Sandstrom
Rt. 4 — Box 95
Seymour, Mo. 65746

Kind of Wood

Early American TREENWARE

Treenware in selected domestic woods
Semi-Fancy Grade: utility, used in most of our standard treenware styles.

Selected because of color, grain and strength, our semi-fancy grade is primarily available most of the time. Great care has been taken to keep the quality the same as our finest grades. Our treenware is designed to give you fitness for purpose, beauty of form and a love of old-time craftsmanship.

Designing Promotional Materials

When designing your own letterhead, brochure or business card, never use a design or picture you have clipped from a magazine or newspaper because it is probably protected by copyright. If you can't draw, you can create unusual artwork by using ideas found in the *Dover Pictorial Archive*

Cornfield Creations

7288 S. Garland Ct.
Littleton, CO 80123
(303) 973-2227

Sue Turner

The Country Memories Collection

Note matching hangtag. . . very professional-looking.

PAMELA J. SPINAZZOLA

Pamela's Studio One
33 MOUNTAIN AVENUE
REVERE, MASSACHUSETTS 02151

(617) 289-7055

ILLUSTRATOR • ENGROSSER-ILLUMINATOR
GRAPHIC DESIGN • GREETING CARD DESIGN

Scherenschnitte
by
ARLENE FRANCE

BY APPOINTMENT
345 N. BROAD ST.   LITITZ, PA. 17543

Kelligraphies

Kelly Cline calligrapher

2904 Ames
Ponca City, OK 74604
405 762-0453

(313) 548-8352

BUTTON MANIA

AURICE (RICKIE) KNOWLES

3293 BACON ○ BERKLEY, MI 48072

147

Many craftspeople design their own business cards. Here are several examples from the author's collection (shown in slightly reduced size). Interesting effects can be achieved by the use of colored ink or card stock, and cards can be any size or shape desired, printed horizontally or vertically. The card for Ayn's Shuttle Shop, for example, is a rectangular card folded in half. On the side you do not see, Ayn has listed the various items she weaves for her shop.

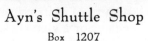

Ayn's Shuttle Shop

Box 1207
Oak Bluffs, Mass.
02557

Wesley House Waterfront

SHOP HOURS - MON. thru SAT.
9:30 A.M. to 9:00 P.M.

books (mentioned in an earlier chapter). A drawing or design can be used in conjunction with typesetting ordered from a printer, transfer lettering you can do yourself, or fancy fonts generated by a computer and laser printer. (Some print shops now offer this service at lower cost than traditional typesetting.)

"Transfer lettering," a product available in artist supply stores, is a transparent sheet that has specially printed, pressure-sensitive letters on the back. You simply place the sheet so that a letter is positioned where you want it, then rub the letter with a rubbing stick to transfer it to your "mechanical," the piece of artwork you will give to your printer. If your final artwork is too large or too small, it can be reduced or enlarged by the printer to fit the size stationery and envelopes you wish to use.

When designing a letterhead or brochure, keep in mind that standard sizes will be less expensive than special sizes. Every cut or fold the printer has to make will cost you extra.

And! Before you print that piece, prepare a dummy mail piece and have the Post Office verify that it weighs what you expect it to (under one ounce). This is particularly important when you are creating a small catalog.

If you don't feel you can prepare your own artwork, perhaps an artist friend can design it for you using your original ideas as a guideline. If you don't have a cooperative friend, check the art department of your local high school, or ask your printer if he knows someone who does this sort of thing.

Preparing Camera-Ready Artwork For a Printer

The most important thing to remember here is that the final print job will be only as good as your artwork, or "copy." The printer will photograph that copy to make a paper plate or other master, and anything your eyes can see, the camera will also see -- only better. Therefore, remove all smudges and excesses of glue, and cover up unwanted lines or errors with a "white-out" solution available in office supply stores. Many pieces of paper can be pasted on a sheet of white paper or poster board (use rubber cement or a glue stick for best results) and the edges of these papers will all disappear into the background if they are white and thin enough not to cast a shadow when a light is shined on it. (If you can see a shadow, so can the camera, and this would show up on your printing as a dark line.)

148

For best results, your artwork should be black on white paper, regardless of the color you want printed. And, unless you understand how to use a reduction/enlargement scale, your artwork should also be the same size as you want your finished copy to be. You can work with colored materials, but remember that red to the camera is the same as black, which means that red letters on a black background would reproduce as a solid black mass. Light blue or yellow will not show up at all, which is good, because it means you can use a light blue or yellow pencil to make the necessary guidelines on your artwork, and they do not have to be erased or covered up before sending it to the printer. India ink is not required for artwork; you can achieve excellent results using a fine point black felt tip pen or other art pen that gives an even line when writing.

To save money on typesetting, you can use the transfer lettering sheets mentioned earlier, or a typewriter. Good results can be obtained with an IBM Selectric or electronic typewriter with carbon ribbon and a variety of font wheels. If you must use a regular typewriter and cloth ribbon, be sure the type bars are clean and use a new ribbon.

If you are lucky enough to have a computer and software that enables you to design pages and change fonts, as I now do -- the job of preparing camera-ready copy will be a snap. For more years than I care to count, I had to do everything the hard way, cutting and pasting until I was blue in the face. Now that I have a computer and the right software, I can do in one day what it used to take me a week to accomplish.

If you'd like to know more about computers but don't know where to start, you'll find just what you need in the special computer chapter included in my second book, *Homemade Money*. I've also added to this edition of *Creative Cash* some tips on how to publish your own books, with or without a computer. (See Chapter 13.)

A final tip about printing. Always get quotes from more than one printer because the difference is sometimes astounding, particularly where catalogs and booklets are concerned. Request prices on different quantities, too, since the difference in price between 100 and 500 copies may be negligible, but the difference between 1,000 and 5,000 can be significant.

If you don't live near a printer, you can always work with them by mail, using United Parcel Service for delivery. I've done this for years. (To find printers, see the *Directory of Book, Catalog, and Magazine Printers* in the Resource Chapter.

- 13 -

Writing and Self-Publishing

"If you are creative enough to produce original craft projects that others would like to copy, and if you are well enough organized verbally to write technical procedures in a lucid, detailed manner, then perhaps you should consider writing craft articles," says crafts editor Sybil Harp. "If you've worked in one medium and have developed a number of ideas and techniques in that medium, you may even be able to write a book. While there are only a handful of people in the craft field who have made a full living from writing articles and books, many have found it an excellent way to supplement their incomes while enjoying the special prestige that comes from being a published author."

Who better to give advice to aspiring craft writers than Sybil Harp, who has helped foster the writing careers of many craftspeople through the years. Pat Virch is one of those people. (You will recall reading about her in Chapter 11.) When she was just getting started in rosemaling, she sent a letter to Sybil, then editor of *Creative Crafts*. Pat said she didn't know how to write a magazine article, but Sybil sent back a letter of encouragement, as she has done with so many other craftspeople since that day. Pat followed her lead and, emulating the style of other articles in the magazine, wrote an excellent two-part article that led directly to her first book on rosemaling.

Advice for Beginning Craft Writers

Always one to give help and advice when needed, Sybil responded warmly to my request for information, offering the following guidelines for would-be craft writers: "There are certain characteristics required of craft writers. Being a good crafts-man is not enough, and simply being a good writer is never enough. Both abilities are required. This does not mean that one must be a highly polished, professional writer; it simply means that the ability to express oneself verbally is essential to the writing of a how-to craft article or book.

"While this may seem self-evident, it is surprising how many proficient craftsmen lack this ability. My own explanation for this is that craftsmen are basically visual people who conceive ideas visually and who learn techniques with their eyes and their hands, rather than through words as verbally-oriented people do. Those who are highly visual may be able to master a technique and teach it to others through demonstration, but when they have to explain a process verbally, they often are at a loss. Frequently, too, craftsmen who are very adept will assume knowledge on the part of the reader that simply isn't there, and as a result will leave great gaps in writing instructions.

"By the same token, writers unfamiliar with crafts will often assume that writing up a crafts project is the same as reporting on anything else. The truth is that very seldom is a noncraftsman able to capture enough of the feel of a technique to write good, usable instructions. Usually articles prepared by professional writers who are not craftsmen are much too sketchy in the instructions and tend to have overtones of the personality profile. Noncraftsmen writers fail to understand that the readers of craft magazines and books are looking primarily for ideas and for detailed technical information."

Ideas and detailed technical information. That's what all craft magazine editors want. And note that "detailed" does not mean "wordy." Editors have to wade daily through what they call

149

their "slush pile" of manuscripts, and wordy articles on overworked craft topics won't interest them. Clearly and concisely written articles, however, are going to excite them a lot, particularly when the writer is explaining new craft techniques and offering well-designed items readers will enjoy making. When such articles are accompanied by sharply focused photographs or crisp line drawings, it can really make an editor's day.

Beginning writers often prepare an article and send it to an editor without first studying the magazine to see if such articles are even being published. Others will take the time to study the contents of several issues before querying the editor to find out if there is some interest in their idea. Unknown writers are usually asked to write articles "on speculation," which means there is no obligation on the editor's part to buy unless the finished article meets with approval. Craftspeople with good ideas and the ability to explain techniques clearly will have few problems here, however, since their articles will probably be accepted with gratitude -- and nice checks.

If you have decided to try your hand at writing how-to craft articles for magazines, before you start writing you should obtain and read copies of several different magazines to gain a basic understanding of the kind of articles needed by each editor, and the type of audience served by each magazine.

Although there is a difference between writing craft technique how-to articles, and merely writing instructions for a project in a craft medium familiar to most readers, editors of both kinds of articles want basically the same things. For that reason, you may wish to re-read at this point the advice given in Chapter 9, "Getting Designs and Ideas Published."

In addition to magazines specializing in crafts or needlework, you might explore a few consumer publications as well, since many are seeking craft articles. You can study this market thoroughly by obtaining a copy of *Writer's Market*, an annual directory that lists the editorial needs of hundreds of magazine editors (as well as book publishers), and is the "bible" of all serious free-lance writers.

Regardless of whether you are writing how-to articles for a craft magazine or a consumer publication, never assume knowledge on the part of a reader. People use how-to-do-it instructions because they want to make the item described. If they already know how to do your craft project, they wouldn't need you to tell them how, so don't let them down by omitting any step in the process, no matter how simple it seems to you as a skilled craftsperson. Beginners in crafts can become confused very easily, and they need to be led step-by-step through the complete process.

Perhaps the biggest hurdle you will have to overcome as a crafts writer is the need for photographs or line drawings. How-to articles must be illustrated, and it will probably prove too expensive to hire someone to take pictures or do line drawings for you. If you plan to do a lot of writing, you ought to think about buying a good camera and learning how to use it correctly. The more you can do for yourself, the more money you can make as a crafts writer.

Writing a Crafts Book

Some craftspeople drift into writing as naturally as a duck takes to water. Once they have established themselves as craft writers and learned the ins and outs of writing instructions, taking photographs, doing drawings, etc., they may go on to write a book. But this kind of success doesn't happen overnight. It takes time to develop competence in doing all these tasks.

It also takes effort to become a capable writer and, according to Dona Meilach, there is only one way to have written a craft book: "...with difficulty, determination, and slavish attention to detail. If you are willing to expend this effort, your toes may begin to curl over the threshold of the publishing world." Dona, author of more than 35 craft books, gained experience as a writer by doing children's books, writing for magazines, and teaching writing classes. Her start as an author came when she and a friend became interested in doing a book on collage since none existed at the time, and after that, her pen never seemed to stop.

Those who are seriously interested in writing and self-publishing will find the book, *Career Opportunities in Crafts* (Crown Publishers, 1977), inspiring reading. Available in many libraries, it explores the opportunities in all fields of crafts and includes an interesting chapter on crafts publishing that gives specifics on how to write for periodicals and deal with book publishers, what to expect in the way of contracts and royalties, etc. It is here that author Elyse Sommer stresses the importance of the five "C's" when writing: Be *correct, constructive, clear, concise,* and *compelling,* she says. "A gift for turning a clever phrase certainly won't hurt a crafts book, but the real "must ingredient" is not extraordinary writing talent but enthusiasm for and knowledge of your subject and the ability to organize material into a cohesive and easily comprehensible whole."

Elyse did not start out to be a crafts writer, but journalism has always been her vocational interest. She worked her way through college by writing

confession stories, and her first published book was an anthology called *Childbirth*. Her first craft book, on decoupage, began as a series of magazine articles, and the response from readers was so good she prepared a book outline and presented the idea to a publisher. Several books followed thereafter. Like many successful authors, Elyse has always promoted and sold her own books by mail.

Craftspeople who teach or lecture often find that a book is the most natural thing in the world for them to do. Margo Daws Pontius, the cornshuckery artisan you met earlier, illustrates my point. After I had interviewed her for the teaching chapter of this book, Margo wrote to say that she had just written her first book, titled *American Cornshuckery in Action*. Because she had already written several articles on her craft, a book was simply the logical thing to do at this point. (You will be amused to know that Margo's children wanted her to title the book "What My Mother Does in the Cornfield," but Margo decided making the best seller's list wasn't all that important.)

Roberta Raffelli also told me how her books evolved as a result of doing craft work. "I have been interested in crafts since I was in high school," Roberta writes, "but it was not until many years later that I decided I would like to do something with crafts for profit. I have always liked to do different with crafts for profit. I have always liked

to do different things in crafts, be creative -- not just do what someone else is doing -- so I started working on a line of animals made from Styrofoam®, chenille bumps, and chenille stems. I made a whole line, including a pink elephant, camels, cats, poodles, rabbits, etc., and then offered my book to a publisher who was then publishing books of this type. Later I did books such as *Magic With Tin Cans*, a book using craft sticks, and a couple on decoupage. Next I designed a nativity scene with large draped figures. These figures were unique inasmuch as they had ceramic heads, hands and feet, for which I had molds made. I then traveled the country for about a year teaching these figures at ceramic shops as a representative of Fiesta Colors."

Roberta, who went on to teach 18th Century decoupage and later wrote a book on Early American crafts, says the only way to get started in this business is "to love it enough to sacrifice for it. You must get acquainted with people in the business, swap ideas about what you are doing, and follow up on every lead that comes along and looks interesting to you. It's your perseverance as well as your talent that leads you to success."

Getting Your Book Published

Finding a publisher for a crafts book may require great patience. Some authors submit pro-

151

posals or complete manuscripts to more than a dozen publishers (one at a time) before they find one who wants it. I recall a friend who said her book had already been sent to seven publishers, and so far, no interest. In cases like this, it is difficult not to get discouraged, but you must remember that a publisher's refusal to take on a book often has little to do with how good or bad it is. More likely, books are refused simply because they aren't the *kind* the publisher is looking for at the time.

Of course, publishers have been known to make bad judgments from time to time, as Dr. Seymour Isenberg can tell you. "When my wife Anita and I wrote our first book, *How to Work in Stained Glass* (Chilton)," he writes, "it got turned down by no less than twenty publishers, all of whom claimed there wouldn't be enough interest in the subject. In time, however, the book took on a life of its own and became a real classic." The Isenbergs went on to write other books and for several years also published a stained glass magazine.

How can you find publishers most likely to be interested in your book? Perhaps at this point I should explain that you could be dealing with two kinds of publishers here, as different from one another as milk and buttermilk. First there are *trade publishers* who publish hardcover or trade paperback books of a kind normally found in bookstores and libraries. Then there are *craft book publishers* who publish the colorful "floppy books" and design leaflets so common in today's craft and needlework shops. Let's look at this kind of publisher first.

Craft Book and Leaflet Publishers. Unknown or inexperienced craft writers with good skills and ideas should consider their opportunities in this field. Start your market research work by browsing the book racks in any craft or needlework supply shop. I wouldn't be surprised to hear you say, "Why, I could do this!" If so, note the publisher's name on that book, then write for a copy of its "Writer's Guidelines Sheet" (just as you would do if you were trying to get information on what a magazine editor might buy.)

Some of these publishers will buy ideas outright while others will pay royalties. My research indicates that outright payment will vary from $500 to $2,000, while royalties may vary from 5-7% of the wholesale price, depending on the individual publisher's policy. One publisher told me she paid a royalty of 8½ cents on a floppy book that retailed for $2.50. "This may not sound like much," she said, "but it adds up when you consider that we'll sell at least 30,000 copies, and maybe a hundred thousand or more. Some titles, in fact, have sold more than a million copies."

Unlike trade book publishers who have a tendency to print a few thousand copies of a book and hope it sells, publishers in the crafts industry have a remarkable distribution system that quickly gets books into the craft and needlework supply stores where consumers can buy them. Publishers and their distributors also promote their books at the various trade shows they participate in each year.

You may not realize it, but many of the needlework design books and leaflets are being published today by women working out of their homes -- creative designers who have launched full-time publishing businesses of their own. Some began by publishing their designs only, then branched out to publish the work of others.

For a complete list of all the publishers in this field, see the *Craft Market Handbook* published annually in June by *Profitable Craft Merchandising* magazine, a subscription-only trade periodical listed in the Resource Chapter. This directory is also your guide to manufacturers, wholesalers and trade organizations in the industry.

Dealing With Trade Book Publishers. Only the most professional manuscripts will be of interest to major book publishers whose first question is apt to be: What does your book offer that is not already available in other books we have published?

The easiest way to make a list of publishers who *might* be interested in your book is to visit any bookstore or library. Note the kind of craft books that have been published recently, and the publishers who have done them. Then, in the library, look for a directory called *Literary Market Place*, which will give you detailed and up-to-date information about all trade publishers. Also in the library, look for the latest edition of *Writer's Market* to see exactly what each publisher on your list is interested in publishing in the coming year. Usually they include special instructions on how to present a book idea. (Note: Do not rely on information in *Writer's Market* if it is not the current year's edition. This book is readily available in bookstores or by mail. See the Resource Chapter.)

Finally, see another directory in the library called *Books In Print* which will give you a complete run-down of all the books that have been published in your field and are still in print. Nearby this directory will be a companion volume called *Forthcoming Books*, which will give you information about books soon to be published. (As you can see, there's a lot of research to be done here. Don't approach a publisher with a book idea until you know how much competition it has from books already in print, or soon to be published.)

You don't have to write a whole book before you start looking for a publisher, by the way. In fact, it's better to find a publisher first and write later. To get a publisher's attention, however, you will have to present a good proposal that includes:

1. A table of contents and an outline of the entire book, with a brief description of the contents of each chapter.

2. One or two sample chapters that illustrate your writing ability, the scope of your knowledge on the subject, and the overall feel of the finished book.

3. A few examples of the types of photographs, drawings, or artwork you will use to illustrate the book.

4. A time schedule indicating when you would plan to deliver the finished manuscript.

5. Information about your background and credits as a writer or crafts designer.

6. A few reasons why you think your book is needed, who would be most apt to buy it and why -- in other words, a sales pitch. If you are prepared to help market your book through lecturing, teaching, writing for craft magazines, etc., be sure to mention this. Publishers are interested in making money on the books they publish and if you can help promote or sell your own book, this could be a deciding factor in their decision to publish or not.

More specific information on submitting book proposals and manuscripts to publishers can be found in books about writing available in your library. One I strongly recommend you read is *How to Get Happily Published*, by Judith Appelbaum and Nancy Evans. It presents a marvelous overview of both the trade publishing industry and one's options as a self-publisher, including a lengthy resource chapter of interest to all writers.

Something many authors complain about is the fact that trade publishers do not continue to promote their books after the first year or so. Understandably, publishers will always have new books to promote, and they cannot continue to wage a sales campaign forever on every book they release. For this reason, it is sometimes more profitable to work with a smaller publishing house because such publishers tend to promote their books harder and keep them in print longer. Such publishers may also be receptive to working with authors who want to sell their own books by mail, or in their classes or workshops. (You should try to get a discount of 50-60% off the retail price so you have enough profit to do some special promotions of your own.)

Or maybe you should just publish the book yourself. It really isn't that difficult.

Publishing Your Own Book

I know a few hundred craftspeople who have become publishers in recent years, and the exciting variety of publications they've issued boggles the mind. Everything from little booklets, patterns, designs and calendars, to newsletters, magazines, directories and books have been published by individuals with no previous experience in this field. Some craftspeople become publishers because they can't find anyone interested in their book, but others simply enjoy the challenge of doing everything themselves and like the idea of getting all the profit.

The book you publish yourself may not get into bookstores, but if it is one that appeals to craft shop owners or lends itself to mail-order selling, it could continue to yield a good profit for many years to come. And if you happen to teach or lecture, just think of all the extra sales you might make.

When Pat Virch wrote her first book, *Traditional Rosemaling,* she decided to publish it herself and found a good printer who put it all together for her. She had 2500 copies printed, and her husband loaned her $5000 to pay for the printing and advertising. Fifty pages in length, the book was advertised for $3 and sold out within six months. "I had enough money then to pay for another printing," she recalls, "so we got brave and printed 5,000 copies this time. Believe it or not, that second printing sold in less than a year and we went on from there and have been reprinting the book ever since." (When I last checked with Pat, she had sold 30,000 copies of this book.)

Pat wrote a second book on rosemaling, and a third book on decorative tinware. She figures she spends around $3,000 a year on advertising, and sells about half her books at retail, with the rest being wholesaled to shops. She admits it was a little frightening at first when she realized she had to promote her own books, but she met the challenge just as she did when she was faced with the problem of learning how to teach.

Before you get the idea that publishing and selling your own book is as easy as I've just made it sound, let me point out that self-publishing has its pitfalls and problems like everything else. As with selling handcrafts, having the best product is useless unless you also have a market for it, so the most important question to consider before trying

153

to publish your own book is: *Will it sell?* Do you really have something of interest to write about, and are there people who will want to buy your book? (You'll have to do some market research to find out. Refer back to Chapter 2.)

Assuming you have answered yes to both questions, then it's time to think about what it will cost to publish your own book -- and how many copies you should print the first time around. Since a book's cost will be directly related to the number of pages and copies you have printed, you'll have to sit down and do some figuring and planning. First, determine the size of your book. Will it be a mini-booklet, something a little larger, or an 8½ x 11 in. paperback? Paper can be cut to any size, of course, but it will always be less expensive to use stock sizes, such as 8½ x 11 in. or 11 x 17 in. sheets (which would fold to an 8½ x 11 in. book). Actual sizes would be a bit less than this, of course, since the printer would trim the edges after the books were put together.

Once you have determined the size of your book, get some paper in the proper size and make a "dummy book," numbering the pages and planning what you might put on each page. For example, imagine a 12-page booklet, plus cover, printed to size 5½ x 8½ in. Take four sheets of paper size 8½ x 11 in., fold them in half, and put them together in book form. The outside sheet would be your cover (and you will need to talk to your printer about "cover stock" -- something a bit heavier than what will be used in the inside of your book). Then number all three sheets (now folded in half) pages one through twelve; open up the pages and flatten them out; and note how the number fall: Pages 1 and 12 are on the same sheet of paper with pages 2 and 11 on the back. Pages 3 and 10 are together, with pages 4 and 9 on the back; 5 and 8 are together, with 6 and 7 on the back. You'll soon understand the importance of this page sequence.

The book you publish yourself does not have to be a drab job in black and white. Paper comes in many interesting colors, and the addition of even one color to your book would add considerably to its appeal if this is important to its sale. Black ink on white paper is the least expensive, of course, but brown ink on ivory stock, for example, might cost only a little extra. (Discuss the possibilities with your printer.) You can also print black ink on white paper and have another color on a few pages throughout the book. This would involve additional negatives, plates, and another run through the press for each page with color, which will add to your printing costs, but it may also add to your eventual profit if books are to be sold through bookstores or craft shops. Color adds life and helps sell a product.

Now back to your dummy book and the way the pages are numbered. In order to save money on your printing bill, you should try to place photographs and color on the same sheets of paper, since this will mean that fewer negatives, plates, and printing runs would be required. That is, plan to have photographs and your extra color on the same sheets of paper in your dummy book -- such as pages 1 & 12, 3 & 10, etc. (Let the printer see your dummy book, to make sure he understands exactly what you expect to receive on the finished print job.)

The least expensive method of putting a book together is to have it "saddle stitched" or stapled, and this can be done even for thick books of 80 pages or more. Spiral-bound books are especially nice for certain types of books that may be used as reference guides since they will lie flat when opened, but this will add considerably to your costs. Even more expensive is the "perfect bound" method, where pages are glued to a flat spine. (This is the method you should use for any book you hope to sell to libraries or bookstores.)

Remember that there will always be an initial charge for plates and negatives, which will be the same regardless of how many books you print. Sometimes the difference between printing 1,000 and 2,500 copies of a book (or anything else, for that matter) will be surprisingly small for this reason. Be sure to get printing estimates for several quantities before deciding how many to print, and keep in mind that it may be wise to pay more for your first printing and see if the book is going to sell, rather than to try to save money by printing an extra thousand copies you may have to store under the bed for years.

Instead of thinking only about the number of books you should print to gain an economical per-book cost, think instead of the number of books you can reasonably expect to *sell* in a six-month period. Personally, I'd rather print fewer books at a slightly higher per-book cost than have an extra 500 books sitting in my basement, tying up my business capital. There are a number of book printers who specialize in small press runs of as few as 100-500 books, and if you request quotes from several of them, I'm sure you'll be able to find a printer who can deliver the book you want at a price you can afford. (Check the Resource Chapter for John Kremer's helpful book, *Directory of Short Run Book Printers.*)

Be sure to remind the printer to save your book negatives, since they will be used again if you decide to reprint. (Also make sure that you can *get the negatives back* should you wish to change printers for some reason.) While book printers will normally hold a customer's negatives for two or

154

three years, and wouldn't destroy them without checking with you first, regular print shops may automatically destroy job negatives after one year unless a customer specifically requests that they be retained.

You can save a lot of money by putting your own camera-ready copy together, and you've already read about how to do this in an earlier chapter. Typesetting is *not* necessary in a self-published book. It may seem more professional to you, but since you are likely to be selling your book by mail in the first place, no one is going to know whether it is typeset or typed unless you tell them, and they aren't going to care one way or the other so long as the book contains the information they want to receive. Rent an electric or electronic typewriter with changeable typefaces, or work with someone who has a computer and can "set type" with a desktop publishing system.

Naturally you will want to copyright your book, and this was discussed in an earlier chapter. Simply write the Copyright Office and request a copyright claim form for a book (Class TX). Place the proper copyright notice on your work before it is printed; then when it is finished, complete the form, enclose your check, and send two copies of the book to the Copyright Office. That's all there is to it. Later you will receive a copy of the form, stamped with the official seal of the Copyright Office.

How This Book was Produced. Since the book you're now reading is a self-published book, you may be curious to know the method I used to create it. I have a PC-compatible computer and use *WordPerfect 5.1* software, which has excellent graphic capabilities and is compatible with another software package I use called *Publisher's PowerPak* (manufactured by Atech and available wherever software is sold). It retails for less than a hundred dollars and offers a variety of inexpensive fonts that can be scaled to any size desired. This affordable and easy-to-learn "desktop-publisher's package" has given me all the power I need to create my newsletter, publish books, and design the brochures, catalogs and other printed materials needed in my business.

I didn't always have it so good. Prior to getting my computer in 1986, I did my newsletter and one book (*Crafts Marketing Success Secrets*) on my trusty IBM Selectric typewriter -- the same one I had used back in the 70s to create five years' issues of *Artisan Crafts* magazine. (Believe it or not, but when I finally traded in my old Selectric for an Adler electronic typewriter in 1987, I got more in trade than I'd paid for it originally. Best business investment I ever made.)

A little typewriter trick I used to give the illusion of typesetting was to create my print masters to a larger size, then have the printer reduce them photographically to 85% of their original size.

For three years after I got my computer, I used an inexpensive word processing program that I found revolutionary when compared to a typewriter, but which couldn't give me a two-column format or fancy fonts. Although the computer made it much easier to write and create my newsletter, I was still doing a lot of cutting and pasting and had to order typeset headlines for everything I printed. I wrote and published one book this way (*Help For Your Growing Homebased Business*). I wasn't happy with the typefaces available in my dot matrix printer, but it was the best I could do with what I had at the time, and no one has ever complained to me that the book wasn't typeset.

The point of my story is that we must all grow in our businesses as time and money allows, striving always to keep learning and improving the way we work. Like many, I resisted computer technology for several years, but once I began to use word processing and database software in my business, I kicked myself for having delayed this important purchase for so long. If you're serious about publishing your own work and selling it by mail, I urge you to buy a computer *now* -- or, if you already have a computer, take a closer look at all the new and inexpensive software and printers now available to desktop publishers.

Promoting and Selling Your Book

Here are some tips on how to let the world know you've published something worth reading:

1. Prepare a press release and send it, along with a review copy of your book, to every magazine that carries reviews on books similar to yours. The resource section of this book includes a fine list of publications to consider. Not everyone will review your book, but many will, especially the craft journals.

2. If your book is one that craft or hobby shops might like to carry, be sure to send a review copy to the journals serving such shops, and advertise it as well in magazines such as *Profitable Craft Merchandising*, which is read by the majority of craft retailers throughout the country. Remember that you will have to give craft distributors a heftier discount than is normally given to retail shops who buy directly from you.

3. The largest book wholesaler in the world, Baker and Taylor Company, might be interested in your book. They publish a monthly *Journal for Academic Libraries*, and each issue contains a bibliographic listing of recently published titles. Write to them for additional information.

You may have little interest in trying to sell to bookstores (they can be a pain in the neck for independent publishers because they expect to be invoiced, take 3-6 months to pay, and often return unsold books for credit); however, whenever you get publicity, independent bookstores and libraries are likely to place orders for your book through Baker and Taylor, so it can pay to make them aware of your self-published titles.

4. It would be wise to investigate the advantages of membership in COSMEP, the Committee of Small Magazine Editors and Publishers, since they publish a helpful newsletter. Through COSMEP you would also be able to obtain helpful books for publishers, plus a variety of mail lists: distribution outlets, libraries, book reviewers and others interested in reviewing new titles.

5. I'm sure you already know you have to constantly advertise and promotes. Read the publicity and advertising chapter again for ways to do this economically.

Magazine Publishing

I've been talking only about book publishing up till now, but I wonder if you're aware of the fact that individual craftspeople are behind many of the fine craft and needlework magazines being published today? I thought you might enjoy having a peek behind the scenes of one of these publishing companies.

Handwoven, a quarterly weaving magazine originally known as *Interweave*, is published by Linda Ligon. If you are thinking about starting a craft periodical of any kind, her story will be enlightening, to say the least.

"It's been over two years now since I started the magazine (laying groundwork, that is) and my feelings are overwhelmingly positive," Linda told me when I first interviewed her for this book. Her idea of doing the magazine grew out of her need to have a challenging job at home. She was also dissatisfied with the periodical literature available for weavers at the time. "I started it when I found myself at home with a new baby (my other kids were 6 and 8 at the time). Day was very ill for a long time after his birth, and there was no way I

could think of going back to my job teaching high school English. Straight housewifing is not for me, nor production weaving. And I don't have the art background to feel like I can go around weaving museum pieces or brilliant commissions."

Linda had her teacher's retirement fund money (about $1700) to start with. She used it to buy a couple of cameras, a used keyboard for photo typesetting, and to pay her first printer's bill. She scrounged mailing lists from guilds and from one friendly mail-order supplier. "The magazine has been in the black from the beginning," she says, "but then I haven't had to support the family with it. I've only just started to think about paying myself anything."

The Ligons live on a little acreage. In 1977 they had a big garden, chickens, ducks, goats and pigs. "My husband, an electrical engineer, goes around building solar collectors and other strange things in his spare time," Linda wrote then, "so our life has always been chaotic, and that fits right in with publishing a magazine in your dining room."

Except for some experience on her high school newspaper, Linda has no background in journalism, so how did she learn to be a publisher? "I got all the magazines off the newsstands that I thought were well done," she told me, "and studied them. Tried to figure out what it was about the writing, design, format, that made them appealing. And I found a sympathetic printer (his bid wasn't the lowest, but he didn't ask me who my boss was, either). And I asked lots of questions."

By the middle of its second year, the magazine had 1600 subscribers, an impressive figure for so young a periodical. "An additional 800 to 1000 magazines are dispersed in other ways," Linda told me. "While these are really modest figures, the growth has been steady enough that I'm optimistic about the magazine's achieving financial viability, not just hand-to-mouth existence."

Problems? Of course. As you might suspect, Linda didn't have enough time for her craft in the early days of the magazine. "If I'm ever to the point that I can afford full-time help," she then dreamed, "things might even out a little and I won't be three months behind on the mail and I can weave. However, much of the problem is of my own making. I'm a Brownie leader, a 4-H leader, parent-teacher council member, etc. Those things are important to me, too, so I make some deliberate choices about my time that I could change if I chose to. My family has been extremely supportive. The older kids have helped prepare mailings, my husband is always a sympathetic ear, and has given good advice on occasion. And they're all very nice to me during my quarterly frenzy."

In speaking of her business just two years after she'd begun, Linda emphasized confidence and a growing sense of self-esteem as the benefits of her experience. "I've grown and learned a lot. I'm more independent and assertive than I ever dreamed of being," she said. "I've learned a lot (not enough, though) about layout and design, about printing presses, selling ads, coping with the post office, bookkeeping, etc. The magazine also provides me with an excuse to go around meeting really neat people. I'm basically a pretty introverted sort, and it has really opened new worlds for me to have to go out and talk to people."

Shortly after I interviewed Linda, she sent a letter saying she was about to launch a second periodical called *Spin-Off*, an annual just for spinners. By then she had moved from the dining room to her own office in the basement and was only one month behind in her correspondence.

Later, when *Handwoven* celebrated its fifth birthday, Linda commented in one of her magazine editorials: *"We've grown from a staff of three to a staff of 13; from a card file of subscribers to a computer with 64 megabytes of customer records. I can't think of a way I would rather have spent the last five years of my life."*

As I was revising this book for reprinting in 1990, I called Linda to get an update on her business. What a success story we have here! From 1600 subscribers in 1977, *Handwoven* magazine has grown to a circulation of 36,000. *Spin-Off*, which began as an annual directory in 1977, is now a bimonthly with a circulation of 14,000. In 1979, Linda diversified her business by launching a book publishing division that includes 50 fiber-related titles with new ones in the works. Two years ago, she launched a third magazine, *The Herb Companion*, a quarterly now circulated to 50,000 readers. (These magazines are available on newsstands, but if you can't find them, see the Resource Chapter for subscription information.)

Why the diversification move from weaving to herbs, I wondered? "It was just something that interested me," says Linda, "and I wanted to grow -- not be so vertical." How does she manage such a large business that's no longer operated at home? "My original goal was to be at home as long as the children needed me," she says, "and I met that goal. Then it was time to move on."

Linda now has a staff of 24. Five years after she began, she moved the business from the basement of her Loveland, Colorado home to an old Victorian home in town. In time those quarters also became too crowded, so this year she relocated the business to a charming 1920s bank building in town that offers the necessary room for comfort and growth.

The Ligons still live on the same acreage, but now they have only a sheep and a bunch of turkeys, says Linda. Husband Thomas has recently created a fantastic computer model of the solar system called "Dance of the Planets," which is receiving wide attention from schools, observatories and amateur astronomers. Linda works 45-50 hours a week on the business, then spends enjoyable weekends at home where she now has time to weave and pursue other personal interests. The children? Two are in college, one of them in Czechoslovakia. Day is now 15. All have worked on the business from time to time, but none has expressed an interest in being involved in it. "They all have their own fish to fry," says Linda.

Have you noticed the similarities in Linda's story and that of Carol Bernier, the successful shop owner? Both these women simply set exciting new life goals for themselves, then proceeded to achieve them one by one -- in spite of the fact that they lacked time, money and experience in the beginning. Linda says she started her business just about the way she quit smoking. Just said, "I will do it" and never gave herself a chance to say, "Yeah, but..."

Linda believes that people, and dependent women in particular, need to be told about the possibilities that exist for them. "I regret that I was 32 years old before it occurred to me I could do anything besides be a teacher. But no one ever told me."

That's one purpose of this book: To alert you to new possibilities in your creative life and guide you along a new road of discovery. The success stories in this book prove that exciting things can be done by ordinary people. Or perhaps I should say ordinary people who have *extraordinary ambitions* and the kind of inner strength it takes to make a special dream come true.

Publishing Newsletters

If publishing interests you, but books and magazines are more than you can handle right now, perhaps you've considered the idea of publishing a newsletter? Thanks to computer technology which has made it so easy to become a home-based publisher, hundreds of creative people are giving newsletter publishing a try these days. But can this be as easy as it sounds, and is it a good way to make extra money at home? Yes...and No.

In his book, *Publishing Newsletters*, Howard Penn Hudson says: "Newsletter publishing is one of the fastest growing businesses in the United States. With more than 100,000 different newsletters in circulation, there's one for almost every interest..."

Many of the new periodicals I see are from creative entrepreneurs who have found a small niche for themselves as some kind of expert. Others are being launched by individuals who simply have a knack for writing, gathering, and dispensing information of one kind or another. Still others are being launched purely as a hobby enterprise, or as a marketing tool or advertising bulletin sent free to customers and clients on an irregular basis.

Many of the individuals who are offering subscription newsletters know little or nothing about the economics of publishing a periodical, or how hard it is to get and keep paid subscribers. Novices publishers tend to look at newsletter publishing in this way: First they pick a subscription rate (let's take $18 for example), figure out their printing and postage costs, and subtract them from gross income to get their "profit."

It sounds good in theory, but doesn't work in practice. Let's say it costs 40 cents to print an issue, x 6 issues = $2.40.) Add bulk mail postage of .167 cents per issue (and this will soon increase) x six issues = $1.00. Together, these costs total $3.40, or $14.60 profit per subscriber. But this is NOT what it will cost you to deliver six issues to a subscriber, and you're NOT going to make this kind of profit on each subscription.

In addition to the basic print and postage costs connected to a newsletter, the publisher must also consider art, typesetting and design costs, as well as the time it takes to write and produce each issue. There may be clip art to buy. Add to this the cost of maintaining the mailing list -- all those additions, deletions and corrections on a continuous basis. (There will always be newsletters coming back postage due with change-of-address information for subscribers who have moved without notifying you). Now add the cost of labels and addressing of each mailing, plus zip sorting for the post office.

Then there's reader mail to be answered, letters to send to get information and articles for each issue, followed by more correspondence or long-distance telephone calls. Add to this the cost of writing, designing and printing the necessary printed materials needed to solicit subscriptions and renewals: promotional flyers, subscription forms, renewal cards, direct mail brochures or catalogs, envelopes, office forms, invoices, and so on.

Last -- and most expensive -- you have the continuing cost of advertising, whether you use classified ads, publicity, or direct mail promotions. Before long, that $18 you're getting from each subscriber has dwindled to perhaps mere pennies of profit. The bloom is off the rose! There's more to this newsletter publishing business than meets the eye.

Back to advertising. Direct mail is the traditional way to get new subscriptions. But first you have to build a mail list through the placement of classified ads or publicity designed to bring you prospect names. (Rented lists are expensive and not as likely to yield subscriptions as names you generate yourself.) Be sure to reread the section in this book on direct mail and consider the percentage of response your mailers are likely to bring. Once you've made a few mailings, you'll have a better idea of the number of subscribers you're likely to get from every 1,000 prospects mailed.

By the time you add all the expenses involved in getting new subscribers, you may find that you're paying more for each one than you're charging for a year's subscription, and then you hang your hopes on renewals. Will most of your readers stay with you? No. Count yourself lucky if half of your first-year subscribers renew. More than likely, only 30% of them will renew, unless you bombard them with repeated renewal notices (which only adds to your cost). Believe me when I say that people are lethargic about renewing subscriptions, even to periodicals they claim to love. There are just too many places where dollars need to be spent these days, and one way to save is to cut back on subscriptions. (And with 100,000 newsletters in print, you can see you have a LOT of competition here.)

I don't want to discourage you from publishing a newsletter if that's what you really want to do, but I do want you to know that this is no way to get rich quick, and it can be quite stressful at times. Listen to the words of one woman who has been publishing a newsletter for several years:

"I keep promising myself one day I will have time for me. Time to sew, do my crafts, teach again, read a book, work in the garden, and a lot of other things. I feel as though I am on a merry-go-round that just never stops, and as it goes round and round, I see posters listing all the things that must be done, and I try to grab one off each time I go round. But as one poster comes down, another takes its place."

That's one of the best descriptions I've ever read of a publishing business. It runs your life because there is always one more deadline to meet, one more job to do, one more new problem to cope with. It's an exciting business, but it's not for everyone. I happen to love newsletter and book publishing and plan to continue for years. . . but there are times when I'd give *anything* if I didn't have to meet that next deadline.

- 14 -

All Things Legal and Financial

Most creative people hate the thought of "all things legal and financial," which is precisely why I put this chapter at the end of the book instead of the beginning. Now that you've seen how much fun a business can be, I think you're ready for the nitty-gritty "legal stuff" that goes hand in hand with even the smallest business based at home.

After reading this chapter, you may find that you've unknowingly broken some law. But don't panic; it may not be as bad as you think. It is often possible to get back on the straight and narrow merely by filling out a required form or paying a small fee of some kind. What's important here is that you take steps to comply with the laws that pertain to your particular business because the fear of being caught when you're breaking a law is often much worse than doing whatever needs to be done to set the matter right.

I must emphasize at this point that I am neither an attorney nor an accountant; which is to say that the advice in this chapter is not meant to be a substitute for such professional advice. I'm merely sharing with you the benefit of my own business experience and research, the latter of which includes the recollection of many "sad tales of woe" passed on to me by my readers. My goal, then, is to acquaint you with the various laws, rules and regulations applicable to homebased businesses in general, and art/craft businesses in particular *as I know them.*

At the least this information will help you avoid trouble and enable you to ask the right questions should you need to consult with a professional adviser sometime in the future. Before doing this, however, I suggest you "do your homework" by reading the special business books described in

159

the Resource Chapter. In these books you'll find answers to many questions you might normally ask an attorney or accountant -- at much less cost, I might add.

In all my years of business, I've never needed an attorney, and I believe it is because I've always made it a point to read the kind of books and periodicals that provide answers to small business and legal problems. I'm also a member of selected organizations which give me access to what is commonly known as "inside information."

As your small business grows, you would be wise to put special information resources high on the list of things you can't afford to be without. Your ultimate financial success may well depend on them.

Back to lawyers. When do you really need one? If you're going to start a simple sole proprietorship (see next section), you don't need an attorney to handle the details. And you don't need legal assistance to file a copyright claim, get a sales tax number, or register your business name with the county or state.

I believe, however, that you *do* need an attorney if you plan to enter into any kind of partnership arrangement, and that includes taking a business partner, signing a book publisher's contract or other royalty arrangement, or entering into a franchise or licensing agreement. Although you can legally incorporate a business without a lawyer, I wouldn't recommend it simply because there are so many details involved.

When looking for a lawyer, ask friends for a reference, just as you would do when shopping for a new doctor. You might also inquire about a lawyer at your bank since it will probably know most of the attorneys with private practices in your area. Note that there are different kinds of lawyers, just as there are doctors who specialize in different fields. If you have a tax problem, you'll need an attorney who specializes in tax laws (or a CPA who is familiar with your type of business).

If your legal problem happens to deal with labor laws, then seek an attorney who specializes in this field. If you want to trademark or patent something, then you should work with an attorney whose specialty is patents and trademarks.

While most attorneys can advise you on the fine print of any contract, if that contract happens to be with a book publisher, take a tip from this author and find an attorney who normally works with such contracts. In this case, it's not so much what's *in* a contract as what *isn't.* (In particular, pay special attention to the return of rights when the work goes out of print, and include a clause that give you the right to purchase books for your own use prior to a publisher's remaindering the

entire inventory to a clearing house for ten cents on the dollar.)

If you need an attorney, but cannot afford one, you may be eligible to receive free legal service from the Volunteer Lawyers for the Arts (VLA), a nonprofit organization with chapters all over the country. In addition to providing legal aid for performing and visual artists and craftspeople, individually or in groups, the VLA also provides a range of educational services, including the issuance of publications concerning taxes, accounting and insurance. (See Resource Chapter for more information.)

The Legal Form of Your Business

One of the first things you need to think about when you start your own business is the legal structure it will assume:

- Individual Proprietorship
- Partnership
- Corporation

Most craftspeople find the sole proprietorship most suitable for their needs but craft partnerships and corporations are also formed quite often. As mentioned earlier, you don't need a lawyer to start a sole proprietorship, but it would be folly to enter into a partnership of any kind without legal guidance.

Which legal form is best for you? A brief look at the main advantages and disadvantages of each type of legal business structure will alert you to factors that should be considered.

Individual Proprietorship.

Advantages: Simplest to form; least complicated to dissolve. You're your own boss here and the business ends automatically when you stop running it. No government approval required to start. Business profits (or losses) taxed as personal income.

Disadvantages: Proprietor is fully liable for all business debts and actions. In event of a lawsuit, one's personal assets are not protected. Also, many one-person businesses fail because there's too much work for one person to do, and not enough money to hire help.

General Partnership. (Two or More People.)

Advantages: Easy to start; no federal requirements involved. Business profits (or losses) taxed as personal income. Written partnership agreement advised, but not necessary. Business ends with withdrawal of any one of the partners. Each partner shares the work load, contributing work, time, or money in amounts agreed to by all. With more people involved in the business, its chances for success are greater than with a single proprietorship.

Disadvantages: The debts incurred by one partner must be assumed by all other partners. If business fails, creditors can attach each partner's personal income and assets, as in an individual proprietorship. Partnerships between or among friends often end the friendship when disagreements over business policies occur.

Limited Partnership. (Two or More People)

Advantages: Liability of one or more partners is limited to the extent of money invested in the business. Profits (or losses) taxed as personal income.

Disadvantages: More complicated to establish; legal contract must be filed with state. Partnership must adhere to laws of the state in which it is organized. Limited partners not permitted to advise in administration of the business -- one or more general partners must be designated to run it. (Note: General partners often take on limited partners when they need additional cash for their business.)

Corporation.

Advantages: Owner-shareholders are not individually liable for the debts of a corporation and, in the event of a lawsuit, personal assets have greater protection. Because a corporation is a legal entity unto itself, it does not die with the retirement or death of its officers, and investments may be transferred from one party to another without affecting operation of the company.

Disadvantages. Complex to establish; certification of incorporation must be filed with state in which business is located. Much paperwork involved in running a corporation, requiring legal and accounting services.

The main disadvantage of incorporation to the small business is the fact that profits are taxed twice: first as corporate income and again when they are distributed to the owner-shareholders as dividends. For this reason, many small businesses elect to incorporate as Subchapter S Corporations, which allows profits to be taxed at owners' regular individual rates. This form of incorporation is for businesses with 35 or fewer stockholders.

NOTE: Although small businesses often incorporate for the limited liability benefits of this legal form of business, it might be less expensive and just as safe to simply buy liability insurance. Too, a corporation does not provide "blanket protection" against lawsuits. Says Bernard Kamoroff, C.P.A. and author of *Small-Time Operator*, "A corporation will not shield you from personal liability that you normally should be responsible for, such as not having car insurance or acting with gross negligence. If you plan to incorporate solely or primarily with the intention of limiting your legal liability, I suggest you find out first...exactly how limited the liability really is for your particular venture. Hire a knowledgeable lawyer to give you a written opinion."

I urge you to add the above-mentioned book to your small business bookshelf. The author, a home-business owner himself, is a warm and witty writer who makes usually boring information absolutely fascinating. The book's subtitle says it all: *How to Start Your Own Small Business, Keep Your Books, Pay Your Taxes, And Stay Out of Trouble!*

Local and State Licensing and Regulations

Since most small businesses are regulated at the local level, you should check with your city and county to see if you need any kind of permit or occupational license to do business. A *license* is a certificate granted by a government agency that gives one permission to engage in a business, occupation, or activity otherwise unlawful. Only certain businesses need a license to operate. A *permit* is similar to a license, except it is granted by local authorities. Some communities require a permit for almost everything; others require it only for businesses involving food, door-to-door selling, and home shops. For more information, telephone your City or County Clerk.

Registering a fictitious, or assumed, business or trade name. When you operate a business under any name other than your own, you are using a "trade name," and it must be registered since trade names cannot be held legally responsible for anything. Thus, if your name happens to be Mary Smith, and you call your business "Knotty But Nice," you would be using an assumed name. On legal documents, and at your bank, it would read, "Mary Smith, d/b/a Knotty But Nice," the "d/b/a/" meaning "doing business as."

The registration procedure may vary from state to state, but basically you simply complete special forms given to you by the County Clerk and pay a small registration fee (a few dollars). There is one small hitch, however. In many states, you must also place a legal ad in a general-circulation newspaper in the county and run it three times. (You can get the correct wording of this ad from either the County Clerk or your newspaper office. It is a simple statement that you are operating under an assumed name.) After the ad has run, the newspaper will give you a "Publication Certificate" which you, in turn, will mail to the County Clerk who will file it with your registration form. This makes your business completely legitimate.

Note: If you don't want your neighbors to know you're running a business at home (perhaps because you're in violation of local zoning laws), the ad you run in the paper does not have to be placed in your home town paper. It can be in any newspaper in *your county*.

In my state, and probably others as well, it is a Class C Misdemeanor (and punishable accordingly) to operate a business that has not been registered with the County Clerk. In case you've been operating illegally and are shaking in your boots right now, let me ease your mind by telling you that no one goes around checking to see if all small businesses have been registered, and a check would not normally be made unless a neighbor has reported you, or you've gotten some local publicity that suddenly brings your unregistered business to the attention of local officials.

If you have not registered your business to date, *do so now*. Since the form you will complete does not ask when you started your business, the County Clerk will assume you've just started it, and there should be no problem.

Some people who have operated their businesses for years with no one being the wiser about their lack of registration have asked me why they should bother to register after the fact. If being lawful doesn't matter to you, maybe you will appreciate the fact that *unless you protect your good business name by registration, it can be taken by another*. And, if another person takes your name and registers it legally as their own, they can order you to cease doing business under that name, no matter how many years you've been operating.

Once you've protected your name by local registration, register it with your state as well, to prevent its use by any corporate entity. Contact your Secretary of State for the proper form.

Zoning Laws. Millions of people now operate businesses in their home, and it's anybody's guess as to how many of these people are violating zoning laws. What you don't know about zoning could put you out of business. On the other hand, what zoning officials don't know about you might remain a harmless secret.

Generally, artists, craftspeople, writers, designers and mail order businesses have few worries about zoning law because such businesses are usually operated quietly, causing no disturbance in the neighborhood. But if you are thinking about opening a studio or shop in your home that will bring customers to your door on a daily basis, check local zoning laws first.

Also read your lease or title papers for information about building restrictions. In many cases, a home studio or shop would be in direct violation of the law, and might even invalidate your present tenant's or homeowner's insurance policy. The use of hazardous substances or chemicals may also be forbidden in one's home or neighborhood and, again, could invalidate one's insurance policy in the event of an accident involving their use. (See "Insurance" elsewhere in this chapter.)

Most residential areas do not allow business signs, of course, and if this is important to the success of your business, it will be necessary to rent a shop or building elsewhere. In addition, large or unusual equipment, such as a gas-fired kiln for example, might require a special permit and, if it is noisy and disturbing to neighbors, you may not be allowed to operate it in your home or garage. And neighbors will surely complain if you are using anything that causes a strong order.

Here's a good example of how small businesses can run into zoning and legal problems when least expected. Betty Christy of Tree Toys explains: "At one point in the past, we were given short notice to get out of our warehouse and had to scurry about looking for a new building. Within 36 hours we had found another warehouse, but we talked to our lawyer first, and our insurance man second. Both of them said, 'Check with the Village because there's a zoning ordinance.' We did, and found that we had to have a fire inspection by someone in the fire department. We had to get three people together at the same time to make the inspection so we could get a temporary permit and move. If the fire department had found us after we moved in, and we hadn't notified them, we would have been in for a fine and trouble."

Most of this book's readers will probably end up doing business out of their own home, so let me conclude this discussion with an emphasis on what's happening nationwide where zoning and homebased businesses are concerned.

Zoning officials across the country are aware of the national work-at-home movement and its incompatibility with zoning laws that were written in horse-and-buggy days. In many places where homebased businesses are totally forbidden, such as Chicago, for example, thousands of people are starting businesses anyway, and zoning officials are simply looking the other way because this is easier to do than change the law. If local laws currently prohibit a homebased business, you have only two choices: operate underground, or fight to get the law changed.

If you choose to operate underground as so many others already do, make sure you don't annoy your neighbors because it will take only one call from them to put you out of business. And don't draw attention to your business with media ads or publicity in your local paper. Zoning officials probabaly will never check on you unless you give them a reason to do so.

Resale tax number and collection of sales tax. With few exceptions, all states requires sales taxes of one kind or another, and in most states there are county and city taxes as well. *If you make anything for sale, of if you buy goods for resale, you are required to register your business with the Department of Revenue in your state.* This is a simple and painless process whereby you will fill out a form in order to receive a special document from the state. It will bear a tax exemption number that is sometimes called a "Retailer's Occupation Tax Registration Number" or, more generally, a "resale tax number." This is a valuable number, indeed, since it will enable you to buy materials for resale without paying sales tax.

This doesn't mean you can run down to the corner hardware store, buy two dollar's worth of something at retail and avoid the tax, but it does mean you will not have to pay sales tax when you purchase supplies at wholesale prices, or buy other goods for resale. Once you have a resale tax number, you will also have to start collecting sales tax on everything you sell directly to consumers, and file the appropriate reports with the state. (It is illegal to collect sales tax and retain it as income.)

A great many craftspeople ignore the sales tax law and sell their wares at fairs without collecting a cent of tax. Some of them get caught, too. At a large craft festival, I once saw officials shut down several craft booths for this reason. But failure to collect sales tax and file returns could result in more than just having your booth closed. According to one authority at the Illinois Department of Revenue, lawbreakers in that state are subject to a penalty of 20 percent over and above any normal tax obligation, and could receive for each offense (meaning each return not filed) from one to six months in prison and a fine of as much as $5,000. Other states may have similar penalties for sellers who ignore sales tax laws, so if you're going to sell at craft shows or by mail, you must apply for a resale tax number.

Many hobby sellers believe that if they sell "just for the fun of it," they're not considered to be in business and thus do not need to be concerned with the collection of sales tax. This is not true. It doesn't matter to the state's Department of Revenue whether you are "in business" in the eyes of the Internal Revenue Service or not; all it is concerned with is *whether you are selling directly to consumers on the retail level.* "Everyone who sells anything to consumers must collect sales tax," says an official in my state's Department of Revenue. "If you hold yourself out as a seller of merchandise, then you're subject to tax, even if you sell only a couple of times a year."

This same official also said that people who do art or craft work only on commission need not be concerned with a resale tax number since they are considered to be performing a service, rather than making a retail sale. This may be true in Illinois, but I believe some states do tax certain services, so you should clarify this point with your own state officials.

If you sell crafts only in local consignment shops, you do not need a resale tax number. In this case, it is the shop -- not the craftsperson -- that is responsible for collecting the sales tax and forwarding it to the state.

Craftspeople who sell only at wholesale prices fall into yet another group. Although they do not need to collect sales tax on their wholesale sales to shops, stores, etc., they *do* need a tax exemption certificate from the state in order to buy their raw materials at wholesale without paying sales tax. And, further, they must always be sure to obtain, for their tax files, the resale tax number of any retail shop or store with which they do business. Just as craftspeople must furnish their resale tax numbers to suppliers when they are buying supplies for resale, so must wholesale buyers furnish craftspeople with their tax-exempt number when they purchase finished crafts for resale.

In summary, if you are working at your art or craft as a business and selling to consumers on a retail level -- at a fair, holiday boutique, home shop or by mail -- you must collect sales tax and file regular reports with the state. "Hobbyists" are not exempt from this law, regardless of how few sales they make.

Better not take chances here. It's not that difficult to collect the tax and file the reports. If your income is low, you may find you only have to file quarterly or annually, instead of monthly as larger businesses do. For additional information, call your state's Sales Tax Bureau, Department of Taxation and Finance.

One more note on this topic: Perhaps you've heard that several states have now passed special use tax laws designed to make mail order sellers collect sales tax on purchases made by customers outside their own state. For years, out-of-state mail order sales were exempt from sales tax. Now, several states are trying to collect tax from businesses that distribute catalogs and other advertising literature in their states, claiming this gives businesses a "physical presence" in their state.

So far, these laws are being aimed at major mail order companies, many of whom are presently engaged in lawsuits with one or more states. Many believe these state laws to be unconstitutional, and only time will tell what effect all of this will have on small businesses that sell by mail.

When you contact your state for information on how to collect sales tax, you may be told that you must collect taxes on sales of goods to other states. Many small businesses who have been asked to "voluntarily register" for the collection of such taxes have elected not to do this in the belief that their state would not be interested in going after a company as small as theirs. The recordkeeping and paperwork involved with the collection and payment of taxes to several states (each with a different tax rate) boggles the mind.

This is clearly a "legal gray area" and what you do about it is entirely up to you. I've been getting my inside information on this topic from a trade newspaper called *DM News*. This publication serves the direct mail/mail order industry and keeps mailers informed on what the various states and larger companies are doing about this problem. From reading dozens of articles in this paper, I've concluded that most states are currently (1) interested only in challenging companies with gross revenues of half a million dollars or more a year; and (2) much too busy fighting with the big companies to have time and money to mess with the "mom-and-pop" craft businesses across the country.

Income Taxes and Recordkeeping

Some craftspeople probably sell their work at fairs and do not report cash earnings from sales on their annual income tax reports. I am reminded of one woman who told me she was "secretly selling" at one craft fair each year, and not reporting her income because she just didn't want to take that step from being a hobbyist to being "in business." But she became so worried about what she was doing that she said she was waking up in the middle of the night imagining that IRS agents would soon be knocking at her door. Her fear eventually forced her to "go legal," and I know she is much happier as a result.

I'm not here to preach honesty to anyone, but I should remind readers that intentional tax evasion or falsification of tax returns can lead to severe penalties. If you are going to break the law, then you must also *be prepared to pay the penalty*. I should also point out that it is sometimes more advantageous to declare one's craft earnings than to try to hide them. There are many legitimate deductions available to the person in business, and it would be wise to explore this area thoroughly with a competent accountant.

For example, in addition to standard business deductions for materials, labor, supplies, postage, shipping, advertising, office supplies, etc., you can deduct the amount spent on insurance related to your business, the expenses incurred when using your automobile for business purposes, and the cost of craft memberships, fees, subscriptions, etc. Office equipment, a computer system, special machinery or tools can be depreciated over a period of years, or written off entirely (up to $10,000 in one year, under present tax law) greatly reducing the self-employment and income taxes that may be due in a particular year.

If you use a room in your home exclusively for business, you can deduct expenses for it accordingly, including a certain percentage of your rent or mortgage, utilities, and general upkeep of your home. (I can't go into the specifics of tax-deductible business expenses here, but my *Homemade Money* book includes detailed information on this topic, and you'll also find such information in *Small Time Operator*.)

The latter book also includes detailed information on the topic of how craftspeople must handle year-end inventory of goods produced for resale, plus calculation of "cost-of-goods" figures, and the difficult and tedious set of laws called "uniform capitalization rules," which are far too complex to be addressed in this book. "Basically, says author Bernard Kamoroff, craftspeople "...may not write off their production expenses until they've sold the goods they produced." He adds, "I suggest you find a sympathetic accountant who will help...".

Women have occasionally told me their husbands didn't want them to work because their extra income would put them in a higher tax bracket, but as attorney Marion Schenk says, "With good accounting you can make quite a bit of money before you have to pay tax. And remember that the tax will only apply to the net profit, not the amount the business grosses in any given year."

One might remind a husband that in the early years of a business, expenses will often exceed income -- at least on paper -- thus resulting in a

164

SCHEDULE C
(Form 1040)

Department of the Treasury
Internal Revenue Service (R)

Profit or Loss From Business
(Sole Proprietorship)

▶ Partnerships, joint ventures, etc., must file Form 1065.

▶ Attach to Form 1040 or Form 1041.   ▶ See Instructions for Schedule C (Form 1040).

OMB No. 1545-0074

1992

Attachment
Sequence No. **09**

Name of proprietor | Social security number (SSN)

A Principal business or profession, including product or service (see page C-1) | **B** Enter principal business code (from page 2) ▶

C Business name | **D** Employer ID number (Not SSN)

E Business address (including suite or room no.) ▶ ....
City, town or post office, state, and ZIP code

F Accounting method: (1) ☐ Cash (2) ☐ Accrual (3) ☐ Other (specify) ▶ ....

G Method(s) used to value closing inventory: (1) ☐ Cost (2) ☐ Lower of cost or market (3) ☐ Other (attach explanation) (4) ☐ Does not apply (if checked, skip line H) | Yes | No

H Was there any change in determining quantities, costs, or valuations between opening and closing inventory? If "Yes," attach explanation

I Did you "materially participate" in the operation of this business during 1992? If "No," see page C-2 for limitations on losses .   .

J Was this business in operation at the end of 1992? . . . .

K How many months was this business in operation during 1992? . . . . ▶

L If this is the first Schedule C filed for this business, check here . . . . ▶ ☐

Part I Income

1	Gross receipts or sales. **Caution:** *If this income was reported to you on Form W-2 and the "Statutory employee" box on that form was checked, see page C-2 and check here* . . . . ▶ ☐	**1**
2	Returns and allowances	**2**
3	Subtract line 2 from line 1	**3**
4	Cost of goods sold (from line 40 on page 2)	**4**
5	**Gross profit.** Subtract line 4 from line 3	**5**
6	Other income, including Federal and state gasoline or fuel tax credit or refund (see page C-2)	**6**
7	**Gross Income.** Add lines 5 and 6 . . . . ▶	**7**

Part II Expenses (Caution: *Do not enter expenses for business use of your home on lines 8–27. Instead, see line 30.)*

8	Advertising	**8**	**21** Repairs and maintenance . .	**21**	
9	Bad debts from sales or services (see page C-3)	**9**	**22** Supplies (not included in Part III) .	**22**	
10	Car and truck expenses (see page C-3—also attach Form 4562) . . .	**10**	**23** Taxes and licenses . . .	**23**	
			24 Travel, meals, and entertainment:		
11	Commissions and fees. . .	**11**	**a** Travel	**24a**	
12	Depletion.	**12**	**b** Meals and entertainment .		
13	Depreciation and section 179 expense deduction (not included in Part III) (see page C-3) . .	**13**	**c** Enter 20% of line 24b subject to limitations (see page C-4) .		
14	Employee benefit programs (other than on line 19) .	**14**	**d** Subtract line 24c from line 24b .	**24d**	
15	Insurance (other than health) .	**15**	**25** Utilities	**25**	
16	Interest:		**26** Wages (less jobs credit) . .	**26**	
a	Mortgage (paid to banks, etc.) .	**16a**	**27a** Other expenses (list type and amount):		
b	Other	**16b**	....		
17	Legal and professional services .	**17**	....		
18	Office expense . . .	**18**	....		
19	Pension and profit-sharing plans .	**19**	....		
20	Rent or lease (see page C-4):		....		
a	Vehicles, machinery, and equipment	**20a**			
b	Other business property . .	**20b**	**27b** Total other expenses . . .	**27b**	

28	**Total expenses** before expenses for business use of home. Add lines 8 through 27b in columns ▶	**28**
29	Tentative profit (loss). Subtract line 28 from line 7	**29**
30	Expenses for business use of your home. Attach **Form 8829**	**30**
31	**Net profit or (loss).** Subtract line 30 from line 29. If a profit, enter here and on Form 1040, line 12. Also, enter the net profit on Schedule SE, line 2 (statutory employees, see page C-5). If a loss, you MUST go on to line 32 (fiduciaries, see page C-5)	**31**
32	If you have a loss, you MUST check the box that describes your investment in this activity (see page C-5) If you checked 32a, enter the loss on Form 1040, line 12, and Schedule SE, line 2 (statutory employees, see page C-5). If you checked 32b, you MUST attach **Form 6198.**	**32a** ☐ All investment is at risk. **32b** ☐ Some investment is not at risk.

For Paperwork Reduction Act Notice, see Form 1040 Instructions.   Cat. No. 11334P   Schedule C (Form 1040) 1992

165

lovely deduction that can decrease one's overall tax liability.

In talking about taxes with the average craftsperson, the question often arises as to whether one is "in business" or working and selling just as a hobby. Either way, how should income and expenses be handled? The following comment found in the *Los Angeles Times* provides one answer to that question: "The Internal Revenue Service has a clear, totally illogical rule about hobbies: If they cost you money, you can't deduct that; but if they make you money, you must pay income tax on that. Heads they win, tails you lose."

This was confirmed by an official in the IRS office in Chicago, who told me that:

1. The IRS defines a hobby as an activity engaged in primarily for pleasure, not for profit.
2. Losses sustained in the pursuit of a hobby are not deductible.
3. If hobby income is under $400, it should be entered on the 1040 form.
4. If income from any hobby activity is over $400, a "Schedule C" form must be filed, and one can then deduct related expenses so long as they do not exceed the amount earned from the activity. (See illustration, next page.)
5. Making a profit from a hobby does not automatically place one "in business," but the activity will be presumed to have been engaged in for profit if it results in a profit in three out of five consecutive years.

Once you are engaged in an activity for profit, you are considered to be "in business" in the eyes of the Internal Revenue Service and, as such, are entitled to deduct expenses in excess of income. If you claim to be in business, but fail to make a profit in at least three years out of five, the IRS may question your tax report, and you would then have to *prove* that you are really trying to make a profit. If you have maintained complete records for your business, that will be a strong point in your favor, as will be the amount of advertising and promotion you have done on your business, and your overall expertise and business image.

In the end, the question of whether your art or craft-related activity will qualify as a business for tax purposes is a complex one, but no one factor, such as failure to achieve a profit in at least three out of five years, can be used by the IRS to disallow your deductions, which may help offset income from other sources and, in effect, help to underwrite your art or craft.

Tax laws are constantly changing, and to put them into a book like this would be futile. This is an area you will have to investigate on your own. One reason I suggest you add *Small-Time Operator* to your bookshelf is that this book is updated annually to include the latest tax and legal information applicable to small-business owners and, in addition, the author offers all readers inexpensive annual update sheets so the book doesn't have to be purchased anew each year.

You can, of course, obtain a package of free information from the IRS. In particular, request:

- *Tax Guide for Small Business,* #334
- *Business Use of Your Home,* #587

Accountants, Bookkeepers, and Tax Preparers. Many business novices hire accountants when they actually need bookkeepers, and tax preparers when they actually need accountants.

Unless you are totally inept with figures, I suggest that you learn how to do your own bookkeeping because these records will tell you far more about the health and profitability of your business than anything else. While a tax-preparer can fill out tax forms and calculate the amount of tax that's due, history has shown that the average tax-preparer lacks an understanding of the nature of home-based businesses and the deductible expenses related to their operation.

Accountants, on the other hand, have a better understanding of tax laws in general, can help you understand your total financial picture, and aid you in making business management decisions, such as whether you should purchase equipment this year or next, hire employees or independent contractors, or incorporate your business.

Note, however, that not all accountants are certified. A certified public accountant, or "C.P.A." is licensed by the state after having passed an exam on completion of four years of college and one or two years on-the-job-training. That's why C.P.A.s charge more for their services than accountants. More important than the C.P.A. title, however, is whether the accountant you choose has other home-business clients or not, and is totally familiar with all the allowable deductions related to such businesses.

Many small businesses, myself included, use an accountant only once a year when tax time rolls around. Since accountants charge by the hour, it's important for you to go to meetings well prepared. Dumping a sackful of receipts on someone's desk at year's end could prove to be very expensive for you. Ideally you will keep your own books and, at year's end, calculate totals of all income and expenses. Then give this information and substantiating paperwork to the accountant who will put all the figures in the right places on the right forms.

TIP: Make sure you always check the figures on your tax return. Many times I have found errors that could be corrected before the IRS computer ejected our return, thus increasing our chances of being audited. Being audited is, to say the least, an inconvenience, even when you have prepared your return honestly. But if you have "fudged" a bit here and there, you're going to find it hard to explain and may be forced to pay penalties or a severe fine. Therefore, always be able to substantiate any deductions you take. Which brings me back to the importance of a good recordkeeping system.

One nice thing about the IRS is that it does not require any special kind of bookkeeping system. Their primary concern is that you devise a system that clearly and accurately shows true income and expenses. For the sole proprietor, a simple system consisting of a checkbook, a cash receipts journal, a cash disbursements ledger, and a petty cash fund is quite adequate.

You might take a look at the *Dome Simplified Monthly* recordkeeping system, which is sold in stationery store. And the *Small-Time Operator* includes a complete set of ledger sheets you can use, even without bookkeeping experience. Here are some other tips:

- Get a receipt for everything, even the fifty cents you spend on paper clips.

- Retain all receipts in orderly fashion, posting expenses and income regularly to avoid year-end pile-up and panic.

- Generally speaking, accounting records should be kept for at least six years after returns are filed. This period will cover the federal income tax statute of limitations and the statutes of various state and local taxing authorities. (Some business records, such as journals, ledgers, copyrights, licenses, etc., should be kept indefinitely.)

Social Security Taxes

When you make a net profit of $400 or more, you must file a Self-Employment Form along with your regular income tax form, and pay into your personal Social Security account. This could be quite beneficial for some homemakers with previous work experience. A woman's re-entry into the business world as a self-employed worker, and her additional contributions to her Social Security account, could result in increased benefits upon retirement. The topic of Social Security is quite complex, and I do not wish to delve into it here. But because so many senior citizens are starting homebased businesses these days to supplement Social Security income, it should be mentioned that there is a limit on the amount one can earn before losing Social Security benefits. The good news is that this dollar limit increases each year, and once past the age of 70, an individual can earn any amount of income and still receive full benefits.

For more information, contact your nearest Social Security office, or call the Social Security Hotline at no charge by dialing 1-800-772-1213. This will enable you to hear automated messages, order information booklets, or speak directly to someone who can answer specific questions.

Individual Retirement Programs

Self-employed people who have not organized their business as a corporation may wish to establish a retirement program called an *Individual Retirement Account (IRA)*. You can invest up to 15 percent of your income (or a maximum of $2000 each year). Currently, this amount may be taken as a deduction against taxes, provided the individual participates in no other retirement program.

When taxable earnings from a business become substantial, greater tax savings are possible for those who establish a *Keogh Plan*. Here, one can shelter from taxes an amount equal to 20 percent of one's profits, up to a maximum of $30,000.

Each of the above plans has its own advantages and drawbacks, so discuss them thoroughly with your banker or accountant before deciding on one or the other.

Important Regulations Affecting Artists and Craftspeople

"Increased concern about consumer protection, employee safety, and environmental protection has resulted in increased regulatory activity by local, state, and federal government," says Gerald Ely, craft specialist with the Agricultural Cooperative Service in Washington, D. C. "Many laws exist which have significance for craftspeople. However, in many cases, craftspeople are either unaware of these laws or poorly informed of the provisions of the laws."

Following is a brief discussion of several laws and regulations you may not know about and who to contact for additional information:

● **The Consumer Product Safety Act of 1972.** This law protects the public against unreasonable risks of injury associated with consumer products. The Act created The Consumer Products Safety Commission (CPSC), which has powers to establish and enforce mandatory safety standards for consumer products sold in the United States.

One of the Commission's most active regulatory programs has been in the area of toys and consumer goods designed for children. Anyone who makes toys should strive to meet certain guidelines in order to meet safety standards. Make sure all toys are:

- Too large to be swallowed
- Not apt to break easily or leave jagged edges
- Free of sharp edges or points
- Not put together with easily exposed pins, wires or nails
- Nontoxic, nonflammable, and nonpoisonous

Under the Consumer Product Safety Act there is a ban of paint and other surface coatings, such as varnish, lacquer and shellac, which contain more than 0.06% lead by weight. A spokesperson for the CPSC told me, "We have no objection to the use of paint or other surface coatings on children's products as long as they comply with the lead-in-paint-ban." Paints sold for household use in the United States must comply with this ban. Only paints intended for specialized uses are exempt, and these paints must bear a label which warns that the paint contains lead, may be harmful if eaten or chewed, and should not be applied to toys, children's articles or furniture.

NOTE: *Do not use artist's paints on children's toys.* These paints are exempt from the lead-in-paint ban, yet are not required to bear a warning label regarding lead.

● **The Federal Hazardous Substances Act.** This relates primarily to, and prohibits the use of, any substance or mixture that is toxic, corrosive, combustible, an irritant, a strong sensitizer, or any substance that may cause personal injury or illness during handling or use, including "reasonably foreseeable ingestion by children."

168

● **The Flammable Fabrics Act.** This act prohibits the introduction or movement in interstate commerce of articles of wearing apparel and fabrics that are so highly flammable as to be dangerous when worn by individuals, and for other purposes. If you are using fabric in your craft work, you will take comfort in knowing that most fabrics comply with the above Act, but to be doubly sure that the fabric you are using to make children's clothes or toys is save, ask your supplier for a *guaranty of compliance with the Flammability Act.* Most fabric manufacturers test their fabrics for compliance and issue a guaranty of compliance that is generally passed along the chain of distribution by using an invoice statement that reads: *"Continuing guaranty under the Flammable Fabric Act filed with the Consumer Product Safety Commission."*

More information about the above three acts is available from The Consumer Products Safety Commission, listed in the Resource Chapter.

● **The Textile Fiber Products Identification Act.** Craftspeople involved with textiles and wearing apparel should be familiar with the labeling requirements of this act. All items made of any textile or fiber (garments, quilts, stuffed toys, rugs, etc.) must have a securely affixed label showing (1) the name of the manufacturer or other person marketing the textile fiber product; (2) the generic names and percentages of all fibers in the product in amounts of 5 percent or more, listed in order of predominance by weight. Examples: "100 percent combed cotton"; "92 percent cotton, 8 percent other fibers." See samples below.

If a product contains wool, it will require additional identification under a separate law known as **The Wool Products Labeling Act of 1939.** In addition, FTC rules require that the labels of all wool or textile products clearly indicate when imported ingredients are used, even if the product is made in the United States. Thus, the label for a shawl woven in the U. S. from imported fibers would read, "Made in the USA from imported products" or some variation of such a legend. Items which originate entirely in the U.S. need only state "Made in the USA" or "Crafted in USA" or some similarly clear terminology. These regulations are also applicable to the terms used to describe such products in mail order catalogs sent to consumers.

● **Care Labeling Laws.** These laws are part of the Textile Fiber Products Identification Act. Any textile, suede, or leather product in the form of a finished article of wearing apparel, or any textile product in the form of a finished household furnishing, must have a label permanently affixed or attached thereto by the manufacturer of the finished item that clearly discloses instructions for the care and maintenance of such item. This includes all wearing apparel, household furnishings, piece goods, yarn, and rugs.

A label should indicate if any item is to be dry cleaned or washed; if it is to be washed, indicate whether in hot or cold water. Indicate whether bleach may or may not be used, and specify at what heat the item may be ironed. (See sample labels below.)

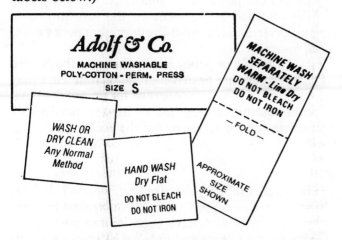

More information on labeling laws is available from the Federal Trade Commission. The various labels required by law can be created by the manufacturer or ordered from suppliers listed in the Resource Chapter.

● **Bedding and Upholstered Furniture Law.** Are you ready for this one? This is an aggravating state law that requires the purchase of a license in order to sell items with a concealed filling. It also requires the attachment of printed tags that bear a manufacturer's registry number. "Concealed filling" items include not just bedding and upholstery, but handmade pillows and quilts; in some states, dolls, teddy bears and stuffed soft sculpture items may also be required to have a tag.

This law has long been a thorn in the side of craftsellers because it makes no distinction between the large manufacturing company and the individual crafts producer who may sell only a few items in selected shops. It is enforced on an arbitrary basis, but it if were to be enforced in every state it would mean that craftspeople would have to purchase a license for each state in which their work is sold. The cost of such licenses vary from state to state --

from $15 to $100, my readers tell me --and must be renewed annually.

In Texas, a reader reports her license cost $15, and she was required to purchase 500 one-cent bedding stamps which then had to be placed on the label of each piece of merchandise offered for sale. "The state directed me to a source for the labels, which have a blank space where you can rubber-stamp contents," she said, adding: "Enforcement is usually through a check of retail stores."

A reader in New York approached this problem by first contacting the Division of Bedding in her state's Department of Health. (Readers in other states might have to call or write State Tagging Law Enforcement Officials, usually listed under bedding, product safety, health, home furnishings, or Department of Health & Environment.) She requested and received samples of what the tag should look like, size requirements, etc., then proceeded to make her own by silk screening them on ribbons that matched her line of garments and pillows. (NOTE: Pillow makers/sellers may be able to get around this law simply by buying pillows that come with the necessary tag.)

A reader in New Holland, Pennsylvania, where bedding officials once came into the area to check for required labels on items in local shops, reports: "Apparently someone from another part of the state, who had been forced to obtain the special license and affix the labels, became aggravated when he or she saw similar items without tags in a bunch of shops. He or she then 'ratted on 'em!'"

A state official told my Pennsylvania reader that they only check something like this if and when they receive a complaint, which explains why the law is arbitrarily enforced throughout the country. Like zoning laws, this particular law seems only to affect those who bring attention to it or themselves, or who are turned in by others who haven't been fortunate enough to go unnoticed.

The only penalty that appears to be connected with a violation of this law is *removal of merchandise from store shelves.* That being the case, you may wish to ignore this law until you are challenged.

169

● **Federal Trade Commission Trade Practice Rules.** Several booklets are available that define the trade practice rules for all industries. Some of interest to this book's readers are:

- *The Jewelry Industry*
- *The Hand Knitting Yarn Industry*
- *The Ladies' Handbag Industry*
- *Catalog Jewelry and Giftware Industry*

NOTE: When an FTC rule has been violated, it is customary for the Federal Trade Commission to order the violator to cease the illegal practice. No penalty is attached to most cease-and-desist orders, but if one violates such an order, he may be fined.

● **The Migratory Bird Treaty Act of 1918.** This obscure regulation has had considerable impact in fines to some craftspeople. It prohibits the sale of feathers of all North American migratory birds. Also, protected under other laws are certain waterfowl and, of course, endangered species. For complete information contact the Department of the Interior.

● **Labeling of Metalwork.** If you happen to work with gold, silver, platinum or combinations of these materials, you should order the brochures available from the National Bureau of Standards, which also has labeling rules for items containing such metals.

Insurance

As soon as you start even the smallest business at home, you need to give special attention to insurance, specifically:

Homeowner's or Renter's Insurance. The policy you have on the personal possessions in your home *will not* cover business equipment, office furniture, supplies or inventory of finished goods *unless* you obtain a special rider. Such riders, called a "Business Pursuits Endorsement" by some companies, are inexpensive and offer considerable protection. Your insurance agent will be happy to give you details.

If you have a computer system, I do not advise that you insure this equipment on the business rider to your house policy. First, coverage may be limited merely to fire or theft. Second, although you may have replacement-value insurance on your personal possessions, a business rider on your policy is exempt from such coverage. In other words, the value of everything covered by the rider would be figured on a depreciable basis, instead of what it would cost to replace it. For this reason, it seems prudent to insure your computer system and software with one of the companies that specializes in such insurance, such as Safeware, listed in the Resource Chapter.

If you regularly travel to craft fairs, you might want to investigate policies designed to protect such property both at home, in your studio, or in transit to and from exhibitions and shows. The American Crafts Council offers such insurance. Write for details.

NOTE: No insurance policy is worth much unless you can document what you owned prior to destruction by fire or other disaster. Thus, you should make a photographic record of all your possessions and keep it, along with all documentation possible as to the value of each item in a safe place -- not your home. (A safe-deposit box will provide the greatest protection.)

Auto Insurance. Be sure to talk to the agent who handles your car insurance, and explain that you may occasionally use your car for business purposes. For example, if you regularly present party-plan sales and had an accident on the way to one of your presentations, would your present policy cover all losses?

Normally, a policy issued for a car that's used only for pleasure or driving to and from work may not provide complete coverage for an accident that occurs during business use of the car, particularly if the insured is to blame for the accident.

Personal Liability Insurance. *Product liability insurance* (see below) protects you against lawsuits by consumers who have been injured while using your product. *Personal liability insurance* protects you against claims made by people who have suffered bodily injury while on your premises.

If you purchase a business rider for your home insurance policy, you should inquire about added coverage for personal liability claims. Ask your insurance agent some specific questions, such as: What coverage would I have if a customer falls while in my home attending a boutique or home sale? What coverage would I have if the UPS delivery person slips on the ice in front of my home while delivering a business package? *Why* these people are on your property may determine the coverage provided by your policy, so be sure to double-check this point.

Also inquire about the availability of an "umbrella policy" which might take over where your present coverage stops. You might be able to purchase a million dollars' worth of insurance on your home and vehicle for as little as $100/year.

Product Liability Insurance. "Product liability is a legal time bomb that could wipe out some craftsmen and retailers, taking not only their businesses but life savings as well," warns a crafts trade paper. "Guarding against this situation is an aspect of your business you cannot overlook," adds another.

If a child swallows part of a craft toy, if a fiber wall hanging enflames, if a ceramic casserole cracks and spills its hot contents into the lap of its user, the maker of the product can be held responsible. Selling through a shop that carries product liability is not the answer to this problem since if a customer sued a shop, the shop's insurance company would undoubtedly turn around and sue the manufacturing craftsman.

In an article in the *Southern Highland Handicraft Guild* newsletter, Alan Ashe points out that:

Some of the things which have caused injury and court cases are: lead-glazed pottery, flameware, stuffed toys with wire or pins in them, knitted items made of yarn or fiber which will burn rapidly, furniture not sturdy enough to hold when a reasonable weight is put on it for support (such as a chair), jewelry that might injure the wearer or another person because of features in its design (sharp points projecting that would cut or injure).

This writer adds that the best way to prevent a lawsuit is to be certain that the items you make have no health hazards and can be safely used.

Michael Scott, in *The Crafts Report,* advises:

...make the product as safe as possible, and alert the customer if special precautions have to be taken. If you inform the customer not to put the glassware in a dishwasher and put the precautionary notice in writing, you have generally met your responsibility, even if she cuts two fingers while taking the broken glass out of the dishwasher. But if the glass breaks and spills hot liquid on someone because you were careless in the production of the item, watch out.

Or, as another adviser puts it: "...brainstorm your products, and try to make them as idiot-proof as possible."

Product liability insurance rates vary greatly from state to state, depending on one's annual gross sales (or anticipated sales), the number of products sold, and the possible risks associated with each of them. (An insurance company will look closely at what your products are made of and consider possible side effects you'd never imagine.)

For more information, check your Yellow Pages for agencies that sell business or commercial insurance policies.

Banking

Many business novices use their personal checking accounts to conduct the transactions of their business. You must not do this because the IRS frowns (to put it lightly) on anyone who co-mingles business and personal income. To do so would probably cause the IRS to rule that yours is not a business but a hobby. This, in turn, would cost you all the deductions previously taken on earlier tax returns.

You do not necessarily need one of the more expensive business checking accounts; just a separate account that enables you to clearly substantiate all business income and expenditures. You can save money on your business checking account by calling several financial institutions and comparing the charges they make for such things as imprinted checks, deposits, checks written, bounced checks, etc. Some banks charge extra for each out-of-state check that's deposited, an expense that would add up for active mail-order businesses.

In selecting the financial institution your business will deal with, also consider that:

■ Savings and loan institutions may pay interest on the amount in your checking account whereas a bank may not.

■ Banks will offer business loans and a commercial line of credit to its business customers, whereas a savings and loan institution offers personal loans only.

■ If at some point you think you may want to have a merchant credit card, so your customers can charge orders on their credit card, make sure your bank offers this service. Not all do, and some of those who do have strict policies against giving a merchant card to a homebased business owner. The charges associated with such credit cards vary greatly from bank to bank, so shop around.

* * *

I know this is quite a lot for you to absorb, especially if you're a complete business novice, so just remember the old saying about how to eat an elephant. (One bite at a time.) You should approach the information in this chapter in the same way, and to make it easier for you, I've included on the next page a handy check list you can photocopy (for your personal use only) as a worksheet of all the things you need to do to "get legal" and stay out of trouble.

Checklist of Legal & Financial
THINGS TO DO

Write for free information from the following sources (addresses in Resource Chapter):

☐ Internal Revenue Service guides for:
    ☐ *Tax Guide for Small Business* - #334
    ☐ *Business Use of Your Home* - #587
    ☐ Any other free info available

☐ Consumer Products Safety Commission for:
    ☐ Requirements for Consumer Product Safety (particularly in area of toys)
    ☐ Info on Flammability Standard for fabrics
    ☐ Use of hazardous substances

☐ Federal Trade Commission for:
    ☐ Textile Fiber Products labeling rules
    ☐ Wool Products labeling info
    ☐ Care labeling information
    ☐ Trade Practice rules for:
        ☐ jewelry
        ☐ knitting yarn
        ☐ handbags
        ☐ catalog jewelry/giftware

☐ Department of the Interior for info on use of feathers in craftwork

☐ National Bureau of Standards, for info on labeling rules for gold/silver items

☐ All suppliers and publishers in the Resource Chapter who offer free brochures or catalogs

☐ Other providers of business services (such as insurance for crafters) listed in the Resource Chapter

Call the following for more information:

☐ Insurance agent - re business rider on house insurance -- and umbrella policy info

☐ Insurance agent - re car insurance

☐ Insurance companies who offer product liability insurance

☐ Local financial institutions - to compare cost of a business checking account

☐ City Hall or County Clerk
    ☐ for info on licenses and permits
    ☐ to register fictitious business name
    ☐ to check on local zoning laws

☐ State Capital
    ☐ Department of Revenue - about sales tax number or tax exemption certificate
    ☐ Registration of business name on state level

☐ Department of Health/Bedding Official, for tag info.

Visit office supply store to check on:

☐ *Dome Simplified Monthly* recordkeeping book
☐ journal and ledger books
☐ standard invoices and other helpful business forms

Other Things to Do:

☐ Look for an attorney (if one is needed). Get references from friends and business associates, or call bank

☐ Get advice on legal form business should take -- whether to incorporate to protect personal assets, or buy liability insurance

☐ Shop for an accountant -- get references

☐ Check out Volunteer Lawyers for the Arts as source of free legal counsel

☐ Make a photographic record of personal and business possessions to be insured

☐ Get a safety deposit box for storage of valuable business papers, photographic record of insured property, computer back-up disks, etc.

- 15 -

Other Things You Should Know

Did you ever fix a terrific meal that called for many different ingredients, then found afterwards that you had a few things left over, like half a package of frozen spinach, the liquid from a can of mushrooms and a wedge of onion? If so, maybe you threw them into a pot and made vegetable soup. Well, this chapter is my "pot of soup" or, if you want to get fancy, a "potpourri" of things that didn't find their way into earlier chapters. The first "ingredient" is a dandy, and enough to spoil your appetite, but it's really important, so don't overlook it.

Hazards in the Arts

"Are the materials you are working with slowly killing you? Or maybe they are just going to make you chronically ill. Scary? I hope so, because many of the materials artists are working with are much more dangerous than is commonly believed." So warns Michael McCann, Ph.D., in his booklet *Artist Beware.*

According to Dr. McCann, toxic substances can enter the body in three ways: by skin contact, through breathing, and through the mouth and digestive system. Many materials can harm the skin directly, causing rashes, burns, and other skin problems. Acute lung diseases result when strongly irritating substances burn the tissues of the air sacs in the lung. Certain fumes are injurious to the kidneys and liver, with effects being cumulative. Symptoms such as weakness, fatigue, palpitations, and pale complexion may be caused by chemical substances that affect the red and white blood cells. Mental problems and nervousness can often be symptoms of physical problems related to chemicals found in art/craft materials. In fact, the entire central nervous system can be affected by certain substances.

You need to realize that anything can be toxic in the wrong place, at the wrong time, to the wrong person, in the wrong amount. This means, in effect, that nearly all materials can be toxic under some conditions. So says occupational and environmental specialist Gail Barazani. In the newsletter, *Hazards in the Arts,* she adds:

> Environmental contaminants, particularly those encountered in the industrial workplace, are creating serious health problems for millions of Americans. Ironically, many of those contaminants are being brought into the home (unintentionally) and into the daily recreational lives of at least one in five of the population in the form of art, craft, and other hobby materials.

Gail urges artists and craftspeople to obtain material safety data sheets (MSDS) for every product used in their work. These should be filed in a special binder along with any other information (labels, package inserts, etc) and correspondence from suppliers. Be persistent in obtaining the MSDS from manufacturers, putting your request on business stationery. Gail points out that if you give workshops as part of your business, the law requires suppliers to accompany their products with an MSDS.

Those who read the various publications for artists and craftsmen have become well aware of the many hazards to health in the long-range use of certain art/craft materials, but the general public remains largely unaware of these dangers to date. For that reason, I urge every reader of this book to become educated on this topic by ordering one or

173

more of the informative publications listed in the resource chapter under "Health Hazards Literature." Meanwhile, let me give you a few examples of what all the fuss is about:

- Aerosol paints, adhesive sprays, fixatives, etc., are dangerous unless used in such a way as not to breathe the vapors.

- Traditional art materials, such as lead paints and pottery glazes, solvents, inks, welding fumes, and wood and plastic dusts from sanding, can also be dangerous.

- Solvents, casting plastics, polyester resins, polyurethane paints, and varnishes constitute "jeopardy materials," and any person using them is taking an unnecessary risk unless proper precautions are used.

It's not just materials themselves that can cause problems, however. Gail Barazani warns that your own home can make you sick. "Making your home airtight to keep out cold winter winds may in fact be a health hazard," she says in her column in *The Crafts Report*. "Although our homes are not sealed environments, pollutant sources exist in most households. If the home is also a craft studio and workplace, the problem can be compounded."

Chronic fatigue, headaches and nausea that cannot otherwise be explained could be due to pollutants in your living and working quarters. If you feel ill for no apparent reason, tell your doctor about the materials you use in your work. (It may be necessary to consult with an internist, neurologist or occupational health consultant, since the average doctor may not take complaints seriously.)

In the Resource Chapter, you'll find a listing for The Center for Safety in the Arts, which publishes *Art Hazards News* and offers numerous information sheets about materials and processes and health effects. Also offered is a list of physicians across the country who are qualified to diagnose work-related illnesses which may go undetected by regular physicians.

174

There are many precautions you can take to avoid health problems related to your craft work. For example, a stained glass artisan told me recently that she stopped her business while she was pregnant. "It's always a good idea to know the health hazards of your business. Stained glass has quite a few. There are several chemicals plus the lead from the soldering. Every year I get a blood lead count and I wear gloves and a face mask for my safety."

Those who work with wood need to be particularly careful about fine wood dust from sawing, sanding or hand carving. All dust is irritating to the mucous membranes in the nose, throat, eyes and respiratory tract. Some people also have allergic skin reactions from the dust of certain woods. In one of her columns, Gail tells the story of a woodcarver who spent a lot of money on doctors trying to find out what was causing her serious, recurring rash. Finally a doctor asked what she did all day, and when he learned that she was working with cocobolo wood, her problem was solved. (Included in the list of allergenic woods, says Gail, are certain members of the birch, pine dogwood, beech, mahogany, mulberry, and myrtle families.)

Regardless of what you do, here are some specific steps you can take to diminish the dangers of any materials you may be using now:

- Do not inhale fumes, sprays, or dusts, and take special precautions to always have adequate ventilation in your work area. Improper ventilation is the major health problem in all the crafts.

- Airborne dusts, sprays and solvent vapors can be dangerous to your whole family. In particular, keep children away from your workshop since they are more susceptible to toxic substances than adults.

- Wear a dust mask when sawing, sculpting, grinding, or carving any materials to keep minute particles of dust from penetrating your lungs. Also wear a face shield or eye goggles. In cleaning up dust, never sweep, Vacuum instead, or wet-mop, or both.

- Be especially careful about personal hygiene. Always wash hands before touching cigarettes or food, and never work with chemical substances in an area normally used for food preparation or eating.

- Wear gloves when using any liquid other than water, but note that rubber does not work in some solvents; plastic must be substituted.

- If a manufacturer does not list the chemicals in a product, and will not tell you what it contains when you write for this information, do not use it. This could mean its contents are hazardous to your health.

Craft Organizations

A study by the National Endowment for the Arts done in the late 70s revealed that there were then some 300,000 craftspeople who belonged to about 2,000 organizations in the United States. The numbers have surely changed since then, but the concept of craft organizations has not.

Such organizations exist on all levels -- local, state, regional and national. While some have full-time staffs and permanent headquarters, others operate through volunteers and, often, in cases like this, an organization's address is likely to change every year as new officers are elected.

For this reason, no one has ever been able to compile a complete list of all the organized craft groups in America, which include associations, leagues, guilds and clubs. You can compile your own list, however, by using association directories in your library and by reading a variety of craft books and periodicals. To get you started, I've listed in the Resource Chapter several well-known regional and national organizations.

Note that most of them publish a magazine or newsletter to keep members up to date on what's happening in their industry. Some of these periodicals are designed for hobby-crafters while others concentrate on offering business and marketing information. Some offer special services such workshops and educational programs, discounts on books and craft supplies, etc.

Why join an organization? "The environment of an association, says crafts author Margaret Boyd, "provides an impetus, a thrust into crafts participation that excites the imagination. It aids craftspeople in gaining a sense of awareness of themselves in regard to their craft work -- helps them determine where their work stands in terms of talent, originality and quality."

Professionals in all fields recognize the value and importance of association membership, and readers of this book should learn what particular organizations can do for them. Some organizations work a lot harder for their members than others, but what many members forget is that they will get only as much out of an organization as they put in. Ultimately, the strength and longevity of any organization is directly related to the degree of help, cooperation, and financial support it receives from its members.

Cooperative Ventures

Occasionally a group of concerned artists or craftspeople will get together to form a special kind of organization known as a "cooperative." A craft cooperative is a nonprofit business organization -- a special tool that craft producers can use in different ways. People with similar desires, problems, or interests may use a cooperative to improve marketing conditions, purchase supplies, secure needed services, etc. For example, the practical result of a cooperative might be the formation of a central workshop, the opening of a shop or gallery, a materials and equipment buying group, the publication of a crafts catalog or directory, the organization of a large annual fair, and so on.

Here are brief profiles of four types of cooperatives my readers have told me about. They clearly illustrate the many benefits of a cooperative venture, and offer ideas on how others might start cooperatives of their own:

● **A Multi-Faceted Urban Crafts Co-op.** In New York City, a group of 10 craftspeople got together

to form a cooperative studio located in a large loft in Manhattan because they figured they could find a better working space if they combined forces and split expenses. Once established, the cooperative quickly grew to include two dozen members.

This cooperative studio provides sufficient space for each craftsperson to work, store heavy equipment, materials, and craftwork, and even has a special gallery area where work can be shown to potential clients and customers. This co-op does not stress sales as a joint venture, but on an individual basis. Individual members sell through shows, shops, fairs and other outlets. The co-op does produce an annual Christmas show, however, with each member contributing a mailing list for invitations. This event has given the co-op valuable television and newspaper publicity.

Members meet monthly to discuss problems that arise in maintaining the cooperative, and each assumes certain responsibilities in its operation. Each member pays a fixed amount each month that covers rent, utilities and other operating expenses. Naturally, this amount is a mere fraction of what each individual would have to pay for a private studio in New York City, yet the cooperative provides its members with a business identity most could not otherwise afford. A sharing of equipment, such as typewriters, saws, kilns, slide projectors, etc. offers obvious advantages, and because the craftspeople work in a studio with a business telephone number and address, they are taken more seriously by clients, vendors and others.

"An invaluable advantage of membership in a cooperative like ours," says one co-op member, "is the separation of working and living quarters, especially for those living in small urban apartments. Having space for heavy equipment, storing materials and work, and not having to worry about ruining furniture and household with one's mess while working is extremely important."

The combined knowledge of individual members contributes to the group's success. One is skilled in bookkeeping, another in legal matters, another in publicity, etc. Members share information about resources, fairs, outlets, galleries and suppliers, and often refer buyers to one another and suggest sales opportunities. Publicity is easier to obtain as a group, and credit advantages are possible when individual members share with others in ordering supplies in wholesale quantities.

176

● **A Cooperative Crafts Show.** For four years, six craftswomen joined together to participate as a group in as many as eight craft shows a year. When they presented their co-op booth idea to show juries, there was no trouble in being accepted.

The group used four six-foot tables to display their work, mixing it up to create an old-fashioned store image. A large sign, country painted with the name of the group, was prominently displayed on an artist's easel. Each member of the group wore an apron with the name of her own individual business either embroidered or painted on.

For the annual Christmas shows the group produced themselves, they would create a flyer containing a one-paragraph description of the work of each craftswoman. Then they would pool all the names on their individual mailing lists and split the printing and postage costs of the promotional mailing. Total sales from just three shows one year were close to $9,000.

● **A Cooperative Crafts Organization.** When Cathy Gilleland, a busy craftswoman with two young children, finally realized she had too many ideas to carry out alone, she formed a cooperative by finding six other women with similar interests. In a couple of months they had by-laws, a Constitution, a Standards Committee, and were putting on a splendid craft show with 40 other creative people.

Four months later, the Co-op had a hundred members, and the group has continued to grow ever since. Now the Co-op produces its own craft shows, has it's own shop, and does regular cable television shows to promote the organization, which serves beginners and professionals alike. Member benefits include a newsletter, regular monthly meetings, frequent field trips and low-cost workshops.

Recognizing the need for information on craft cooperatives, Cathy wrote a booklet detailing this group's experience. (See *How to Start and Run a Successful Handcraft Co-Op In Your Own Community* in the Resource Chapter). "I highly recommend that other craftspeople follow in our footsteps," she says. "I've met so many wonderful, talented people and watched them grow in their craft endeavors. A lot of excellent networking occurs in our group."

● **A Cooperative Crafts Shop.** In Holly, Michigan, a crafts supply store on the verge of going out of business was suddenly saved by quick thinking on the part of Ann Lang, a store employee and owner of a homebased business called Annie Things Possible.

Taking a cue from her business name, Ann suggested that the owner lease space in the store to craftspeople in the area who needed a retail outlet for their work. It wasn't difficult to find four other women who wanted to "set up shop" in the store, and before long word had spread and the customers began to appear.

By year's end, the owner was able to take down the "For Sale--Bobbies Hobbies" sign and replace it with "Bobbies Shop of Shops." Today, many creative people sell their work with success through the Shop of Shops Co-op that was eventually formed.

After two years of successful operation and lots of changes in how the cooperative was being operated, Ann wrote a how-to booklet to help other individuals start a similar organization. (See Resource Chapter.) It details the cooperative's formation and business practices and discusses the various problems the group encountered and eventually solved.

It would be hard for the average individual to imagine all the little problems and irritations that can erupt in a group like this, so Ann's account of them in her booklet is as much a guide to what NOT to do as it is a guide on how to make a cooperative run smoothly. "The most important things we learned from this experience," she says, "is that there can be only ONE boss if a co-op is to survive."

That "boss" is the store's owner, who has complete control over the financial responsibilities and operations of the Shop of Shops, from utilities to bank deposits. Her insurance covers the building, but each owner insures his or her own merchandise. There are committees to manages the advertising fund, plans marketing strategies, and settle the occasional disputes common in any organization.

Individual sellers in the co-op are responsible for the display, pricing and tagging of their merchandise. All sales go through the shop owner's cash register, which is balanced each day. Sellers can pick up their earnings on a weekly or monthly basis, as desired.

The overall theme of the shop is a blend of country/Victorian/nostalgia. Each seller's items must be distinctly different from others in the shop while also keeping to the shop's merchandise theme. (Items are juried and questionable merchandise is removed.) Each seller works in the shop, usually about one day every two months.

"The wonderful part of the whole setup," says Ann, "is that we share a camaraderie as crafters and artisans, hoping each of us will succeed. Those of us with small children have the freedom to work at home while also marketing our merchandise downtown."

Is There a Computer In Your Life?

If you already use a computer in your crafts business, I don't need to tell you about the wonders of technology and how it can make one's life easier. If you've reached the point where you're at least thinking about a computer, but are still stalling on its purchase, you will probably see yourself in one or more of the categories below:

- You don't think you can afford a computer at this time.
- You're not convinced that a computer will do that much for you.
- You don't have enough time to learn to use a computer because you're too busy as it is.
- You're concerned about your ability to learn computer technology and don't want to appear stupid.

During the first six years of my present business, I used all four of those excuses to delay my own computer purchase. But the day finally came when I realized my business could no longer survive, let alone grow, without the help of computer technology. My mail list was out of control and I was a nervous wreck because of it. And, with writing the main thrust of my business, I knew I also had to find a better way to produce my newsletter and self-published books in the future.

I'm not going to bore you with the details of my computer-learning experience, except to say that I had a long talk with my equipment as soon as I plugged it in and turned it on. "Listen," I said, "I haven't got time to learn all this stuff because I've got a business to run and deadlines to meet. I've got to get my subscription list on computer in just one month, so don't give me trouble, okay?"

Seriously, I believe my positive approach to learning, coupled with the knowledge that I *simply had to do this thing -- or else --* made all the difference. Later, after I'd accomplished my immediate goal and was feeling comfortable at the keyboard, my husband said he never could have done what I'd done in only a month with no help from anyone. I told him he was right -- not because he wasn't bright enough to learn, but only because he lacked a reason to do so. (He still has no interest whatsoever in messing with the computer.)

I fell in love with computer technology the moment I first saw my words appear on screen. How exciting it was to suddenly discover that now it took only the flick of a finger to move whole paragraphs around, delete this, add that, and -- wonder of wonders -- check what I'd written for spelling errors. Later, after I'd spent almost a hundred hours trying to master my *dBASE III+*

software (one of the toughest programs on the market), I knew I had it whipped. "If I can figure this out," I thought, "I can learn anything."

Let me tell you briefly how I use the computer to make my business and personal life easier, more efficient, and less stressful. My database software is used to manage my newsletter subscription list and thousands of customer and prospect names which are regularly mailed. (Harry was really thrilled when he realized that computer technology meant he no longer had to sort all our mailings by zip code.) Other special database files include my massive PR list, all the resources in my books, and inventory records of our personal possessions and a number of other things I like to keep organized. I do all my bookkeeping on the computer, so the annual job of gathering tax records is now a snap instead of a nightmare. And how comforting it is to know that such information is now permanently safeguarded on floppy disks in the safe deposit box, should we suffer a fire or other disaster.

I use my word processing software to manage hundreds of files -- articles, speeches, special reports, office forms, form letters, workshop handouts, press releases, my catalog copy and brochures, etc. -- to say nothing of my newsletter, magazine columns, books in progress and idea files galore. Now that I'm finally a full-fledged "desktop publisher" with sophisticated word-processing software, typesetting capabilities, a scanner and a laser printer, I figure I owe technology a mighty big thank you. Frankly, I don't know how I ever got along without it. The change in the quality of my writing and publishing output is as dramatic as the switch from a kerosene lamp to electricity.

You will not be surprised, then, to hear me encouraging you to enter the computer age if you have not already done so. It's natural to feel overwhelmed by technology, but with only the desire to learn and a little common sense, anyone can learn to use a computer for fun and profit. There are many books on the market today to help beginners get started, and many places where computer classes are being offered. If you have a computer, but haven't yet learned to use it well, or lack the proper software to do what needs to be done, you should start reading computer magazines on a regular basis. (The two I've learned the most from are *Home Office Computing* and *PC Computing*.) If, after reading a couple of magazines, you feel like a complete idiot because you can't understand all that technical jargon, cheer up. Most competent computer users today -- myself included -- felt the same way in the beginning. It's amazing how, bit by bit, it all begins to fall into place and make sense. You just have to stick with it and have a desire to learn.

In writing the special computer chapter that appears in *Homemade Money*, I interviewed a number of computer users in my network who shared their start-up experiences with me and explained how computers had sparked business ideas or changed their personal lives.

Two women turned their home computer into a moneymaking machine when they created a menu-planning service. Several individuals, when trying to work with computer programs inadequate for their needs, learned how to write programs from scratch, thus launching themselves into the business of helping others as computer consultants or programmers. Some people, on finding how easy it was to gather and organize certain kinds of information for printing, began to sell that information in the form of newsletters, special reports, directories or books. (In fact, several of those publications are listed in this book's Resource Chapter.)

One craftswoman expanded her business by offering mail list services to local fraternal organizations. Another woman discovered unknown artistic talents when she began to play around with the graphic capabilities of her computer. She went on to publish a book of computer cartoons and now admits that the computer actually unlocked her sense of humor. And a friend who failed typing in High School (and was a poor speller to boot) found that the computer unleashed all sorts of ideas she could at last put on paper. "My typing problem was keeping them locked in," she told me. "The word processor thus was the key to my discovery that I could write articles or do a newsletter."

Another woman told me that the computer simply made her feel younger. By keeping up with computer technology she has, in her words, "...conquered my own mythical beast by learning how to use this machine to do me some good. That is a major confidence-builder for me. It means the brain cells will still accept new concepts and skills and that's exciting for the entrepreneurial housewife."

In a future book I will explore the many ways that craftspeople are using computers to manage their growing businesses or help them be more creative. Therefore, if you'd like to share your computer experience with me, I'd be happy to hear from you.

Meanwhile, remember that we're now living in a new age of technology. People who elect to remain in the old world by avoiding computers are apt to end up on the short end of the stick someday. Imaginative, creative people who remain open to opportunities are the ones who will be in demand when the new century rolls around. I intend to be one of those people. How about you?

Epilogue

It's time to add the final seasoning to my "pot of soup." Time to take it off the fire, dish it up, and hope everyone likes it. Time to leave you with a few last words of encouragement, a philosophical thought or two, and a couple of reminders about luck and success.

Until now, you may have lacked the courage to get your craft ideas off the ground, but now that you've seen how other people have accomplished their goals, I hope you feel more confident and adventurous, and are ready to capitalize on your creativity.

About that courage I mentioned. . . In one of her lectures to women across the country, Dr. Joyce Brothers once commented that the only difference between being a neurotic and a creative artist is *courage*, adding that the creative person is capable of turning adversity to advantage, whereas a neurotic would wallow in self pity.

No one really knows why some people are more creative than others, but I believe all people are inherently creative, whether they realize it or not. Everyone seems to have his or her own definition of creativity, like Miriam Fankhauser, who says: "To be creative is to dare to try something new with no manual at your side." (Well, you can cheat a *little;* your use of *this* manual doesn't mean you're not creative.) Miriam adds, "Don't be afraid to dare to try. It is essential. And don't be afraid to fail. It is all part of learning and succeeding next time. Only by making mistakes do we learn how to find solutions and come up with something really fine."

Carol Bernier encourages all women to develop their talents but adds, "Don't expect to succeed at everything. Instead, concentrate on the fields that seem to work out for you. Work hard; don't be nonchalant."

And Ruby Tobey advises, "Keep on keeping on. Keep on working at your chosen art or craft -- you will be surprised at how much you improve, and how the new ideas keep coming as you work."

Why do women work so hard at certain things? Money, sure. But many work just for self-fulfillment, as we have seen, and those who work with crafts seem to derive special pleasures and satisfactions that are often difficult to explain. Making things by hand obviously feeds the soul, and although it is nice to please others with the work that has been created, pleasing oneself is really what it's all about.

As Jude Martin writes: "My greatest happiness is sitting on the floor, making a basket or designing a one-of-a-kind crocheted vest, or trying to learn to quilt or make toys. No matter how fragmented life becomes, I can go back to these and restore my perspective and peace of mind. I cannot envision ever leaving crafts; I feel there will always be something I can make for the pleasure of trying an idea."

179

As for success, remember it's a journey, not a destination. (I don't know who first said that, but I've always liked it.) Your attitude toward success is very important, of course. If you think it's impossible to achieve your goal, it probably will be. On the other hand, if you're confident of your ability and convinced you will succeed in time, you probably will. It can never hurt to assume a determined attitude when you set out to do anything, so long as you can accept failure as a possibility. And, even when we occasionally fail, we can justify our failures simply by accepting the fact that through failure we can correct our mistakes.

Or, as Margaret Thompson puts it, "You may fail, but you will learn something, even if it's your own limitations." She adds that "It's all out there for the taking" and suggests that you "take a course at the 'Y', read a book, buy a kit, get involved." In her life, Margaret says, happiness is busy-ness. Successes, great or small, have been a lucky by-product of her trying and failing, then trying once again.

Did I just mention luck? Yep. Luck does play an important role in success, according to Max Gunther, author of *The Luck Factor* (Macmillan Pub. Co.). He has some interesting theories about luck, and here's one that seems especially appropriate now: "The luckiest people I know haven't lived their lives in a straight line but in a zigzag. You've got to be ready to jump off in a new direction when you see something good." Gunther also believes that people who would "catch good luck" are generally those who have taken the trouble to form a great many friendly contacts with other people.

Perhaps your luck is going to improve now that you have the opportunity to make some good craft contacts and form some new friendships with creative people like yourself.

Since *Creative Cash* has concentrated on the topic of selling one's work, it seems only fitting to close on the subject of money. Making money from your needlework and crafts is what I hope you'll soon be doing, of course, but don't get so carried away by the idea of financial success that you lose track of your real goals. As Jude Martin says, "I have been called a 'soft sculptress,' when I know that I am a toymaker. Keeping your head on straight about your goals will do much to make them come faster and be more successful."

Finally, I want to remind you that the happiest years of your life are not necessarily going to be the years in which you make the most money, but rather the years in which you accomplish the things that are most important to you. My wish is that this book will open many new doors of discovery for you -- so many, in fact that it will take you the rest of your life just to explore the possibilities.

I hope someday you'll tell me about your accomplishments.

P. S.

As I've mentioned in this book, I have been publishing a newsletter since 1981. Actually, my quarterly report is more a "mini magazine" than a newsletter, except that it contains no advertising. I hope you'll want to subscribe to *National Home Business Report* so we can stay in touch in the future. Many successful craft business owners benefit from the small business and marketing information in each issue. Be sure to sample a current issue to see how you might benefit, too. (See periodicals section in the resource chapter.)

If you enjoyed this book, I know you'll appreciate and benefit from my other books as well. If you did not purchase *Creative Cash* directly from me, be sure to drop me a line so I can send you my free catalog and get your name on my regular mailing list.

When you write, just mention that you're a *Creative Cash* reader. Contact me at P. O. Box 2137, Naperville, IL 60567.

Barbara

Resources

Harry S. Truman once said, "The only things worth learning are the things you learn after you know it all." Although you now know a lot about selling crafts, I hope you will continue your education by exploring the many information sources listed in this chapter.

Do understand, however, that this chapter has been included as a special service to readers, and is not considered an endorsement of those listed herein. The author accepts no responsibility for any unfavorable action or transaction that might occur as a result of using the information published in this book.

Note: Every attempt has been made to insure that descriptive information and source addresses are correct and up to date. If your mail is returned however, and you especially want to contact that resource, *send Barbara a self-addressed, stamped envelope and ask for the new address*. It will be sent as soon as it becomes known to the author.

Each time this book is reprinted, this chapter will be updated according to information in file at that time.

When writing to anyone mentioned in this book, please mention *Creative Cash* in your correspondence. Thank you!

Guide to the Resource Chapter

Section I: Art & Craft Periodicals

This is by no means a complete listing of all the periodicals in this field (which may number 300 or more), but rather a listing of those publications best known to the author and believed to be of maximum interest to this book's readers. Magazines generally available on newsstands have not been included here unless they were mentioned in the text.

Listings are in alphabetical order and include a wide range of magazines, newsletters, newspapers, bulletins and show listings, many of which are issued by homebased publishers. Additional information is always available on request. Sample copy prices have been indicated when known to the author. Subscription rates have not been included because they're always changing. **Please mention this book in your correspondence with publishers.**

Note that this list of periodicals, added to those published by organizations in Section II, will serve as an excellent mailing list for your press releases. Periodical directories in your library will yield the names and addresses of other magazines and newsletters you may wish to add to your PR mail list.

 FOR ADDRESSES OF PERIODICALS LISTED IN THIS SECTION, SEE SECTION VII, ADDRESS LIST #1

☐ *Aardvark Territorial Enterprise.* A fascinating catalog-newspaper for everyone with an interest in needlework. Unusual craft-oriented information, rubber stamps, supply sources and aardvarks, of course. Send $2.00 for a sample issue.

☐ *Book Marketing Update.* John Kremer, editor and publisher. This 32-page bimonthly newsletter is an invaluable source of contacts, tips, resources and real-life self-publishing examples for crafters who are interested in self-publishing. Write for subscription information and catalog of all books and special reports for publishers.

☐ *Classified Communication.* Agnes Franz, editor/publisher. This monthly newsletter includes information that will help you write less expensive and better-pulling classified ads.

☐ *The Cloth Doll.* Colleen Bergman, editor & publisher. Outstanding quarterly magazine for cloth doll and fabric artists; with how-to articles, features, columns, marketing information, book reviews, and lots of reader-shared experiences and information. Sample, $3.50.

☐ *Country Handcrafts.* Deborah Hufford, editor. This consumer crafts magazine offers yet another market for craft and needlework designers who offer patterns and projects. A sample and copy of "Designer Guidelines" are available for $2.98.

☐ *Crafter's SourceLetters.* Teri Hales, editor/publisher. There are three newsletters offered in this series, one for crafters, one for stitchers and one for sewers. A subscription includes free annual source directory, classified ads and source-finding service. Samples are $5 each. **Note:** Suppliers should send their press releases/catalogs to Teri to receive free publicity.

☐ *Craft Marketing News.* Adele Patti, editor. A monthly newsletter for craftsellers that includes shop listings, special information for craft designers, articles, and reader mail. Sample, $3.00.

☐ *Craftmaster News.* Published by Marsha Reed, this bimonthly newspaper is primarily a show/fair-listing periodical; includes detailed entry info and contact sources for West Coast events, plus feature articles. Sample, $3.00.

☐ *Crafts.* Judy Brossart, editor. A popular monthly for crafts enthusiasts (on newsstands) that features the how-to projects of America's best craft and needlework designers (many of whom are members of the Society of Craft Designers). Request Designer's Guideline Sheet. This magazine has carried Barbara's column, "Selling What You Make" since 1979.

☐ *The Crafts Fair Guide.* Published by Lee Spiegel. A large quarterly listing of West Coast art/craft shows, with evaluations provided by participating craftspeople. One of the best publications in its field. Single issue, $15.

☐ *Crafts 'N Things.* Julie Stephani, editor. Published eight times a year. Another excellent market for designers interested in selling their how-to projects and design ideas. Write for Designers' Guideline Sheet. Available on newsstands.

☐ *Crafts Plus.* Susan Huxley, editor. This magazine reaches Canada's largest audience of "home arts hobbyists" with an interest in crafts and needdlework. Advertise here to reach 360,000 readers in rural areas, or request writer's guidelines to submit project ideas. (Single issue $2.95 Canadian funds.)

☐ *The Crafts Report.* Christine Yarrow, editor. Newsmonthly of marketing, management and money for crafts professionals. Has excellent ad sections for buyers and sellers, plus nationwide listing of fairs, workshops, conferences, reviews, and the best crafts marketing articles you'll find anywhere today. (P.S. This is a paying market for craft business writers--request writer's guidelines for more information.) Sample, $3.00.

☐ *Craft Supply Magazine.* Tammy Keck, publisher. This quarterly "Industry Journal For the Gift Producer" is one solution to the problem of where to find wholesale suppliers who will sell to homebased craft businesses. The February issue is an **Annual Directory**; the other three issues provide supplemental information. Issues include marketing articles and a "Product Showcase" where new suppliers can get free editorial mentions. For subscription information and a free sample of the report, send request on business letterhead.

☐ *The Creative Machine.* Sewers will love this 32-page quarterly newsletter published by Robbie Fanning. It contains a little of everything--tips and tricks, industry and product news, books, reader mail, Q&A sections, etc. You can sample an issue for $3.50.

☐ *The Dream Machine.* Published since 1990 by John Moreland for creative people interested in marketing their inventions. Articles and departments address legal issues, patents and trademarks, and marketing strategies. Sample copy $4 from The Dream Merchant. (#1)

☐ *Fiberarts.* Ann Batchelder, editor. Bimonthly dedicated to the needs and interests of professional or would-be professional fiber artists, with emphasis on contemporary weaving, crochet, knitting, basketry, stitchery, fiber sculpture, and clothing.

☐ *Fine Woodworking.* Dick Burroughs, editor. Beautifully-printed bimonthly magazine for serious woodworkers--the only one of its kind. (A good source for the best books and videos in this field -- request catalog.)

☐ *Handwoven.* Linda Ligon, editor and publisher. Full-color bimonthly magazine that features a sharing of techniques, ideas and news; with weaving projects, feature articles, columns, book reviews and supply source. Sample, $4 ppd.

   Note: Interweave also publishes selected fiber-related books. Says Linda, "We look for manuscripts that provide information you won't find in other books in print. We look for authors who not only are clear and direct and have a good grasp of their materials, but who are fun to read, too." The book catalog is free on request.

☐ *The Herb Companion.* Linda Ligon, editor and publisher. This colorful bimonthly magazine offers a wide range of information on growing and using herbs, with emphasis on aromatic and culinary plants. Sample, $4.00.

☐ *Homeworking Mothers.* Published by Georganne Fiumara, who started a Mothers' Home Business Network in 1984. This periodical serves as a lifeline to working mothers who want both a happy family and a successful home business. Send SASE for free brochure.

☐ *Let' Talk About Dollmaking.* Gloria Winer, editor and publisher. This quarterly newsletter is filled with good gossip, networking, sources for hard-to-find dollmaking supplies (quantity discounts available), and occasional marketing articles. Sample and catalog, $2.00.

☐ *McCall's Needlework & Crafts Magazine.* Gary Boling, editor. A good market for your craft and needlework projects; now part of the company that owns *Crafts* magazine. Request Designer's Guidelines sheet. Available on newsstands.

☐ *National Home Business Report.* Barbara Brabec, editor & publisher. Crafters who want their businesses to grow will subscribe to this 28-page quarterly (in publication since 1981) to learn more about managing their homebased business and marketing with limited funds. This networking publication includes feature articles, reader mail, many special departments, small business resources, and more. Your press release on small business products, services and publications is welcome and may lead to valuable publicity. Subscribe for $24/year U.S. ($28 Canada) or sample a recent back issue for $6 ppd.

☐ *Nutshell News.* A highly regarded monthly magazine for serious devotees of minitura who want to connect with others in this industry.

☐ *Potpourri from Herbal Acres.* Phyllis V. Shaudys, editor and publisher. An excellent networking newsletter that shares a wealth of information (and addresses) in every issue. Send business-size SASE for subscription information and details about companion books Phyllis has written. (If your business is herb-related, this newsletter is a must.)

☐ *The Professional Quilter.* Jeannie M. Spears, editor & publisher. This quarterly magazine is edited for women who are running a small business related to quilting. Features articles on business, marketing, record-keeping and more. This publisher also has several books and reports for professional quilters. Request free descriptive flyer.

☐ *Quilter's Newsletter.* Bonnie Leman, editor. A full-color monthly magazine that features patterns, how-to information, biographical articles and historical research on the art of quilting. Free brochure.

☐ *The Ronay Guides.* Camille Ronay, editor and publisher. Individual directories list some 2300 art shows, fairs and festivals and juried art competitions in the Southeast by state: GA, FL, AL, TN, SC, NC. Updated guides listing new events are published during the year. Also available from this source: *The Professional Artist's Guide,* which lists associations, centers and guilds in all states, national art, craft & gift markets, juried shows/competitions, shops & galleries and more. In addition, Camille offers an "Exhibitor Pack" advertising service that will put your flyers directly in the hands of exhibiting craftspeople through the Southwest. Request more information on all of the above from The Ronay Guides.

☐ *Rug Hooking.* Mary Ellen Cooper, editor & publisher. Five magazine issues per year include instructional articles on hooking, designing and hand-dyeing. Send SASE for information on this publication and related books.

☐ *SAC Newsmonthly.* Wayne Smith, Editor and publisher. This newspaper includes hundreds of art/craft show listings, plus feature articles. Sample $2.50.

☐ *The Sewing Sampler--Business Edition.* Editor Kathy Sandmann publishes this quarterly newsletter for the small manufacturer/designer interested in business and marketing information. Includes wholesale sources for all types of sewing supplies. Sample back issue, $3.00. Also available from this source: other newsletters and books for home sewers. Request catalog.

☐ *Sew News.* A monthly magazine (on newsstands) for people who sew--with informative articles, news and product information. Includes marketing column, "Sew to Success." Writers and designers should request Writer's Guideline sheet to propose articles or how-to projects for publication. For subscription information call toll-free (800) 289-6397.

☐ *Sharing Ideas.* Dottie Walters, editor/publisher. When you're ready to speak professionally about your art or craft, this bimonthly magazine (and fantastic networking tool) will introduce you to the world of professional speaking. Sample copy and information about related books and tapes, $5.00.

☐ *Spin-Off.* Linda Ligon, publisher. A quarterly magazine for spinners, with in-depth articles and information related to the craft. Sample $3.50.

☐ *Stitches Count.* A quarterly newsletter for counted thread enthusiasts, edited and published by Suzanne Weyer and Nancy Hoerner, who also write a regular column for *Crafts* magazine.

☐ *Sunshine Artists, USA.* A monthly magazine jam-packed with entry information on street, park, mall and arena shows nationwide and in 7 foreign countries. Includes critiques of individual shows, marketing articles and more. Sample copy, $5.00.

☐ *Teaching For Learning.* Charlene Anderson-Shea, editor. This semi-annual newsletter is for fiber teachers interested in networking and success strategies. Includes tips on how to get publicity, build self-confidence, motivate students, etc. For list of available back issues, send SASE.

☐ *Treadleart.* A bimonthly magazine edited and published by Janet Stocker. For fabricrafters interested in sewing machine art. Articles on technique, patterns, new product info, book reviews, reader mail. Also available: a retail *Sewing Supply Catalog* ($2 ppd.) of books, threads, notions, patterns; and a wholesale *Sewing and Quilting Supply Catalog.* (Request copy on business letterhead.)

☐ *West Coast CRAFTLINK.* A Canadian newsletter published quarterly by Karen Booy & Donna Astbury. Features upcoming craft events and articles. Also available: a directory of Canadian suppliers who will sell wholesale to craftspeople. Request details from West Coast Craftlink.

184

Section II: Organizations

Each of the following organizations offers special benefits of membership, and most publish outstanding periodicals for artists and craftsmen. Write to each organization of interest and request a brochure. This list is given merely to whet the appetite of readers who will find lengthier lists of national and regional organizations in library directories such as *Encyclopedia of Associations.*

For addresses, see ADDRESS LIST #2.

☐ **American Crafts Council (ACC).** A nonprofit, educational, cultural organization serving a national membership. Publishes *American Craft* and other publications for craftsmen. ACC offers a broad range of group insurance plans-- major medical, hospital indemnity, life insurance, short term disability, Medicare Supplement, and a Studio policy that protects against loss to both unfinished and finished works, at home or away.

☐ **The American Quilter's Society.** A membership society for anyone who loves quilts. Membership includes *American Quilter,* a full-color quarterly magazine, free admission to the National Quilt Show and Contest, discounts on books, a newsletter, pin and card.

☐ **American Society of Artists, Inc.** A national organization whose membership benefits include a quarterly publication, *ASA Artisan* and a lecture and demonstration service. Send SASE for information.

☐ **Center for the History of American Needlework** (CHAN). Main goal is to legitimatize and document the importance of needlework in America. Activities include special needlework shows and exhibitions, publication of booklets, and the building of a resource library that includes books, periodicals, catalogs, patterns, pamphlets, slides, photos and items of needlework. Members receive CHAN's quarterly newsletter.

☐ **The Center for Safety in the Arts.** A national clearinghouse for information on hazards in the arts. Publishes *Art Hazards News.* Send SASE to receive a publications list and information about hazards in the visual, graphic, and performing arts and crafts.

☐ **COSMEP** (The Committee of Small Magazine Editors and Publishers). This is *the* international association of small magazines and presses. Membership is open to any press or periodical, including self-publishers, and includes a helpful newsletter. COSMEP also offers a variety of helpful marketing/promotion mail lists.

☐ **Council of American Embroiderers.** Members receive *The Flying Needle* magazine, have access to a book and slide library and correspondence courses. The Council also sponsors regular seminars, an annual Study Retreat, and biennial juried "Needle Expressions" exhibition of original fiber art.

8½ x 11" PB, 392 pgs., $23.95 ppd.

The home-business "bible" — a powerful success tool that has changed the lives of thousands—your survival guide for today's economy.

More than 85,000 copies in print!

Homemade Money

How to Select, Start, Manage, Market and Multiply the Profits of a Business at Home

"I am pleased to see this expanded edition incorporate innovative marketing and promotional concepts into its information base. Developers and entrepreneurs truly have a single source document that addresses every issue relevant to operating a home business. My access to accurate and timely advice and information is greatly enhanced by the writing of the 5th edition of Homemade Money."

**– H. Sam McGrier, Assistant District Director,
U. S. Small Business Administration, Chicago, Illinois**

Weighing in at 2 lb. 7 oz. with 392 pages, this NEW FIFTH EDITION of *Homemade Money* is the heftiest, *meatiest* home-business book in print! You may have read earlier editions of this book, but they bear no resemblance to this latest edition. It's ALL NEW! *Add it to your home-business bookshelf today to realize greater profits tomorrow!*

SOMETHING SPECIAL FOR EVERYONE:

● Dreamers with ideas and talent needing help and encouragement to get started

● People without jobs who must find a way to earn money right now

● Corporate dropouts seeking greater satisfaction through self-employment

● "Sideliners" needing know-how and guidance to grow their part-time businesses

● Established homebased entrepreneurs and other self-employed individuals eager to increase sales and profits through better business management, marketing and diversification

● Teachers and seminar leaders who want to give their students the best home-business information available

---

"In every endeavor we undertake, we realize that there must be an investment required of us. I often tell individuals who ask me how they can succeed in their homebased business that 'you wouldn't take a final test without preparing, would you? Then you must not consider starting a business without research.' What Barbara has provided is the Cliff Notes of business entrepreneurship. HOMEMADE MONEY is fantastic! I recommend it as their primary assignment."

– Marcia Stuckey, Exec. Dir., Nebraska Home-Based Business Association, Kearney, NE

Seven Good Reasons to Buy

❶ SIXTEEN JAM-PACKED CHAPTERS—eleven of them brand new, the rest totally revised and expanded.

❷ 67 MORE PAGES than earlier editions. Large size (8½ x 11") format.

❸ EXPANDED A-TO-Z "CRASH COURSE in Business Basics"—literally a 76-page book-within-a-book that includes reliable information verified by professionals in the fields of law, taxes, accounting, banking, insurance, copyrights, patents and trademarks. Tells beginners in both the U.S. and Canada how to get started on the right legal foot while reminding established business owners of potentially dangerous and legally expensive business pitfalls they may be overlooking. (This chapter could save you hundreds of dollars' worth of tax and legal advice!)

❹ THIRTY FULL-PAGE CHARTS and ILLUSTRATIONS to help you (1) select a profitable business or diversification idea; (2) design necessary printed materials; (3) avoid missing important legal tax deductions; and (4) fully understand the many low-cost marketing and promotional ideas available to you.

❺ NEW RESOURCE CHAPTER of nearly 300 vital references for U.S. and Canadian readers—books, periodicals, organizations, government contacts and library references.

❻ Colorful and informative SIDEBAR MATERIAL throughout the book—extra juicy tidbits of information to enhance your understanding of topics discussed in the text.

❼ HOME-BUSINESS HUMOR—to make the medicine go down. True stories shared by Barbara and her readers add to the book's appeal and make the learning fun!

(MORE INFORMATION AT RIGHT ➡)

"Reading HOMEMADE MONEY is like sitting at the kitchen table with Barbara Brabec, talking about starting and marketing a homebased business. Hardly a day goes by that I do not send a future home business owner to the public library to pick up this bible for home business."

– Mary Jane Shearer, Program Coordinator, Prince George's Community College, Largo, MD

The grandmother of home-business newsletters—
and one of the most powerful home-business networks
in existence . . . is now known as

Barbara Brabec's
Self-Employment Survival Letter

TO SURVIVE IN BUSINESS, you must stay current with your industry and the people in it, know what's new, what's changing, what's working, what isn't and why. That's what this newsletter is all about.

SUBSCRIBE NOW to learn how others are operating homebased income activities and what they're doing to realize greater profits in today's tough economic climate.

THE MARKET IS FLOODED with home-business newsletters that feature standard how-to articles or rehashed business information aimed at beginners. If you need start-up support, you'll find it in *Homemade Money*. But if you're looking for a continuing supply of FRESH BUSINESS INFORMATION AND INSIDER TIPS FROM PROS, you'll find them in *Barbara Brabec's Self-Employment Survival Letter*. It's published by an industry leader and edited for serious business owners and all other self-employed professionals who work at or from home base.

A typical issue will share information from the editor and twenty or more business owners. There may be as many as fifty new resources. Complete contact information is always given to encourage networking, ordering, and other business-to-business connections.

ISSUES ARE ENTIRELY AD-FREE. You will never find money-making opportunities, MLM offers, "get-rich schemes" or mail order circular programs promoted in this high-quality business bimonthly.

EDITORIAL CONTENT

- Industry & Trade News
- Editor's Reports
- Business Trends
- Reader Mail
- Tax & Legal Updates
- Business/Office Management Tips
- Computertalk/Desktop Publishing
- Marketing & PR Strategies
- New Business Resources
- Networking Contacts

Homemade Money
Table of Contents

". . . buy this book! Barbara offers the kind of advice that can help you every step of the way."
– MOTHERS MATTER

Home Business Humor

AS SOON AS YOU START A BUSINESS AT HOME, you will never again have enough time to do everything you want to do. As someone once said, "If it weren't for the last minute, nothing would ever get done." You'll stop polishing your copper-bottom pots, forgotten food will turn green in the refrigerator, and you'll soon adopt the attitude, "If I can't see it, I don't need to clean it." Gourmet cooking will quickly fall by the wayside, and if you have been preparing fantastic meals for years prior to starting a business, the oven is not the only thing that's going to heat up when you start throwing quickie meals on the table.

A homebased business will also curtail your social life. Either you'll be working in the evenings or on weekends, or you'll simply be too tired to think about entertaining guests, let alone cleaning house for them. Before long, you'll find yourself identifying with the Tupperware rep who shared this insight on housekeeping: "When I can write my name in the dust on my coffee table, it proves one thing—*that I'm literate.*"

© 1994 by Barbara Brabec

Add to your business knowledge

with these informative MINI REPORTS and RESOURCE LISTS (Information not included in Barbara's books.

How to Develop and Profit From Your Mail List. You've got some great names from ads or publicity . . . but are you managing your list properly? In this 5,000-word report, Barbara shares over 30 years' experience in managing mail lists. How to compile a good list with or without a computer . . . determine the value of present lists for remailing or rental . . . cut list rental maintenance costs and avoid pitfalls in renting or trading lists. Includes tips on computerizing a list, with field structure help, coding systems and general database management guidelines. **(#R1, $5)**

Publishing Home-Business Directories. Can you make money doing this? Maybe. Avoid common pitfalls with this money-saving report that details the experiences of publishers in Barbara's network who tell what worked and what didn't. Includes tips on how to find home-business owners, get them to send listings, obtain paid ads to offset printing costs, and distribute printed directories. **(#R2, $5)**

Independent Contractor Information Package. You are on dangerous ground if you use independent contractors to produce goods manufactured by individuals in their homes, particularly if those goods are sewn, and especially if they are garments for women or children. For invaluable insight on the legal difference between employees and independent contractors—and whether you're likely to be sued by the Labor Department for breaking the law—read *The Judge's Decision in the Silent Woman Case* (an official court document unavailable from any other source) and

---

A Classic in its field.

85,000 copies sold

If you want an . . . in the how-to's . . . time living from . . . of extra money . . . this inspiring bo . . . its fifth edition . . .

The book *Fa* . . . has been compl . . . Originally a sele . . . edition of *Creat* . . . selection of Boo . . .

Who's Working at Home and Why

— an excerpt from *Homemade Money* © 1994

With job security a thing of the past, millions of people who once thought they would have a job for life are wondering if they're going to get the pink slip. Many still-employed corporate workers are taking steps to position themselves for self-sufficiency should the paycheck suddenly cease, and a growing number of ex-corporate employees are now working for their former employees as independent, homebased consultants.

Job loss may continue to be a factor in one's decision to start a business at home, but many choose to work at home because they

How about you?

- think they can make more money working for themselves;
- are tired of their job;
- want a new challenge;
- want to spend more time with their families;
- desire a change of lifestyle.

About Barbara Brabec

Barbara Brabec is one of America's best-known small-business writers. Her newsletter has been in publication since 1981 and two of her books (described inside) have become classics in their fields. Both books have more than 85,000 copies in print and both are recent book club selections.

Barbara has contributed to several books and her articles have been published in dozens of small-business periodicals. Constantly quoted in the national press as a home-business expert, she has given countless radio and newspaper interviews. Her television credits include a week-long appearance on ABC-TV's *Home* show in a "Homemade Money" series named after her book. She has also appeared in FNN's "Americans Creating Tomorrow" series; on CNBC's "Money Talk" show and WCIU's "Ask An Expert." America's first family of finance, Ken and Daria Dolan, frequently recommend *Homemade Money* on their radio show and in their newsletter.

As a speaker and seminar leader, Barbara has participated in many of the major home-business conferences in the United States, and has also shared her viewpoints in Nova Scotia, British Columbia and Saskatchewan. As North America's only home business humorist, Barbara has recently found new audiences for her talks, and her next book may well be a funny one.

● **Telephone Consultations** with Barbara are available at $60/hour. For more information or to arrange an appointment, call (708) 717-4188.

Note: The rate for newsletter subscribers is just $50/hour for appointments scheduled in advance. Subscribers who need only a few minutes of Barbara's time can use her "Ten Minutes—Ten Bucks" consultation service any time.

● **Free Article Excerpts** from *Homemade Money* and *Creative Cash* are available to editors. Request listing of available articles (600–1,000 words) and "Quick Tips" that are perfect for newsletters with limited space.

● **Free Workshop Handouts** are available to teachers and seminar leaders on both home-business and crafts marketing topics. Indicate your special needs when you request the free listing. (Include your telephone number.)

● **A Speaker's Kit** is available to program sponsors.

□ **Counted Thread Society of America.** Society's purpose is to encourage and promote the practice and knowledge of counted thread embroidery in all its forms. A quarterly magazine is published for members. Also available: *Handbook for Designers of Counted Thread* (see BOOKS section).

□ **Embroiderer's Guild of America.** This is the American offshoot of the Embroiderer's Guild of England, and is an educational, nonprofit organization that sets and maintains high standards of design and workmanship in all kinds of embroidery and canvas work. Members receive the quarterly magazine, *Needle Arts.*

□ **Handweavers Guild of America, Inc.** Nonprofit organization of weavers, spinners and dyers. Members receive *Shuttle, Spindle & Dyepot* magazine. Organization also publishes a *Suppliers Directory* and U.S. textile collections directory.

□ **International Guild of Candle Artisans.** Offered are workshops, national convention, round robin groups and monthly publication, *The Candlelighter.*

□ **The Knitting Guild of America.** For those wishing to advance the quality of workmanship and creativity in their endeavors. Membership includes the quarterly journal, *Cast-On,* and opportunities to exhibit in retail markets and an annual convention.

□ **Minnesota Crafts Council.** Membership includes a subscription to *Craft Connection,* a bimonthly tabloid designed to foster a sense of community among Midwestern craftspeople.

□ **Montclair Craft Guild.** This nonprofit organization (over 1100 members in New Jersey and the Northeast) has created, in association with Bollinger Insurance, Ind., a uniquely designed insurance package for craftspeople nationwide. The insurance package includes broad protection for your premises, product liability at your place of business and at craft shows, and "all peril" replacement cost coverage for craft property. Membership in the Guild is a requirement to obtain the insurance (affordable to most craft businesses). Membership includes subscription to *Showcase* newsletter. For insurance details, call the Craft Insurance Hotline: (800)526-1379; in New Jersey, call (800)772-2252. For membership info, write to the Guild.

□ **National Quilt Association, Inc.** Organization has chapters in the U.S. Membership benefits include instruction at meetings, exhibitions, annual juried show, and quarterly *Patchwork Patter.* The association has also published a book, *Teaching Basic Quiltmaking.* (See BOOKS section.)

□ **National Society of Tole & Decorative Painters, Inc.** Members receive a quarterly, *The Decorative Painter.* Aim of this nonprfit organization is to preserve and enrich all forms of decorative painting. They hold an annual convention and publish an annual directory.

□ **National Woodcarvers Association** (NWCA). Thousands of woodcarvers nationally network through this organization's bimonthly, *Chip Chats.*

□ **Ohio Arts & Crafts Guild.** A nonprofit service and informational organization for practicing artists and crafts-people at all levels of achievement. Members receive *Creative Ohio* magazine, directory of Ohio festivals/competitions, and insurance options. The annual two-day OACG Conference provides excellent networking/learning opportunities.

□ **Ontario Crafts Council/Craft Resource Centre.** Membership includes the bimonthly magazine, *Ontario Craft,* and access to valuable publications such as *Suppliers of Craft Materials* and *Shops & Galleries* (in Canada). This organization has established Canada's largest and most comprehensive reference library in the crafts field. In the Centre is a Guild Shop featuring exceptional work by Canadian craft makers.

□ **The Professional Knitwear Designers Guild.** This organization was formed to assist professional knitwear designers or those desiring to become professional designers. Members receive a newsletter and other benefits. Send SASE for a membership brochure. (#3)

□ **Sewing & Fine Needlework Guild.** For those wishing to advance the quality of workmanship and creativity in their sewing endeavors. Mmembership includes 4 issues of *Sewing & Fine Needlework* magazine and opportunities to exhibit in retail markets and the annual convention.

□ **Society of Craft Designers.** A professional organization for designers, writers, book and periodical publishers, editors, teachers and others who wish to sell in the crafts and needle-work industries. The annual educational seminar enables beginners to learn from the experts and make valuable editorial, publishing, and manufacturing contacts. Members receive a newsletter.

□ **Stained Glass Association of America.** Aim is to promote the finest development of the stained glass craft. Membership includes the quarterly magazine, *Stained Glass.*

□ **Stumpwork Society.** Members network through the *Stumpwork Society Chronicle* newsletter. Founder Sylvia Fishman has an abiding interest in conservation and restoration, and offers a special "Threads of Nostalgia" slide lecture. You can sample the newsletter for $2.50.

□ **Surface Design Association.** Group's aim is to improve communications among artists, designers, industry, and teachers working in surface design on textiles and related media. Members receive *The Surface Design Journal* (sample, $6 ppd.) and a newsletter.

□ **United Maine Craftsmen.** A nonprofit, educational organization with membership open to all. Publishes an annual membership directory of Maine craftsmen, shops and supply sources, as well as a periodical, *The Craft Tradesman.*

□ **Volunteer Lawyers for the Arts.** A nonprofit legal aid organization that provides free arts-related legal assistance to artists and arts organizations in all creative fields who cannot afford private counsel. Has affiliate offices in 42 cities nation-wide. This organization publishes a wide variety of publications, such as *Legal Guide for the Visual Artist, Trademark and the Arts, VLA Guide to Copyright for Visual Artists,* and more. Write for a descriptive brochure.

185

Trade magazines are not meant to be read by hobbyists, but serious craft sellers will find such publications a gold mine of information, and the key to finding necessary supplies and materials at wholesale prices. **NOTE:** Send requests for information on your business letterhead; otherwise, you may not receive a response.

For addresses, see ADDRESS LIST #1 OR #2, as indicated by the number in parenthesis after the description.

☐ **American Craft Association.** This is the "trade arm" of the American Crafts Council. It sponsors six of the country's major craft fairs (retail/wholesale marketplaces) in West Springfield, Mass., Baltimore, Minneapolis, New York, Atlanta, and San Francisco. Open to craft sellers nationwide, but the standards are high. (#2)

☐ *Apparel Industry Magazine* and *Apparel Industry Sourcebook.* The sourcebook published by its companion magazine is a national directory of suppliers and contractors to the apparel industry. (#1)

☐ **Beckman's Gift Shows.** Professional craftspeople find the Beckman shows to be excellent markets. Exhibitors must produce domestic handcrafted giftware. Details available from Industry Productions of America. (#2)

☐ *Craft and Needlework Age.* Monthly issues of this magazine emphasize particular aspects of the crafts industry, with trade show news and product information. (#1)

☐ *Craftrends.* This monthly trade magazine serves sewing and craft chain stores, and features new products, resources and some reviews. (*Sew Business* magazine, which used to be published separately, merged with *Craftrends.*) (#1)

186

☐ *Gift & Tableware Reporter.* Monthly magazine edited for dealers in the gift and tableware market. Publishes an annual directory, *Gift Guide.* (#1)

☐ *Gift Basket Review.* The only trade magazine for the gift basket industry. (#1)

☐ *Gifts & Decorative Accessories.* A monthly magazine for retailers, and an excellent overview of what's hot in the gift industry. Subscription include the annual *Gifts & Decorative Accessory Buyer's Guide,* which lists thousands of manufacturers, importers, distributors; plus sources for manufacturing and assembling materials, gift boxes, bags, tags, etc.; trade names, trade show information, industry associations, and more. (#1)

☐ **Hobby Industries Association (HIA).** A major trade association in the hobby/crafts field. Produces annual trade shows in which manufacturers, publishers and service companies market to wholesalers, retailers, institutional buyers and professional craft producers. (Very strict entry qualifications for this show.) (#2)

☐ **Miniatures Industry Association of America.** This organization promotes the interest of those engaged in buying, selling, and manufacturing miniatures merchandise. Membership includes a newsletter, listing in a trade show directory, and access to two annual trade shows. (#2)

☐ *Profitable Craft Merchandising.* Published monthly for craft retailers, wholesalers and manufacturers; also read by designers, teachers and mail-order sellers in the crafts industry. Publishes annual directory, *The Craft Market Handbook,* which lists manufacturers, wholesalers and publishers in the industry, plus manufacturers' representatives, trade organizations, and trade names of products. (#1)

☐ **The National Needlework Association.** A nonprofit association formed to advance needlework quality, understanding and marketing in the U.S. Membership includes manufacturers, distributors, importers and retailers. TNNA produces three major trade shows annually, and publishes *National Needlework News.* (#2)

☐ *The Yellow Pages of American Crafts.* This publication looks like a magazine, but is in fact a directory published by *Niche, The Magazine for Progressive Retailers.* Professional craftspeople can receive one free listing in this directory in a crafts category of their choice (baskets, fiber, gifts, miscellaneous, wood, etc.). Additional listings are $10 each, and display ad space is available. The directory itself is $10 ppd. To order, or for a free listing form, contact Yellow Pages of American Crafts. (#1)

Most of the publications described in this section can be ordered by mail from a source named in the listing. Prices have been checked, but are always subject to change.

If a listing carries no ordering information, it means you should look for this particular publication in a bookstore or library.

For addresses, refer to the ADDRESS LIST indicated in parenthesis after the description.

□ *Artist's Market*. Published annually, this directory lists 2,500 buyers of graphic and fine art. Available in bookstores or by mail from Writer's Digest. (Elsewhere in this section, you'll find a description of other books available from this source. Request a free catalog.) (#1)

□ *The Artist's Complete Health & Safety Guide*, by Monona Rossol, a health hazards expert. Explains how to make studios and materials safe for use. In bookstores, or order from Writer's Digest. (#1)

□ *Business Forms and Contracts (in Plain English) for Craftspeople*, by Leonard D. DuBoff. A companion to *The Law (in Plain English)* listed elsewhere. Describes every conceivable type of form and contract used by craftspeople, including copyright, tax records, leases, consignment agreements, warranties, sales and commissions. Includes many example forms. $15.90 ppd. from The Crafts Report. (#1)

□ *Cart Your Way to Success: A Peddler's Play in Three Acts*, by Gail Bird. This book explains "pushcart merchandising," which the author has done for ten years (selling a line of Russian Punchneedle Embroidery and supplies). She says many shopping malls now offer attractive carts, kiosks or other structures on a temporary basis and are often willing to strike deals with artists and craftspeople. Her book gives "the tricks of the trade." $21.95 pd. from Gail Bird. (#3)

□ *The Complete Crafter's Handbook*. This is a directory of show promoters and over a hundred shops nationwide that take products on consignment, purchase outright, or rent space. Compiled by Maureen Davis. (#3)

□ *The Consignment Workbook*, by Sue Harris. After two years of operating her own consignment store, the author wrote this guide to help other shop owners succeed. You'll find tips on money, equipment, supplies, contracts, forms, leases, store layout, computers, advertising, banking, and more. $15 ppd. from Sue Harris. (#3)

□ *The Crafts Business Encyclopedia*, by Michael Scott (as revised by Leonard D. DuBoff; 5th edition, Harcourt Brace Jovanovich). A "bible" of the industry, this book answers hundreds of A-to-Z crafts business and marketing questions. In bookstores, or order by mail from The Crafts Report. (#1)

□ *Crafts Marketing Success Secrets*, by Barbara Brabec. A companion guide to *Creative Cash* published in 1986. A sharing of previously-published, profit-oriented information and ideas from the author and more than a hundred crafts professionals across the country. Of special interest: stories of success and failure in party-plan businesses, holiday boutiques and other cooperative marketing ventures; plus lengthy chapters on selling to shops, at fairs, wholesale outlets, or a shop of your own. $11.95 ppd. from Barbara Brabec Productions. (#1)

□ *The Crafts Supply Sourcebook*, by Margaret Boyd. (Betterway, 1993). Includes 2600 product listings arranged in two sections: general arts, crafts and hobbies; and needlecrafts, sewing and fiber arts. Listings include complete ordering information. Although designed primarily for use by individuals who need mail order supply sources, this book also includes valuable wholesale data for those in business. In bookstores, or $19.95 ppd. by mail from Barbara Brabec Productions. (#1)

□ *Creative Cash*. Additional copies of this book (a great present for a friend) are available for $16.95 ppd. from Barbara Brabec Productions. (#1)

□ *The Creative Woman's Getting-It-All-Together (At Home) Handbook*, by Jean Ray Laury. A collection of ideas and proposals for accomplishing both personal and family goals -- for creative women in the fiber/fabric fields. $10.95 ppd. from Hot Fudge Press. (#1)

□ *Design and Sell Toys, Games & Crafts*, by Filis Frederick. This book, now out of print, is an excellent guide worth tracking down through your library. Includes a wealth of info about the most popular toys and games of our time -- how they were created and marketed.

□ *Directory of Art Publishers, Book Publishers and Record Companies*. If you think your work is appropriate for greeting cards, calendars, postcards and record covers, here's the directory you need to find buyers. More than a hundred listings--what companies want. Also available from the same source: *Directory of Galleries for the Fine Artist,* and *Fine Art Representatives & Corporations Collecting Art*. Details from Art Network. (#1)

□ *Directory of Book Printers*, by Marie Kiefer. Ad Lib Publications, 1991. Lists 1,000 printers who specialize in bound publications -- from catalogs to cookbooks to consumer guides and directories. $13.95 ppd. Request free catalog from Ad Lib Publications. (#1) from Open Horizons Pub. Co. (#1)

□ *Directory of Craft Shops & Galleries*. Published by Adele Patti. Revised annually. The 10th edition includes over 1,000 craft marketing opportunities by state, with descriptions of the specific handcrafts wanted by buyers. Includes catalog markets, sales reps, and craft home-party organizers who accept handcrafted items. $11.45 ppd. from Craft Marketing News. (#1)

□ *Directory of Seasonal Holiday Craft Boutiques,* by Adele Patti. Complete descriptions of boutiques nationwide as well as comments from the organizers and crafters who participate in these marketing opportunities. Many of these boutiques accept work on consignment from crafters in other areas. Third edition, $9.95 ppd. from Craft Marketing News. (#1)

☐ *Directory of Show Listing Periodicals.* This information, compiled by Barbara Brabec, will put you in touch with nearly 50 publishers who offer newsletters, magazines, special show guides or pamphlets describing art/craft events in particular states. This listing is your key to getting advance show information regionally or nationally -- all types of events -- fairs and festivals, mall shows, flea markets, and more. You can sample publications of interest prior to subscribing. This listing is $3.00 ppd. from Barbara Brabec Productions. (#1)

☐ *Directory of Wholesale Reps for Craft Professionals.* Sharon Olson has compiled this handy marketing guide, which lists over 100 companies interested in hearing from crafts-people with wholesale product lines. Listings include crafts wanted, commissions taken, and tips from sales reps them-selves. Regularly updated; ask publisher for price of latest edition. Northwoods Trading Co. (#1)

☐ *The Fabric and Fiber Source Book -- Your One-and-Only Mail Order Guide,* by Bobbi A. McRae. (Taunton Press, 1989). In addition to the supply sources you'd expect to find, there are also listings for educational opportunities, publica-tions, services and museum collections -- even computer programs for textile design. More than 650 detailed listings in all. Available in bookstores or by mail for $14.95 ppd. from the author at Fiberworks Publications.

Also available from this source: *The Fiberworks Direc-tory of Self-Published Books on the Fiber Arts* ($12.95 ppd.); *Fiberworks Quarterly* (newsletter); and *Nature's Dypot,* a resource guide for spinners/weavers/dyers. $9.95 ppd. (#1)

☐ *Handbook for Designers of Counted Thread.* Contains all the practical know-how of how to chart, find a printer, where to sell. Includes info on copyrights and taxes. $10.25 ppd. from Counted Thread Society. (#2)

☐ *Homemade Money--The Definitive Guide to Success in a Homebased Business,* 4th Revised edition, by Barbara Brabec (Betterway Books). Covers all aspects of working at home, including several marketing chapters, an A-to-Z "Crash Course in Business Basics" (detailed financial, legal, tax info), a chapter on the use of computers in homebased businesses, and a 500-listing resource chapter completely different from the one in this book. $21.95 ppd.

NOTE: A brand new edition of this book will be published in late February, 1994, and the new subtitle will be *How to Select, Start, Manage, Market and Multiply the Profits of a Business at Home.* Inquire about price of that edition from Barbara Brabec Productions. (#1)

☐ *How to Be a Weekend Entrepreneur, Making Money at Craft Fairs, Trade Shows and Swap Meets,* by Susan Ratliff. 1991. A step-by-step approach to building a profitable weekend business. $13 ppd. from Marketing Methods Press. (#1)

☐ *How to Get Happily Published,* by Judith Appelbaum. Excellent overview of the whole publishing world. Includes a section, "The Self-Publishing Option," with three chapters devoted to the pros/cons of self-publishing. Also has one of the best resource chapters available to writers, editors, publishers and others in the publishing industry. Check bookstores or libraries for the latest edition of this book.

☐ *How to Design/Write/Craft for Profits,* by four SCD designers. Until the publication of this book, beginning designers had no source of printed information on how to break into the crafts industry as a professional. This candid guide explains how to make contacts, find product sources, submit to editors, build self esteem, and more. No other book for designers offers the degree of inspiration, motivation and organizational tips to be found in this much-needed handbook, $14.35 ppd. from Co-Op Publications. Also inquire about the book's companion newsletter, *The "How-To" Marketing & Business Quarterly.* (#1)

☐ *How to Publish, Promote and Sell Your Book,* by Joseph V. Goodman. A handy guide, offered by a printer that regularly prints books for small publishers. Includes book jobbers, addresses of review media, etc. $7.25 ppd. from Adams Press. (#4)

☐ *How to Put On a Great Craft Show First Time & Every Time* by Dianne Hendricks Spiegel & Lee Spiegel. Covers all aspects of producing a show or improving the quality of shows you already may be presenting. $15 ppd. from The Crafts Fair Guide. (#1)

☐ *How to Start and Operate a Mail-Order Business,* by Julian L. Simon (4th ed., 1987, McGraw-Hill). A classic in its field. Sound advice, basic techniques, and up-to-date info on new developments in the industry. Includes a section on the fast-growing field of catalogs, a list of 500 mail order products known to sell well, and much more. Available in bookstores and libraries.

☐ *The Law (In Plain English) For Craftspeople,* by Leonard D. DuBoff with Michael Scott, (Madrona Publishers). Covers issues of concern to craftspeople who need to acquire business skills and a grasp of legal principles relating to the sale and use of their work. $8.90 ppd. from The Crafts Report. (#1)

☐ *Pattern Designer Directory.* 2nd Edition. Adele Patti compiles this directory of craft designers to help craft sellers figure out which craft or needlecraft patterns they can use commercially without fear of violating designers' copyrights. The directory lists some 200 designers and book publishers who have answered specific questions on copyrights and given their guidelines on how patterns may legally be used to create finished items for sale in both retail and wholesale markets. $12.95 ppd. from Craft Marketing News. (#1)

☐ *Photographing Your Craftwork,* by Steve Meltzer. This hand-on guide is for craftspeople who need quality slides or photographs to send to juried shows, magazines, shops or galleries. $10.95 ppd. from Madrona Publishers. (#1)

☐ *The Self-Publishing Manual,* by Dan Poynter. The most comprehensive and informative book beginning self-publishers can read. Covers all areas of publishing, from preparation of a manuscript to printing, getting book reviews, distribution, promotion, etc. $15.95 ppd. *Publishing Poynters* is the author's promotional newsletter. Mention this book to get a free copy and more information about the many other books and publishing services offered by Para Publishing. (#1)

□ *Selling to Catalog Houses,* by Ron Playle. This booklet, published in 1989, explains the type of products that sell well in catalogs, how to price them, invoice companies, and find the catalog houses most likely to be interested in your products. Info is applicable both to handcrafts and self-published books. $13.45 ppd. from Craft Marketing News. (#1)

□ *Sewing For Profits* by Allan & Judy Smith. A small business guide written especially for homebased sewers. $12 ppd. from Success Publications, which offers other books and reports of interest to creative individuals. (#1)

□ *Small-Time Operator – How to Start Your Own Business, Keep Your Books, Pay Your Taxes, and Stay Out of Trouble,* by Bernard Kamoroff, CPA. This excellent book is updated annually to include the newest information on state and federal laws and taxes. Includes ledger sheets and worksheets to set up your bookkeeping system. (Annual updates are available once you buy a copy of the book.) In bookstores or by mail from Bell Springs Publishing. (Request price of latest edition.) (#1)

□ *Teaching Basic Quiltmaking,* by the National Quilt Association. How to teach adults, develop a course outline and lesson plan, with a section covering recordkeeping and other details related to the business of teaching. $12 ppd. from National Quilt Association. (#2)

□ *You Can Make Money From Your Arts and Crafts,* by Steve and Cindy Long. This book offers some good information on selling at craft shows, and may be most helpful to craftspeople who are woodworking toymakers like the authors, who write from personal experience. $17.45 ppd. from Mark Publishing. (#1)

□ *Yes You Can Teach! – a Handbook For Teaching Adults* by Florence Nelson. Out of print for several years because of a fire that destroyed the publisher's inventory, this manual is once again available. It will be helpful to beginners who don't know how to get started teaching. $6.50 ppd. from Elizabeth Nelson. (#3)

□ *Writer's Market.* Published annually, this is the professional writer's "bible." It lists 4,000 buyers of freelance materials, as well as listings of agents, contests and awards for writers. Includes articles and interviews with top professionals. Available in bookstores or by mail from Writer's Digest. Request catalog for price of current year's edition. (#1)

Section V
Other Publications

This is a sampling of the many unusual and helpful "little publications" available to craftspeople today -- most of them published by craftspeople themselves. Included are booklets, special reports and article reprints.

Also included here are free pamphlets and catalogs offered by government agencies and other businesses.

For addresses, see the ADDRESS LIST indicated in parenthesis after the description.

□ *The Bead Directory.* 1992, Expanded 2nd Edition. This is the most comprehensive collection of bead resources available. Includes bead suppliers, societies, bazaars, books, associations, classes, conferences, magazines/newsletters, museums featuring bead collections, and more. $16.95 ppd. from The Bead Directory. (#4)

□ **Calligraphy Information.** For a special information package on calligraphy, send a LSASE to receive samples of Ken Brown's calligraphy prints and information about his kits and publications. His newsletter, *Brownlines,* features successful calligraphers and shares tips on techniques. This information will guide you to ways to profit from your calligraphic skills. Write to Ken Brown Studio. (#3)

□ **Consignment Forms.** If you don't wish to create your own form, you may order 50 copies of the form pictured on page 65 for $6.50 ppd. from The Unicorn. From this same source-- for $3--you can get a catalog of some 1600 books related to textile arts and crafts. (#4)

□ *A Co-Op That Can Co-Operate!* by Ann Lang. Instrumental in the establishment of a successful co-op shop, Ann has written a helpful booklet that includes start-up tips, discussion of problem areas, and how to establish general guidelines and business practices for such a group. $6.95 ppd. from Ann Lang. (#3)

□ *The Cooperative Approach to Crafts.* $2.00 ppd. Ask for Program Aid No. 1001 from the Agricultural Cooperative Service. (#4)

□ *The Cooperative Approach to Crafts for Senior Citizens,* by Gerald Ely & William Seymour. Discusses the possibilities that exist for a craft organization, and initial steps to be taken in establishing such a cooperative. $1.25 ppd. Ask for Program Aid No. 1156 from the Agricultural Cooperative Service. (#4)

□ **Copyright-Free Design Books.** Request the free catalog offered by Dover Publications. It describes the many design books in the Pictorial Archive Series which can be used without permission from the publisher. (#4)

□ **Copyright Pamphlets.** The Copyright Office offers a variety of helpful publications explaining all areas of copyright law. They are free on request. Registration forms can be ordered by mail, or by telephoning (202) 707-9100. (#4)

☐ **Crafting For Cash Reports** by Joanne Hill. This crafts marketing expert offers 30 reports that could be helpful to your business. Examples: *The Basics of Good Displays, How to Purchase Supplies Wholesale, Pricing Your Product for Profit.* Each report is $1 ppd. from Joanne Hill. (#3)

☐ **The Craft Party Plan Report**, by Susan Scharadin. A step-by-step outline for organizing and conducting craft selling parties in one's home. $5 ppd. (A business kit including agreements and business specifics is also available.) Contact Susan Scharadin. (#3)

☐ **Crafts Marketing Articles & Mini Reports by Barbara Brabec.** Included in the author's special series are "Developing and Manufacturing a Product" and "Niche Markets Crafters Might Consider" ($2 each); "Copying and Copyrights" and "Tag & Label Suppliers & Product Safety Guidelines" ($3 each). Complete catalog of Barbara's books and reports free from Barbara Brabec Productions. (#1)

☐ **Federal Trade Commission Rules & Regulations.** Several free pamphlets are available from the FTC on request, as discussed in the text. (#4)

☐ *General Information Concerning Trademarks* and *General Information Concerning Patents.* Two free booklets available from the Patent & Trademark Office. (#4)

☐ *A Guide to Marketing Crafts Through the Home Party System,* by Jo Mucha & Marion Boyer. Gives specific advice and detailed answers for the most commonly-asked questions troubling the novice in the areas of product liability, inventory investments, cash flow difficulties, display techniques, and job descriptions. $6.50 ppd. from Village Vendor. (#4)

☐ **Hard-to-Find Needlework Books.** Looking for special books on knitting, crochet, lace, quilting, embroidery, canvas, dolls, and more? Send $1 for an introductory catalog, which will place you on Bette S. Feinstein's mailing list. Bette also offers a search service for special books in the field you may be seeking. (#3)

☐ *How to Establish and Profit from Running Your Own Teaching Studio at Home,* by Sylvia Landman. A comprehensive correspondence course and consultation service for at-home teachers. For details, send SASE to Self-Employment Consultants. (#4)

190 ☐ *The How-To-Get-Wholesale Report.* Author Margaret Boyd (see BOOKS section) offers this special report to help crafters understand the secrets of buying supplies at wholesale. $5.50 ppd. (#3)

☐ *How to Save Money on Office Supplies.* This free booklet will introduce you to the wide variety of office supplies and materials you can order by mail from the Quill Corporation. (#4)

☐ **Internal Revenue Service Pamphlets.** Free on request. Of special interest would be "Tax Guide for Small Business," #334; and "Business Use of Your Home," #587. (#4)

☐ **The Marketing Options Report Series for Craftspeople,** by Constance Lagan. Send $1 plus SASE to receive a brochure describing a series of reports that may be helpful in your crafts business. Examples: *How to Sell Your Craft Know-How to Libraries; How to Sell Your Articles and Designs to Magazines; How to Start a Craft Co-Op.* Each report is $6 ppd. from Constance Lagan. (#3)

☐ **Money-Making Audio Tapes** by Sylvia Landman. *How to Sell by Mail Order, Arts/Crafts in the Marketplace, Couples in Business,* and more. $10.95 ppd. Send SASE for catalog of other tapes, home-business books, and special reports available from Self-Employment Consultants. (#4)

☐ *Show Business —How to Organize a Successful Arts and Crafts Show,* by Kay Weber. Helpful little booklet with tips and help from one who has done this many times. $5.00 ppd. from Kay Weber. (#3)

☐ **Small Business Guides.** Since 1959, Pilot Books has been publishing helpful little booklets on a wide variety of topics. Some of interest to this books's readers would be *Organizing and Operating Profitable Workshop Classes, Starting a Business After 50; The Flea Market Entrepreneur* and others. Each of these booklets are $4.95 ppd. from Pilot Books. A free catalog is available on request. (#4)

☐ **Stencils and Stencil-Cutting Service.** If you need stencil patterns for painting, embossing, quilting and decorating, send for the catalog offered by Needlearts International ($2.00 ppd.). This company also offers custom cutting services for those who need their own designs cut in quantity. (#4)

☐ *The Whole Work Catalog.* If you'd like to have a reliable source for small business books and tapes by mail, look no further than this catalog. It includes many titles difficult or impossible to find in bookstores, and speedy service is guaranteed. The catalog is free on request from The New Careers Center. (#4)

NOTE: If you have self-published a small business guide, and are looking for mail-order dealers, send details to Tom Ellison, who may wish to include your title in his next catalog.

☐ **U. S. Small Business Administration Pamphlets.** A wide range of management and technical publications designed to help small businesses are available free. For a list, ask for free bulletins, #SBA 115A, and for-sale booklets, #SBA 115B. (#4)

☐ *Your Guide to the Home Boutique Bonanza,* by Barbara Griffin. This informative booklet explains how to organize and run a successful home holiday boutique, based on the author's own experience. $4.50 ppd. Barbara offers other booklets and a newsletter on the topic of sewing for children. Send SASE for her catalog. (#3)

Bags, Cartons and Mailers

☐ **Action Bag Company.** Your source for gift wrap, tissue paper, retail shopping bags, regular polybags, shipping supplies and more. Free catalog.

☐ **Associated Bag Company.** Write for free catalogs which describe this company's line of: plastic zipper bags, bubble bags and sheets for packaging, shipping and mailing envelopes, corrugated shipping boxes and other containers. (This is also a source for press-on packing list envelopes mentioned in the text, and vinyl sheet protectors for notebooks.)

☐ **Gaylord Specialties Corp.** Wide range of colorful wrapping supplies and ribbons, plus tote bags and sacks that can be imprinted with your business name. Request info on your business letterhead.

☐ **U. S. Box Corporation.** Offers a catalog of stock packaging -- folding and set-up boxes, mailing containers, boxes with acetate covers, air cushion bags and padding. (Minimum order $150.)

☐ **20th Century Plastics, Inc.** Catalog features vinyl products, including zipper bags that can be imprinted.

Office Supplies

☐ **The Drawing Board.** Offers a wide variety of supplies, business forms, standard stationery, etc. Free catalog.

☐ **Grayarc.** Office forms, shipping labels, foil labels that can be imprinted, and other supplies. Free catalog.

☐ **Quill Corporation.** A leading mail order distributor of office supplies and equipment. Free catalog.

☐ **The Stationery House.** Stationery, letterheads, envelopes, business cards. Free catalog.

☐ **Vermont Business Forms Co.,** The craftsman's source for creative business cards. Samples, $1.

Craft Tags, Labels & Photos

☐ **Charm Woven Labels.** Offers regular cloth labels in a variety of styles. Free color brochure.

☐ **Kimmeric Studio.** Craft Hang Tags; 96 designs -- country, folk, traditional. Brochure and samples, 50 cents plus large SASE.

☐ **Quantity Photo Company.** A by-mail source for photos in quantity, for promotional purposes. Black and white or color. Free brochure.

☐ **Sterling Name Tape Co.** This company will create labels for you, or adapt your own artwork (logo, etc.) for the custom labels you need. You can order as few as 100 labels.

☐ **Widby Enterprises.** Offers a large selection of standard labels, including care labels. For information and samples, send large SASE to attention of Don Widby.

Craft Fair Display Units

☐ **Armstrong Products, Inc.** Multi-media displays designed with the artist's needs in mind. Aluminum construction, modular. Free catalog.

☐ **Elaine Martin, Inc.** Canopies for outdoor shows, folding tables, folding carts, indoor booths, and more. Write for brochure.

☐ **Tri-Conn, Inc.** Offers a variety of interesting craft fair display units. Quick assembly, lightweight. Free brochure.

Computer Resources

☐ *Home Office Computing.* This monthly, on newsstands or available by subscriptions, is one of the best publications for home-business owners who use computers in their businesses, or would like to.

☐ **Computer Insurance.** Homeowner policies and riders generally do not cover computers used by business; a specific business policy may be necessary. Request a brochure from Safeware, The Insurance Agency.

ArtNetwork
P. O. Box 399
Renaissance, CA 95962-0369

Aardvark Territorial Enterprise
P. O. Box 2449
Livermore, CA 94551

Apparel Industry Magazine
   and Sourcebook
180 Allen Rd., Suite 300
Atlanta, GA 30328

Book Marketing Update
Open Horizons Publishing Co.
P. O. Box 205
Fairfield, IA 52556-0205

Barbara Brabec Productions
P. O. Box 2137-CC
Naperville, IL 60567

Bell Springs Publishing
P. O. Box 640
Laytonville, CA 95454

Classified Communication
Box 4177
Prescott, AZ 86302

The Cloth Doll
P. O. Box 1089
Mt. Shasta, CA 96067

Co-Op Publications
P. O. Box 5573
Wakefield, RI 02879

Country Handcrafts
P. O. Box 572
Milwaukee, WI 53201

Craft and Needlework Age
225 Gordons Corner Plaza
Box 420
Manalapan, NJ 07726

Crafter's SourceLetters
CraftSource
Box 575749
Murray, UT 84157

Craft Marketing News
The Front Room Publishers
P. O. Box 1541
Clifton, NJ 07015

Craftmaster News
P. O. Box 39429
Downey, CA 90239

Crafts
PJS Publications, Inc.
P. O. Box 1790
Peoria, IL 61656

The Crafts Fair Guide
P. O. Box 5508
Mill Valley, CA 94942

Crafts 'N Things
Clapper Publishing Co. Inc.
701 Lee Street, Suite 1000
Des Plaines, IL 60016

Crafts Plus
130 Spy Court
Markham, Ontario L3R 5H6

The Crafts Report
P. O. Box 1992
Wilmington, DE 19899

Craft Supply Magazine
225 Gordons Corner Plaza
Box 420
Manalapan, NJ 07726

Craftrends
6201 Howard Street
Niles, IL 60648

The Creative Machine
Open Chain Publishing
P. O. Box 2634
Menlo Park, CA 94026

The Dream Merchant
1209 Torrance Blvd., Suite 201
Torrance, CA 90501

Fiberarts
50 College Street
Asheville, NC 28801

Fiberworks Publications
P. O. Box 49770
Austin, TX 78765

Fine Woodworking
Taunton Press
Box 355, 63 S. Main St.
Newtown, CT 06470-9977

Gift & Tablewear Reporter
Billboard Publications, Inc.
1515 Broadway
New York, NY 10036

Gifts & Decorative Accessories
51 Madison Avenue
New York, NY 10010

Gift Basket Review
1205 Forsyth St.
Jacksonville, FL 32204

Handwoven
Interweave Press
201 East 4th St.
Loveland, CO 80537

The Herb Companion
(same address as Handwoven)

Homeworking Mothers
P. O. Box 423
East Meadow, NY 11554

Hot Fudge Press
19425 Tollhouse Rd.
Clovis, CA 93611

Let's Talk About Dollmaking
P. O. Box 662/B
Point Pleasant, NJ 08742

Madrona Publishers, Inc.
P. O. Box 22667
Seattle, WA 98122

Marketing Methods
2811 N. 7th Avenue
Phoenix, AZ 85007-1125

Mark Publishing, Inc.
5400 Scotts Valley Drive
Scotts Valley, CA 95066

McCall's Needlework & Crafts
Magazine
(same address as Crafts)

National Home Business Report
P. O. Box 2137-CC
Naperville, IL 60567

Northwoods Trading Company
13451 Essex Ct.
Eden Prairie, MN 55347

Nutshell News
Kalmbach Miniatures
P. O. Box 1612
Waukesha, WI 53187-1612

Open Horizons Publishing Co.
P. O. Box 205
Fairfield, IA 52556

Para Publishing
P. O. Box 4232-121
Santa Barbara, CA 93140-4232

Potpourri from Herbal Acres
Pine Row Publications
Box 428
Washington Crossing, PA 18977

The Professional Quilter
Oliver Press
Box 1628
Wheatridge, CO 80034

Profitable Craft Merchandising
P. O. Box 1790
Peoria, IL 61656

Quilter's Newsletter
Box 394
Wheatridge, CO 80033

The Ronay Guides
A Step Ahead, Inc.
2950 Pangborn Rd.
Decatur, GA 30033

Rug Hooking
P. O. Box 15760
Harrisburg, PA 17105

SAC Newsmonthly
P. O. Box 159
Bogalusa, LA 70429

The Sewing Sampler
P. O. Box 39
Springfield, MN 56087

Sew News
(same address as Crafts)

Sharing Ideas
Royal Publishing, Inc.
P. O. Box 1120
Glendora, CA 91740

Spin-Off
(Same address as Handwoven)

Stitches Count
1456 N. Albert St.
St. Paul, MN 55108

Success Publications
2812 Bayonne Dr.
Palm Beach Gardens, FL 33410

Sunshine Artists, USA
1736 N. Highway 427
Longwood, FL 32750-3410

Teaching for Learning
511 Hahaione St., No. 18-C
Honolulu, HI 96825

Treadleart
25834 Narbonne Ave., Suite 1
Lomita, CA 90717

West Coast CRAFTLINK
Box 547
Fort Langley, B.C. VOX 1JO
Canada

Writer's Digest/North Light Books
1507 Dana Avenue
Cincinnati, OH 45207

Yellow Pages of American Crafts
Suite 200 Mill Centre
3000 Chestnut Avenue
Baltimore, MD 21211

American Craft Association
21 S. Elting Corners Rd.
Highland, NY 12528

American Crafts Council
72 Spring Street
New York, NY 10012

American Quilters Society
P. O. Box 3290
Paducah, KY 42002-3290

American Society of Artists, Inc.
P. O. Box 1326
Palatine, IL 60078

Center for the History
of American Needlework
P. O. Box 359
Valencia, PA 16059

The Center for Safety in the Arts
5 Beekman Street, Suite 1030
New York, NY 10038

COSMEP
P. O. Box 703
San Francisco, CA 94101

Council of American Embroiderers
P. O. Box 428
Plymouth, MI 48170-0428

Counted Thread Society of America
1285 South Jason St.
Denver, CO 80223

Embroiderer's Guild of America
335 W. Broadway, Suite 100
Louisville, KY 40202

194 Handweavers Guild of America, Inc.
120 Mountain Avenue, B101
Bloomfield, CT 06002

Hobby Industries Assn. (HIA)
319 E. 54th St.
Elmwood Park, NJ 07407

Industry Productions of America
Beckman's Gift Shows
P. O. Box 27337
Los Angeles, CA 90027

International Guild of
Candle Artisans
867 Browning Avenue South
Salem, OR 97302

The Knitting Guild of America
P. O. Box 1606
Knoxville, TN 37902

Miniatures Industry Association
of America (MIAA)
Box 2188
Zanesville, OH 43702

Minnesota Crafts Council
528 Hennepin Ave., Rm. 308
Minneapolis, MN 55403

Montclair Craft Guild
P. O. Box 111
Emerson, NJ 07630

National Needlework Assn. (TNNA)
650 Danbury Road
Ridgefield, CT 06877

National Quilt Association, Inc.
P. O. Box 393
Ellicott City, MD 21041

National Society of Tole &
Decorative Painters, Inc.
Fifth & Main, Box 808
Newton, KS 67114

National Woodcarvers Association
7424 Miami Avenue
Cincinnati, OH 45243

Ohio Arts & Crafts Guild
P. O. Box 3080
Lexington, OH 44904

Ontario Crafts Council
Craft Resource Centre
35 McCaul Street
Toronto, Ontario M5T 1V7

The Professional Knitwear
Designers Guild
c/o Shirley MacNulty
P. O. Box 1612
Carolina Beach, NC 28428

Sewing & Fine Needlework Guild
P. O. Box 1606
Knoxville, TN 37901

Society of Craft Designers
6175 Barfield Rd., Suite 220
Atlanta, GA 30328

Stained Glass Assn. of America
P. O. Box 22642
Kansas City, MO 64113

Stumpwork Society
P. O. Box 122
Bogata, NJ 07603

Surface Design Association
P. O. Box 20799
Oakland, CA 94620

United Maine Craftsmen
RR 2 Box 1920
Manchester ME 04351

Volunteer Lawyers for the Arts
1 East 53rd St., 6th Fl.
New York, NY 10019

Gail Bird
110 Jennings Ave.
Patchogue, NY 11772

Margaret Boyd
P. O. Box 6232
Augusta, GA 30906

Ken Brown Studio
P. O. Box 637LB
Hugo, OK 74743

Ayn Chase
Ayn's Shuttle Shop
Edgartown, MA 02539-2264

Betty Christy
Tree Toys
P. O. Box 492
Hinsdale, IL 60521

Maureen Davis
11 Drummers Lane
Bethel, CT 06801

Bette S. Feinstein
96 Roundwood Rd.
Newton, MA 02164

Barbara Griffin
Barb Griffin Designs
2843 Trenton Way
Ft. Collins, CO 80526

Sue Harris
RD 1 Box 350
Petersburg NY 12138

Joanne Hill
Crafter's Link
59999 Myrtle Road
South Bend, IN 46614

Constance Lagan
Creations by Connie
35 Claremont Ave.
N. Babylon, NY 11703

Ann Lang
Annie Things Possible
309 S. Saginaw
Holly, MI 48442

Sandy Mooney
Batik by Sandy
6293 River Rd.
Flushing MI 48433

Elizabeth Nelson
Teacher!
P. O. Box 120633
St. Paul, MN 55112

Susan Scharadin
20 Windswept Rd.
Breinigsville, PA 18031

Linda Markuly Szilvasy
P. O. Box 871
Metamora, IL 61548

Ruby Tobey
2305 W. 32nd South
Wichita, KS 67217-2044

Pat Virch
1506 Lynn Avenue
Marquette, MI 49855

Kay Weber
300 Ross Lane
Belleville, IL 62221

Colette Wolff
Platypus
Box 396, Planetarium Station
200 W. 82nd St.
New York, NY 10024

Suppliers, Government Contacts & Other Businesses

Action Bag Company
501 N. Edgewood Avenue
Wood Dale, IL 60191

Adams Press
25 East Washington St.
Chicago, IL 60601

Agricultural Cooperative Service
U. S. Department of Agriculture
Washington, DC 20250

Armstrong Products, Inc.
P. O. Box 979
Guthrie, OK 73044

Associated Bag Company
P. O. Box 07120
Milwaukee, WI 53207

Baker & Taylor Co.
P. O. Box 4500
Somerville, NJ 08876

The Bead Directory
P. O. Box 10103
Oakland, CA 94610

Charm Woven Labels
P. O. Box 30027
Portland, OR 97230

Consumer Products Safety Comm.
Bureau of Compliance
5401 Westbard Avenue
Bethesda, MD 20207

The Copyright Office
Library of Congress
Washington, DC 20559

Department of the Interior
Div. of Law Enforcement
U. S. Fish & Wildlife Svc.
Washington, DC 20240

Dover Publications
31 E. 2nd St.
Mineola, NY 11501

The Drawing Board
P. O. Box 660429
Dallas, TX 75266

Federal Trade Commission
Div. of Legal & Public Records
Washington, DC 20580

Gaylord Specialties Corp.
225 Fifth AVenue, Suite 443
New York, NY 10010

Grayarc
Greenwoods Industrial Park
P. O. Box 2944
Hartford, CT 06104

Home Office Computing
730 Broadway
New York, NY 10003

Internal Revenue Service
Washington, DC 20224

Kimmeric Studio
P. O. Box 3586
Napa, CA 94558

Elaine Martin Co.
P. O. Box 261
Highwood, IL 60040

National Bureau of Standards
Technical Building., B167
Standards Develop. Svc. Sec.
Washington, DC 20234

Needlearts International
19411 Village Dr.
Sonora, CA 95370-9228

The New Careers Center
Box 339
Boulder, CO 80306

Patent and Trademark Office
U. S. Department of Commerce
Washington, DC 20231

Pilot Books
103 Cooper St.
Babylon, NY 11702

Quantity Photo Company
119 W. Hubbard St.
Chicago, IL 60610

Quill Corporation
100 Schelter Rd.
Lincolnshire, IL 60069-9585

Safeware
The Insurance Company
2929 North High Street
Columbus, OH 43202

Self-Employment Consultants
1090 Cambridge St.
Novato, CA 94947

The Stationery House
1000 Florida Avenue
Hagerstown, MD 21740

Sterling Name Tape Co.
Box 1056
Winsted, CT 06098

Tri-Conn, Inc.
143 Golden Hill Street
P. O. Box 190
Bridgeport, CT 06601

20th Century Plastics, Inc.
P. O. Box 30022
Los Angeles, CA 90030

U. S. Box Corporation
1298 McCarter Highway
Newark NJ 07104

U. S. Small Business Administration
SBA Publications
P. O. Box 15434
Ft. Worth, TX 76119

The Unicorn
1338 Ross St.
Petaluma, CA 94954-6502

Vermont Business Forms Co.
Business Card Division
RD 4, Box 2478
Montpelier, VT 05602

Village Vendor
604 Calico
Portage, MI 49081

Widby Enterprises
4321 Crestfield
Knoxville, TN 37921

Index

197

samples of,